Get Set for America

Get Set for American Studies

Edward Ashbee

Edinburgh University Press

Edinburgh University Press Ltd
22 George Square, Edinburgh

Typeset in Sabon by
Hewer Text Ltd, Edinburgh, and
printed and bound in Finland by
WS Bookwell

A CIP record for this book is
available from the British Library

ISBN 0 7486 1692 6 (paperback)

CONTENTS

ACKNOWLEDGEMENTS

I would like to thank Kelly Arland, Philip Davies, John Dumbrell, Jon Herbert, Ian Ralston and Amy Voyle-Morgan for their help and assistance. I am also very grateful to Ann Vinnicombe for her careful and scrupulous work. Her efforts strengthened many of the chapters. I am, of course, solely responsible for errors and omissions.

Edward Ashbee,
Copenhagen Business School,
January 2004

PART I
What is American Studies?

1 WHY STUDY THE UNITED STATES?

This section of the book considers the reasons why the US is worthy of study. It also assesses the significance of the US in shaping the contemporary world and surveys the development of American Studies as a university subject.

During the 1980s, there was widespread talk of American decline. In *The Rise and Fall of the Great Powers*, Paul Kennedy of Yale University suggested that empires, and the imperial nations that are at their core, overreach themselves. After a period of growth, their resources and capabilities are exhausted. Weighed down by the military expenditure required so as to secure and maintain their territory, great powers inevitably face the prospect of long-term decline and displacement by rivals. The fate of the British Empire can be cited as an example. Unless it adjusted its policies and priorities, the US – Kennedy warned – would also run 'the risk of what might roughly be termed "imperial overstretch"'.

A 'HYPERPOWER'

A decade after the publication of *The Rise and Fall of the Great Powers*, the picture appeared to have changed dramatically. Those who had challenged Kennedy's thesis and talked instead of an American revival seemed vindicated.[1] By the end of the 1990s and at the beginning of the new century, notions of decline had given way to descriptions of the US as a 'hyperpower' or global 'hegemon'. The collapse of the Soviet

3

Union and the communist bloc at the end of the 1980s eliminated the only serious contender for global dominance. Although there were fears that Iraq could become a quagmire for allied forces, and warnings that 'rogue states' such as North Korea and terrorist organisations – most notably Al-Qaeda – still posed a threat to American national security, there were no credible rivals for power. The end of the Cold War placed the US, for either good or ill, in a position of undisputed hegemony. As Phyllis Bennis has noted:

> But never before, not in the ancient Persian Empire . . . not in the eras of the Roman, the Ottoman, the British, or the Portuguese empires, had the colossus of any existing imperial center so thoroughly dwarfed the combined capabilities of the rest of the world. (Bennis 2003: 137)

The US's military strength is, in itself, a compelling reason to study American institutions and processes. The country plays a pivotal role in shaping the character of global politics and international relations. The future of Europe, Asia and the other continents cannot be considered without an understanding of American attitudes, perceptions and goals.

ECONOMIC POWER

However, the US is an economic as well as a military colossus. Its Gross Domestic Product – the sum total of goods and services produced during the course of a year – amounts to more than 20 per cent of total world output. The American economy is larger than that of the next three countries (Japan, Germany and the United Kingdom) added together (Snyder 2003: 29). Furthermore, the impact of US economic might can be felt across the globe. Only the relatively small numbers who live in societies insulated from the market are unfamiliar with American brands such as Coca-Cola and Levis. Over 85 per cent of computers across the world use Microsoft Windows or Unix and are powered by Intel or Motorola processors. About 75 per cent of global internet traffic passes through the US at some point (Prestowitz 2003). Indeed, the process of 'globalisation' has become almost synonymous with 'Americanisation'. The overseas investment plans of US companies can determine the fate of communities, regions and countries in both Europe and across the world. Financial indicators such as the Dow Jones and NASDAQ indexes – which record the rise and fall of share prices – are watched with close attention both inside and outside the US.

America also has a role as an economic pacesetter. For much – although not all – of the twentieth century, the development of American technology was far ahead of that in other countries. The US led the way in terms of innovation. Automated mass production, the assembly belt and the use of management techniques associated with *Taylorism* – which were pioneered in US industries – provided a model that was emulated throughout much of the developed world.

CULTURAL EXPORTS

The US is also important because of its impact on global culture.[2] From the early twentieth century onwards, American cultural 'exports' – most notably those generated by the US music and film industries – structured the perceptions and aspirations of successive generations. Even in their formative years, the output of companies such as RCA and the Hollywood films studios dwarfed that of competitors across the globe. Today, American films account for about 85 per cent of box-office receipts in Europe and more than 80 per cent across the globe (Prestowitz 2003).

AN IDEA

America is, however, also important because it does not only refer to a geographical territory. It is also tied to particular representations and images. America is – to a greater extent than any other country – an idea. Although the themes upon which this idea is constructed are often contradictory, it rests on notions of escape, beginning again, self-expression and self-realisation. They incorporate an implied, or sometimes overt, contrast with the seemingly restrictive cultures of more traditionalist countries.

Much of this has been evoked in American music and cinema. In some instances, the medium was the message. Jazz, the blues, rock and roll, and later musical genres such as rap and hiphop, defied established strictures and were, in themselves, a form of liberation. Films offered vistas that were absent in the 'old World'. There was the competitive individualism of city life, the hope of upward mobility and the lure of material wealth. There was a sense of freedom for those tied to the tightly bound family and neighbourhood structures that characterised many of the countries of both Europe and Asia. All this was often tied to a discovery of 'self'.

These ideas are most evident in the 'road movie' that has long been a perennial feature of American cinema. Although also drawing on the drug culture and the experimental forms of living that are associated with the late 1960s, Dennis Hopper's film *Easy Rider* (1969) evokes long-established American images. Like cowboys riding towards the west, Hopper and Peter Fonda set out on Harley-Davidson motorbikes. As they do, a watch is cast away, marking a deliberate rejection of time and the constraints of ordered society. The open road that they take is seemingly unbounded, offering freedom, opportunity, fulfilment, and the chance to come to terms with both identity and self. However, *Easy Rider* has a sudden and brutal ending, perhaps suggesting that these forms of escape and the promise long-offered by America were being lost as the country was increasingly gripped by intolerance and reaction. A more recent road movie, *Thelma and Louise* (1990), which is set in the south-west, has also provoked discussion. Hailed by some as a feminist manifesto, it follows two women who become fugitives seeking freedom and an escape from the law. They discard and throw away the trappings of their former existence. However, there is – in the end – only one form of escape

ATTITUDES TOWARDS THE US

'. . . some of our students take American Studies because they are critical of America; others because they are fascinated by the USA.' (King Alfred's College, Winchester)

Although few question the extent to which the US has influenced and in many instances, reshaped the fate of countries around the world, there is much less consensus about the nature and character of its impact.

For those who see the US in positive terms, it has long symbolised individual freedom and represented a beacon of hope to those living under repressive forms of government. Its military forces fought alongside the allies in the final year of the First World War. They played a pivotal role in rescuing Europe from Nazi oppression in the Second World War. The American policy of *containment* – adopted in the early years of the Cold War – prevented the expansion of Soviet communism beyond the boundaries of eastern Europe. Forty years later, President Reagan's commitment to a new generation of missile technology and his administration's backing for anti-communist guerillas in countries such as Afghanistan contributed to the collapse of the Soviet bloc and the 'westernisation' of countries such as Hungary, Poland and Russia itself.

Over the centuries, the US has also offered the opportunity to escape from poverty and degradation to countless numbers. Generations of immigrants have crossed the Atlantic and Pacific Oceans. In the US, their communities prospered and laid the basis for a diverse but – at the same time – stable society integrated around a shared commitment to the principles of democracy, freedom and self-reliance.

There are, however, those who are bitterly critical of the US and its policies. American backing for Israel and the war in Iraq have, in particular, provoked bitter resentment across the Islamic world and, especially, among supporters of the Palestinian cause. Indeed, for many radicals, the US is an imperialist power. American policy, it is argued, is based upon economic self-interest. It is structured around reshaping the world so as to acquire resources and create expanded markets for US commercial interests. From this perspective, both the Gulf War of 1991 and the war against Iraq in 2003 were aggressive ventures motivated primarily by hopes of acquiring access to the oilfields of the Middle East and *neo-conservative* hopes of remaking the world in America's image.

Others point to different forms of economic and cultural imperialism. From this perspective, national economies and established cultures are being undermined and destroyed by the relentless logic of *'McWorld'*. Distinct traditions, languages and histories are being displaced across the globe by an anonymous corporate ideology and cultural nihilism structured around worldwide commercial enterprises such as McDonald's, Starbucks and Microsoft.

The process of 'McDonaldisation' has provoked protests, bringing together campaigners from both the left and the right. In France, José Bové, a farmer and longtime activist, emerged as a household name and, for many, a national hero. In August 1999, a McDonald's was due to open in Millau, a town in the south-west of the country. In a protest action, co-ordinated by Bové, it was dismantled by protesters. A crowd loaded the rubble on to trucks and tractors, drove it through town and dumped it outside the town hall.

Nonetheless, despite the seeming rise of anti-Americanism, attitudes towards the US are often far from straightforward. They require 'unpackaging' or 'taking apart'. Throughout the Cold War years, when US military might – and its nuclear 'umbrella' – seemed to offer protection against Soviet expansionism, many in western Europe backed American foreign-policy goals but were, at the same time, disdainful about the cultural character of the US. For significant numbers of Europeans, Americans were loud and unsubtle. They had, it was said, no understanding of – or respect for – history and tradition. Hollywood and US television seemed to threaten long-established customs. In the Middle East and other Islamic countries, attitudes appear to be different but also contradictory. Brian Keenan, an Irish lecturer and writer, who was held for years as a hostage by Islamic radicals in the Lebanon, has recalled that although his captors were bitterly hostile towards American foreign policy, they were also drawn to – and fascinated by – American cultural forms.

ENCOUNTERS AND 'INTERMINGLING'

The study of the US is therefore important because its foreign policy, economy and different forms of cultural expression have – for good or ill – shaped the character of other countries across the globe. At the same time, however, the study of America is also important in itself. The US has a cultural wealth that is at times neglected in European representations of the country. Although – as conservatives stress – built upon the basis of European thinking, American forms of cultural expression have a distinct character and draw upon a number of themes.

- The US is, as President John F. Kennedy dubbed it, a 'nation of immigrants'. The immigrant experience – and the dilemmas posed by the process of adjustment to another society – informs many American literary narratives and commentaries.

- The scale of the continent and the opening up of the west unleashed profound emotions including both awe and a growing belief in the ability of individuals to conquer a pristine 'wilderness'.

- Tied to this, there was a sense of the US as a frontier society. It was shaped – according to a number of accounts – by the process of westward expansion as the territory under European settlement shifted towards the Pacific Ocean. Since then, observers suggest, American thinking has been characterised by feelings of restlessness and a need to seek out other forms of exploration. Outer space represented, according to the opening words of *Star Trek*, the 'final frontier'.

- The apparent mobility and freedom of American society laid the basis for the *American dream*. This refers to the belief that individuals can – through their own efforts – climb the economic ladder and accumulate material riches. Some accounts go further and depict the 'dream' in terms that go beyond economic success. America, they suggest, offers opportunities for self-realisation, a casting off of the past and even, perhaps, a form of 'rebirth'.

• Faith in the ability of individuals to reshape their circumstances led to a stress upon the lone hero. Whereas some European narratives emphasise broad structural forces and see people's actions as a response to their class or family circumstances, there is – in place of this – an emphasis upon the role of human agency in determining events.

• American history – and the different forms of cultural expression that have emerged in the US – also rests on the encounters and relationships between different groupings and traditions. As the University of Plymouth notes in its course specification:

The history of the United States of America has been the history of migration. The intermingling of peoples, with their different languages, religions, cultures and expectations, has made America a dynamic society.

The process of 'intermingling' has sometimes been creative and co-operative. In 1908 Israel Zangwill, a playwright, described the process by which immigrants were assimilated and 'Americanised' as a 'Melting Pot':

America is God's Crucible, the great Melting Pot where all the races of Europe are melting and reforming! . . . German and Frenchman, Irishman and Englishman, Jews and Russians – into the Crucible with you all! God is making the American. (Quoted in Glazer and Moynihan 1967: 289)

Zangwill was offering a profoundly optimistic vision of the American future and the country's capacity to assimilate immigrants. All could be drawn and remade in the American image.

At other times, however, 'intermingling' has been profoundly oppressive. Many observers have talked of the mass murder – or genocide – of native Americans (or 'Red Indians' as they were termed a generation ago). Irish immigrants were regarded for much of the mid-nineteenth century as a degenerate underclass. African-Americans were subject to institutionalised discrimination, particularly in the southern states, until the latter half of the twentieth century.

However, although 'intermingling' has always been a defining characteristic of American society, it has sometimes remained unacknowledged and hidden. Despite slavery and segregation – which relegated African-Americans to a legally subordinate status and separated them out from white society – black musical forms and patterns of religious worship had a profound impact on white culture. The blues that emerged in the Mississippi Delta and cities such as Chicago, for example, informed the later development of rock music.

THE DEVELOPMENT OF AMERICAN STUDIES

American Studies initially had little academic kudos in Europe. It was regarded as both marginal and – in the eyes of some – a form of US propaganda. Why, then, did it grow? The expansion of American Studies in European universities was, in part, a consequence of the US's growing importance during the decades that followed the Second World War. As Norman Podhoretz – an editor of *Commentary*, the influential neoconservative periodical – asked rather cynically:

Does Finland have a great literature . . . Does Afghanistan? Does Ecuador? Who knows or cares? But give Finland enough power and enough wealth and there would soon be a Finnish department in every university in the world – just as, in the 1950s, departments of American Studies were suddenly being established in colleges where, only a few years earlier, it had scarcely occurred to anyone that there was anything American to study. (Quoted in Pells 1997: 102).

There were, however, other reasons for the growth of American Studies. In West Germany and the countries of Scandinavia, employment prospects in some of the more highly paid occupations became increasingly dependent upon a knowledge of English and a familiarity with the English-speaking world. The Fulbright Program also played a part. Established in 1946 under legislation proposed by Senator J. William Fulbright of Arkansas and largely funded by the US government, it was an educational exchange programme. It sought to 'increase mutual understanding between the people of the United States and the people of other countries'. It allowed – and continues to permit – US students and scholars to study abroad. At the same time, the programme funds non-Americans who are studying in the US. Approximately 250,000 'Fulbrighters', 94,000 of whom have been from the United States and 155,600 from other countries, have participated since its founding.

However, despite US government funding for programmes and initiatives, American Studies began to acquire an increasingly critical edge. It did not simply celebrate the US and its achievements. This shift in the character of the discipline was tied to four processes.

First, as Richard Pells argues in *Not Like Us*, the character of American Studies in European universities differed from the way in which the discipline evolved within the US. Americanists in Europe had a perspective that was shaped by their own background and experience. They introduced a comparative dimension that considered and evaluated the building blocks of both American and European societies. They also studied the ways in which the US affected the different countries of Europe. Seen in comparative terms, the US was not always seen as superior or more advanced. Instead, some of its structural weaknesses were highlighted. As Pells notes, these efforts were not always well received in the US:

So from Washington's vantage point, the European Americanists seemed ungrateful, even insubordinate, when they converted American Studies into a movement that questioned, and thereby enabled people to resist, America's influence. (Pells 1997: 133)

Second, from the late 1960s onwards, the subject was increasingly influenced by radical critiques of the US. Widespread opposition to American intervention in Vietnam created a context within which the US was depicted as an aggressive and imperialist power. At the same time, there was an increasing identification with those who appeared to have been neglected or 'silenced' in mainstream accounts of US history and culture. A growing number of studies considered the history of African-Americans, 'Chicanos' (Mexican-Americans) and native Americans. Scholars turned to look at the evolution of the trades unions and chart the development of the women's movement.

Third, the subject broadened its field of study. It was influenced by the emergence of cultural studies as an academic discipline. This, in particular, shaped the development of American Studies as a discipline within the US itself. What is cultural studies? It rests upon a broad understanding of 'culture'. Although the concept had formerly been restricted to the 'high' culture of literature, art and traditional music, it increasingly encompassed almost every aspect of everyday life. Dialect, patterns of speech, popular television programmes such as *South Park* or *The Simpsons*, blockbuster movies, new styles of music such as hiphop or gangsta rap, all became legitimate subjects of study. Those studying these forms of cultural expression assessed the assumptions that underlay them. In particular, they considered their relationship with race, gender and sexuality.

Last, the discipline became – particularly within Europe – more self-reflective. It began to consider and evaluate its own approaches and methodologies. Histories of the US that had formerly been much respected and widely used were subject to growing criticism. These texts, it was argued, said more about the writers – and the context within which they undertook

their work – than about the subject or theme under consideration. Scholars increasingly asserted that these histories re-
flected the assumptions, aspirations and prejudices of those
who penned them.

Some accounts went further. Notions of 'reality' or an
absolute 'truth' were discarded as observers stressed the idea
that knowledge did not simply exist but was instead constructed. From this perspective, our perceptions and understandings are built entirely upon models and simulations. Life
is, in this sense, like a soap opera. In a celebrated, but
impenetrable account, Jean Baudrillard, a French cultural
theorist, suggested that 'all of Los Angeles and the America
surrounding it are no longer real, but of the order of the
hyperreal and simulation' (quoted in Hall et al. 1999: 245).
Paradoxically, however, Disneyland – which evokes the ordered certainties of traditional American small-town life – is
for many people rather more 'real'.

Alongside this, there was a turning away from what were
later to be dubbed 'master narratives'. Increasingly it was said
that the diverse and contrasting experiences of different groupings, particularly women and minorities, could not be reduced
to a single overarching explanation. The US could not be
understood, for example, simply through its experience as a
frontier society. Furthermore, many of the concepts and
categories that had hitherto been taken for granted began
to be questioned. The concept of 'race', for example, came
under scrutiny. Increasingly, scholars asserted, it was a social
construction rather than a biological category. Skin pigmenta-
tion or other physical attributes were only significant because
societies attached cultural importance to them and associated
certain ascribed characteristics with them.

SUMMARY

American Studies is an important academic discipline because
of the military, economic and cultural significance of the US.
The idea of America has, in itself, shaped popular thinking

across the globe. However, the settlement of the American continent and the character of the encounters between different racial and ethnic groupings have created a society that is, in itself, worthy of exploration. For its part, American Studies has evolved as a subject. It is increasingly prepared to look at the US – and its own approaches – in a critical way and challenge the concepts and categories that are often taken for granted. It has also broadened its scope so as to consider popular cultural forms such as television, film and music.

NOTES

1. During the 2003 Iraq war, Kennedy himself again warned that the US faced the prospect of 'imperial overstretch':

   It possesses the world's single largest national economy but faces huge trade and budget deficits and economic rivalries from an equally large European Union and a fast-growing China. It has taken on military commitments all over the globe, from the Balkans and Kuwait to Afghanistan and Korea. Its armed forces look colossal (as did Britain's in 1919), but its obligations look even larger. (Kennedy 2003)

2. In his study, *Not Like Us*, Richard Pells challenges the received wisdom. He suggests that the Americanisation of Europe and other continents was largely symbolic:

   The American impact, reputedly destructive of local and national traditions, was always restrained by Europe's disparate institutions and customs . . . To a considerable extent, Europeans resisted the standardization and homogeneity allegedly inflicted on them by their European masters. Instead, they adapted America's products and culture to their own needs.' (Pells 1997: 279)

ATTITUDES TOWARDS THE US: SEPTEMBER 11th AND AFTER

In recent years, perceptions of the US have shifted. At the beginning of the new century – as Table 1.1 suggests – significant majorities in Britain, France, Germany and Italy saw the US in positive terms. Opinion in Russia was very different partly perhaps because of resentments tied to the decline in its own global status.

As Table 1.1 indicates, opinion shifted as the US war on terrorism broadened out so as to encompass a commitment to the removal of Saddam Hussein and 'regime change' in Iraq. Despite the sense of shared shock and an initial wave of sympathy that had followed the terrorist attacks of 11 September 2001, attitudes towards the US took an increasingly negative form. For significant swathes of opinion in western Europe, the prospect of war in Iraq appeared to be a cavalier act of imperialism. In the Islamic nations, opposition to the Iraq war fused with hostility to other US policies in the Middle East. In Moslem eyes, the US was complicit in the repression of Palestinian national hopes because of its backing for the hardline Likud government in Israel. Against this background, by March 2003, the proportion of the population holding a favourable opinion of the US sank to an all-time low.

Table 1.1 Proportion of the population holding a favourable view of the US (percentages)

	1999–2000	2002	2003
Britain	83	75	48
France	62	63	31
Germany	78	61	25
Italy	76	70	34
Spain	50	—	14
Poland	86	79	50
Russia	37	61	28
Turkey	52	30	12

Source: adapted from The Pew Research Center for the People and the Press (2003), *America's Image Further Erodes, Europeans Want Weaker Ties*, 18 March, people-press.org/reports/display.php3?ReportID=175

Only some countries – most notably Britain and a number of nations in eastern Europe such as Poland,

Hungary and the Czech Republic – held out against the trend. Although – as war approached – significantly greater numbers of people in these countries saw the US in negative terms, there was markedly greater support for the US, and the war in Iraq. On this basis, Donald Rumsfeld, the US Secretary of Defense, drew a distinction between attitudes in what he dubbed the 'old' and the 'new' Europe. Asked about opposition to the Iraq war in Europe, he replied: 'You're thinking of Europe as Germany and France. I don't. I think that's "old Europe" . . . the center of gravity is shifting to the East . . . You look at vast numbers of other countries in Europe. They're not with France and Germany [regarding Iraq], they're with the United States' (quoted by M. Baker (2003), 'US: Rumsfeld's "Old" and "New" Europe Touches On Uneasy Divide', *Radio Free Europe / Radio Liberty*, www.rferl.org/nca/features/2003/01/24012003172118.asp).

THE UNITED STATES AND 'AMERICA'

American Studies almost always refers to the study of the United States. However, the term 'America' is a description of two continents. As Felipe Fernandez-Armesto records, those in other American countries complain 'that the citizens of one country have usurped the appellation of Americans', Felipe Fernandez-Armesto (2003), *The Americas: The History of a Hemisphere*, London: Weidenfeld and Nicolson. His book offers a challenging but useful introduction to the history of north, central and south America and the different ways in which the continents have been understood over the centuries.

2 AMERICAN STUDIES: COURSE CONTENT

American Studies is a **multidisciplinary** and **interdisciplinary** subject. It is multidisciplinary insofar as it rests upon a range of different subjects including history, politics, international relations, literature and popular culture. It is interdisciplinary when it brings the disciplines together so as to gain a greater understanding of a particular topic or theme. This section of the book offers an introduction to the different disciplines, and outlines the core concepts, institutions and processes that students may encounter. It also examines three interdisciplinary themes.

HISTORY

The first native Americans (or American 'Indians') are believed to have crossed from Siberia to Alaska during the last Ice Age. While some of the tribal societies that evolved were nomadic, others had a more settled character.

Although adventurers crossed the Atlantic from 1492 onwards – when Columbus landed in the Bahamas – and Spanish conquistadors seized the central American isthmus, the first permanent European settlement in what became US territory was founded at Jamestown (Virginia) in 1607. The Jamestown venture was a commercial expedition by an English company and it gave rise – over the decades that followed – to a hierarchical society governed by wealthy planters and merchants.

Many labourers initially made the journey as indentured servants. They paid the cost of their passage by agreeing to four- or five-year labour contracts. Nonetheless, despite the hardships that this entailed, there were opportunities for land ownership that were absent in England and significant numbers prospered.

In 1620 Puritan settlers landed in Massachusetts. In contrast with the Virginia settlers, they had a spiritual mission. They sought a 'purified' faith that eschewed the corruption, worldliness, and ritual of the European churches. They sought to construct God-fearing communities that might serve as a model to Christians across the globe. As John Winthrop, who became Governor of the Massachusetts Bay colony in 1830, told the others, 'we shall be as a City upon a Hill . . . The eyes of all people are upon us.'

By the early eighteenth century, the American colonies had an established character. Although subject to rule by the British crown and dominated by WASPs (white Anglo-Saxon Protestants) drawn from the British Isles, they attracted growing numbers from other European countries such as Holland, Germany and Sweden. While there were small numbers of free blacks, the slave population also grew and by 1770 represented about a third of the population in the southern states.

Table 2.1 The population of the American colonies, 1610–1790

Year	Population
1610	350
1650	50,368
1700	250,888
1750	1,170,760
1790	3,929,214

Source: adapted from University of North Florida (2003), *USDOC, Historical Statistics of the United States, Colonial Times to 1957, Series Z1; USDOC, Historical Statistics of the United States, Colonial Times to 1970, Series A 1–5*, www.unf.edu/~jperry/3622mat1.doc.

The right to vote was, as in England, tied to property ownership. However, because land ownership was more widely distributed, this extended the franchise to significant numbers of white men. While governors were appointed by the British authorities, there were also colonial assemblies that had a broadly representative character. There was increasing talk of rights, liberties and forms of government that were – at least to some degree – accountable to the people.

Independence

As the eighteenth century progressed, British policy seemed to threaten American interests. In 1763, a royal proclamation prohibited settlement west of the Appalachian mountains. Large numbers of troops were stationed in the colonies and they were – from 1764 – supported by revenue from a Stamp Act. Trade was regulated through the Navigation Acts and duties imposed. For their part, the American colonists had evaded or circumvented many of these measures. They had, for example, bought smuggled tea rather than pay the duties required by Britain. However, in 1773, the Tea Act provided financial relief for the British East India Company's tea exports so as to undermine the boycott. This, in turn, led to the 'Boston Tea Party'. Patriots, as American radicals were becoming known, threw chests of tea into the harbour.

The British authorities responded with repressive measures. Although there were still many loyalists in the colonies who feared mob rule and radical excesses, Patriots established the Continental Congress – which met for the first time in Philadelphia in September 1774 – bringing together representatives from most of the colonial assemblies.

Against this background, British troops sought to capture rebel leaders and supplies leading to skirmishes. A Continental army was formed by the colonists under the command of George Washington, although local militias played a pivotal role in the fighting. At the beginning of July 1776, the Congress approved the Declaration of Independence, written principally by Thomas Jefferson. It was an indictment of British rule and an assertion of rights and the importance of accountable government:

We hold these truths to be self-evident, that all men are created equal, that they are endowed by their Creator with certain unalienable rights, that among these are Life, Liberty, and the pursuit of Happiness. That to secure these rights, Governments are instituted among Men, deriving their just powers from the consent of the governed. That whenever any Form of Government becomes destructive of these ends, it is the Right of the People to alter or to abolish it, and to institute new Government.

Table 2.2 American war of independence – major battles

Date	Battle	Development
1775	Lexington	Attempts to capture Patriot leaders and supplies – American losses
	Concord	
	Bunker Hill	
1776	Trenton	American victories
1777	Saratoga	
1777–8		American forces beleaguered at Valley Forge
1778		Alliance concluded between the Americans and France
1780		British victories in the south
1781	Yorktown	British surrender

The Articles of Confederation – which established ties between the states and laid for a form of central government – were passed by Congress in 1777. They were only ratified by all the states in 1781.

Following the American and French victory at Yorktown, the British recognised American independence in the 1783 Treaty of Paris.

Origins and development of the United States

The political structures established under the Articles of Confederation were, however, weak. This led to the calling of a constitutional convention in Philadelphia (1787). The delegates, who later became known as the 'Founding Fathers' or 'Framers', agreed to the US Constitution. In 1789, George Washington took office as the first president. In 1791, the first ten amendments – the Bill of Rights – were added to the Constitution.

In 1803, the Louisiana Purchase doubled the size of the nation and added to the opportunities for westward expansion across the continent.

A three-year war with Britain began in 1812. Despite early losses and divided opinion about the war, the British were defeated at the Battle of New Orleans.

Reflecting growing American self-confidence, the US insisted – in the 1823 Monroe Doctrine – that the European powers should not interfere – or seek further colonies – in the Americas.

The industrial revolution 'took off' in the north-eastern states. During Andrew Jackson's presidency (1829–37), westward expansion continued, forcing the native-American tribes from the lands that they had traditionally occupied. At the same time, there was a significant increase in the numbers voting in elections. Although the franchise was still largely confined to white men, the era of mass politics began at this time.

In 1845 Texas – which had been a separate republic since 1836 – was annexed. War with Mexico and gold discoveries opened up California. In a celebrated phrase, the conquest of the continent – from the Atlantic to the Pacific – was now said to be the US's 'manifest destiny'.

Civil War

Although abolished in the north, the southern states retained slavery. There were growing tensions between the northern and southern states. In part, these were economic in nature. They were, however, fuelled by abolitionist sentiment in the north and concerns about the future of the territories that had been settled through westward expansion.

The victory of the Republican Party candidate – Abraham

Lincoln – in the 1860 presidential election added to southern fears that slavery was under threat and triggered the secession of South Carolina from the US. It was followed by ten other states that collectively formed the Confederate States of America. Naming Jefferson Davis as its president, the Confederacy was committed – above all else – to the preservation of slavery. For its part, the north denied the rights of states to secede from the union. Fighting broke out after southern forces fired on Fort Sumter, a federal government garrison in Charleston (South Carolina) harbour. Over the four years of civil war that followed, 618,000 were killed by enemy fire, typhoid and dysentery.

The south surrendered at Appomattox in April 1865. The southern states were placed under military occupation. Constitutional amendments built upon the Emancipation Proclamation that had been issued during the war, and ended slavery. However, the hopes associated with Reconstruction were not fulfilled. White hegemony was progressively re-established and segregation, by which African-Americans are denied the right to vote and at the same time relegated to separate and profoundly unequal facilities, was imposed across the south. In 1896, the US Supreme Court ruled, in *Plessy* v. *Ferguson*, that segregation was constitutional.

Industry, immigration and the closing of the 'frontier'

The 1862 Homestead Act allowed settlers in the west to claim 160 acres of land as their own if they had lived on it and farmed it for at least five years. At the end of the decade – in 1869 – the transcontinental railroad was completed linking the east and west coasts. These developments created the conditions for the expansion of the territory under settlement and the emergence of towns and cities across the country. By 1890, there were no substantial areas of unsettled land and – according to the Census Bureau – the frontier had 'closed'. There was a parallel and brutal process. Native Americans were forced onto reservations and most of the buffalo – on which many of the tribes depended – were killed off. At Little

Big Horn (1876), the Sioux and Cheyenne wiped out General George Custer's forces. The final battle between the US and native Americans was at Wounded Knee in 1890. At least 150 Sioux and 25 soldiers were killed.

At the same time, during the closing decades of the nineteenth century, industrialisation accelerated. Real Gross Domestic Product (GDP), or national output adjusted to take accounts of changes in the price level, doubled within twenty years. The process was based around 'heavy' industries such as coal, iron and steel and was tied to the emergence of national companies and a market that stretched across the US. It also gave rise to the 'Gilded Age'. Vast fortunes were made and family names such as Rockefeller, Carnegie and Vanderbilt became synonymous with wealth. At the same time, in the cities, millions still lived in squalor and poverty.

Table 2.3 Real GDP ($bn) (chained 1996 dollars)

Year	Real GDP (billions of 1996 dollars)
1800	$7.19
1810	$10.30
1820	$14.10
1830	$20.30
1840	$30.20
1850	$44.90
1860	$73.80
1870	$99.20
1880	$161.00
1890	$216.00
1900	$311.00

Note: 'chained' dollars are based upon the prices of goods and services but are adjusted to allow for both inflation and price falls. This permits meaningful comparisons to be made between different years.

Source: adapted from Economic History Services (2003), *What was the GDP then?*, www.eh.net/hmit/gdp/gdp_answer.php

It was also an era of mass immigration. Traditionally, immigrants were drawn from countries such as Ireland and Germany. By the early twentieth century, increasing numbers were drawn from eastern and southern Europe.

Table 2.4 Immigration rate by decade, 1871–1920

Year	Total immigrants	Rate per 1,000 of the US population
1871–80	2,812,191	6.2
1881–90	5,246,613	9.2
1891–1900	3,687,564	5.3
1901–10	8,795,386	10.4
1911–20	5,735,811	5.7

Source: adapted from J. W. Wright (1999), *The New York Times Almanac 2000*, New York: Penguin, p. 306.

The scale of the differences between rich and poor, the corruption associated with urban politics, and fears that mass immigration might lead to the dissolution of the nation, contributed to the rise of progressivism. The progressive movement sought to place constraints upon 'trusts' (anti-competitive structures such as cartels and monopolies), restructure the political process through greater participation, and use the power of government to promote social reform.

The interwar years

After a short-lived recession (1920–1) the 1920s were – for many – a period of relative prosperity. Per capita GDP – a measure of average living standards – increased significantly. In particular, consumer industries – symbolised by the automobile – came of age. However, agricultural prices fell and the rural population was largely excluded from the boom. There were also cultural tensions. Prohibition was imposed and immigration severely restricted.

Table 2.5 Per capita GDP, 1910–30

Year	Per capita GDP
1910	$4,850
1920	$5,410
1930	$6,105

Source: adapted from Economic History Services (2003), *What was the GDP then?*, www.eh.net/hmit/gdp/gdp_answer.php

The decade ended in depression. As the growth of demand slowed up, company stockpiles grew. Large numbers had purchased shares contributing to feverish price rises on the stock market. Indeed, such prices bore no relation to the earnings that companies might make over the years to come. On 29 October 1929, the bubble burst. There was panic selling of shares and their prices tumbled. Those who believed that they held – through share ownership – significant wealth found themselves penniless. Against this background, banks were forced to close and companies' investment plans were slashed. Unemployment rose from 3.2 per cent of the work-force in 1929 to 24.9 per cent in 1933.

In 1933, Franklin D. Roosevelt became president. He introduced the Emergency Banking Relief Act, the Agricultural Adjustment Act and other measures ushering in the New Deal. Although Roosevelt's Republican predecessor, Herbert Hoover, had taken some initial steps, the New Deal led the federal government to become much more involved in economic and social affairs. A second New Deal began in 1935 when steps were taken to strengthen the position of organised labour and provide employment – through the Works Progress Administration (WPA) – for those who were out of work.

War and afterwards

Following the Japanese attack on the US naval base at Pearl Harbor in December 1941, the US joined the Second World War. The wartime alliance brought the US together with Britain and the USSR. The conflict came to an end in 1945 with the defeat of Germany (May) and Japan (August). The Japanese surrender followed US atom bomb attacks on the cities of Hiroshima and Nagasaki.

The wartime alliance quickly fell apart as fears grew about Soviet expansionism in eastern Europe and Asia. In 1947, the US committed itself – through the Truman doctrine – to a policy of containment. It pledged itself to support 'free people' across the world. The countries of western Europe began to receive large-scale financial assistance from the US through Marshall Aid. In 1949, the USSR gained the atomic bomb. Against this background, the anti-communist mood in the US became much more pronounced. The drive against alleged Soviet agents and communist sympathisers became known as 'McCarthyism' after the Wisconsin senator who spearheaded it.

A long and sustained postwar economic boom laid the basis for suburbanisation and the emergence of a substantial middle class. At the same time, long-established certainties were challenged. In *Brown* v. *Board of Education* (Topeka, Kansas, 1954), the US Supreme Court ruled that segregation in public schools was unconstitutional. The judgement was followed by direct action. In 1955 the bus boycott in Montgomery, Alabama, marked the beginnings of the civil rights movement. A decade of protests – involving sit-ins, the freedom rides and marches – led to the passage of the 1964 Civil Rights Act and the 1965 Voting Rights Act.

In 1964, President Lyndon Johnson talked of a Great Society and announced the War on Poverty: 'Our aim is not only to relieve the symptom of poverty, but to cure it and, above all, to prevent it.' The 'War' rested on the Economic Opportunity Act, the Job Corps, 'Head Start' programmes for children from disadvantaged backgrounds, and extended health provision through the creation of Medicare (for the elderly) and Medicaid (for the poor). Johnson's presidency was, however, increasingly dragged down by its escalating commitment to war in Vietnam.

The late 1960s are widely seen as an era of radicalism and rebellion. The civil rights movement gave way to calls for black power. Opposition to the war in Vietnam became a mass movement. Traditionalist attitudes towards gender roles and sexuality were challenged by feminism and gay campaigners. New youth cultures emerged alongside shifts in the character of popular music. In what some observers depict as a backlash against cultural and political change, Richard Nixon, the Republican candidate, was elected in 1968 and won an overwhelming re-election victory in 1972. However, his administration became mired in the Watergate scandal, forcing Nixon to resign in August 1974. His resignation – and the Vietnam War – contributed to widespread public disillusionment with office-holders. Trust in government fell significantly and the presidency was weakened.

The Reagan revolution, the 'new economy' and 9/11

Despite an initial recession, Ronald Reagan's period of office (1981–9) is remembered for sustained economic growth. Some observers attribute this to the supply-side economic policies – which included significant tax cuts – pursued by his administration. By 1984, when Reagan was re-elected, his campaign advertisements were boasting that 'it's morning again in America'. His second term was, however, tarnished by the 'Iran-Contra' affair that seemed to suggest that Reagan's 'hands off' style of management had allowed subordinates to pursue their own ideas and plans.

Although Bill Clinton – the Democratic Party candidate – won the presidency in 1992 and 1996, albeit on a centre-right platform, the conservative 'revolution' initiated by Reagan continued to reshape the American public policy agenda. In 1994, the Republican Party won majorities in both houses of Congress. Although the outcome of the 2000 election was declared a month after the vote took place, George W. Bush – who campaigned on the basis of 'compassionate conservatism' – gained the presidency.

While conservatives – who stressed low tax rates, deregulation, self-reliance and limited government – won the economic argument, they were less successful in the social and cultural arena. Although there were significant differences between the major cities and more rural areas, society seemed to be shifting in a more liberal and pluralistic direction. Public opinion was largely unmoved by calls for Bill Clinton's impeachment and became more tolerant of alternative lifestyles. Calls for same-sex marriage began to gain a hearing.

The September 11th attacks transformed perceptions of the Bush presidency. Subsequent military intervention in Afghanistan led to the removal of the Taliban regime that had provided sanctuary for Al-Qaeda operatives. In 2003, the US constructed a 'coalition of the willing' and – claiming that Saddam Hussein's regime possessed 'weapons of mass destruction' – invaded Iraq.

GOVERNMENT AND POLITICS

The American system of government rests upon the US Constitution of 1787. The Constitution – which consists of seven Articles and twenty-seven later amendments – established three branches of government and specified their roles. In place of centralised rule, which could have led to the tyranny associated with many of the European monarchies at the time, there was to be a separation of powers.

- Laws would be made by Congress. The Constitution also granted the legislature specific (or enumerated) powers. These are listed in Article I, Section 8, and included the power 'to regulate commerce' between the states.

- Under the terms of the Constitution, Congress was to consist of two chambers: the House of Representatives – which was to be elected every two years – and the Senate. In the early years of the US, senators were appointed by the different states. However, the seventeenth amendment to the Constitution (1913) established that senators should – like those serving in the House – be elected directly by the people. Senators serve six-year terms.

- The US president who heads the executive branch of government was to be elected every four years. The Constitution assigned him some specific powers. He was to be commander-in-chief of the armed forces. He could nominate federal judges, ambassadors and senior government officials. He could sign treaties with other countries and veto proposed laws passed by Congress.

- There was to be a supreme court and other – 'inferior' or lower – federal courts.

The separation of powers between the legislative, executive and judicial branches of government was reinforced and extended by checks and balances. The founding fathers who wrote the Constitution ensured that the powers of each branch was limited or constrained by the other branches.

- Although the president is commander-in-chief, only Congress can declare war.

- The president's ability to conclude treaties was constrained by a provision that their ratification required a two-thirds majority in the Senate.

- Many of a president's appointments – including those of federal court judges and senior government officials – also need Senate confirmation, albeit by only a simple majority.

- Presidential vetoes can be overridden if there is a two-thirds majority in both houses of Congress.

The US Constitution also rested upon two other principles. First, it established the federal character of the US. Power was not only separated – or in some accounts shared – between different branches of the national government but also divided between the national government and individual states. Second, the first ten amendments to the Constitution which were added in 1791, and known as the Bill of Rights, placed important constraints upon government institutions by guaranteeing individual liberties.

- The first amendment, for example, established freedom of speech and religion.

- The fourth amendment prohibited 'unreasonable searches and seizures'.

- The fifth amendment demanded that those facing punishment for an alleged crime be granted 'due process of law'.

- The eighth amendment forbade the imposition of 'cruel and unusual punishments'.

However, although the wording of the Constitution has remained largely unaltered, the character of the US political system has changed radically over the past two centuries. In particular, the power of the federal government has grown. Correspondingly – as conservative observers emphasise – the states and the individual citizen have lost their former rights.

Why has this happened? In part, it is because some of the words and phrases in the Constitution have a loose or elastic character. For example, alongside the enumerated powers assigned to Congress in Article I of the Constitution, it also allowed Congress 'to make all laws which shall be necessary and proper for carrying into execution the foregoing powers, and all other powers vested by this Constitution in the Government of the United States'. In another loosely worded phrase, it also permitted Congress to raise taxes for the country's 'general welfare'. These clauses laid the basis for a growing number of 'implied powers' alongside those directly specified in the Constitution.

Congress

What are the defining characteristics of Congress?

- To become law, bills must be passed by the House of Representatives and the Senate. The legislative process is long, complex and difficult. The overwhelming majority of bills never become law. In 1996, for example, 6,808 bills were introduced, but only 337 were adopted (Davidson and Oleszek 1998: 278). Once passed in an identical form by both chambers, bills are then passed to the president, who has the power of veto.

- Both chambers have oversight responsibilities. They monitor the actions of the administration and the work of the executive departments and agencies that constitute the federal bureaucracy. The Senate Foreign Relations Committee's scrutiny of the White House's military operations in southeast Asia in the latter half of the 1960s is often cited. However, observers are divided about the overall effectiveness of oversight activity.

- Congress has the power to remove leading officials including the president by initiating *impeachment* proceedings. Two presidents – Andrew Johnson and Bill Clinton – have been impeached but were later acquitted.

1. *The House of Representatives*
The House is directly elected by the people in single-member constituencies drawn up on the basis of population.

Those who serve have to be twenty-five years old or more, and have been a US citizen for at least seven years.

Since 1911, the House has had 435 members. Each represents – following the 2000 census – an average population of 646,952.

The House is a large and heterogeneous chamber. Its members face re-election every two years. Members therefore have to be district oriented.

The leader of the majority party in the House takes the post of Speaker. In contrast with his or her British counterpart, the Speaker is an active and influential partisan.

2. *The Senate*
Each state elects two senators regardless of size.

The Constitution stipulates that senators must be thirty years old or more and have been citizens for nine years or more.

Although senators serve six-year terms, there is a rolling system of election. One-third is elected every two years.

While the vice-president is – according to Article I of the Constitution – 'president' of the Senate, he takes the chair only if a tied vote seems likely. In these circumstances, he holds a casting vote.

The customs of the chamber ensure that each senator has much more influence than the individual House member. There are opportunities to block – or filibuster – legislation. Under Senate rules, debate can only be curtailed – and a filibuster prevented – if there is a three-fifths majority of the full Senate.

The Senate has 'advice and consent' powers. It can confirm or reject the appointment of senior federal officers such as cabinet secretaries, federal judges and ambassadors. It also has responsibility for the ratification of treaties.

Congress has been subject to criticism. Those in the House of Representatives – who face elections every two years – must campaign on a more or less permanent basis. There are also, it is said, too many barriers hindering the passage of legislation. Members of Congress are instead geared towards the immediate needs of the constituents they represent in their home district or state. This has led to pork-barrel politics. Members seek amendments to legislation that allocate funding, resources and the provision of employment to their own constituency. This, it is said, distorts legislation and corrupts government programmes. In the aftermath of the *Challenger* space shuttle disaster in 2003, Senator John McCain suggested that $167 million of 'pork' had been added to legislation funding the National Aeronautics and Space Administration (NASA) and that this may have had an impact on NASA's safety programmes (*Pianin* 2003). The making of public policy is therefore biased towards local and special interests at the expense of the national interest.

The president

Table 2.6 US presidents, 1953–present

President	Party	Election(s)	Period of office
Dwight D. Eisenhower	Republican	1952 1956	1953–61
John F. Kennedy	Democrat	1960	1961–3
Lyndon B. Johnson	Democrat	1964	1963–9

Richard M. Nixon	Republican	1968	1969–74
		1972	
Gerald R. Ford	Republican		1974–7
Jimmy Carter	Democrat	1976	1977–81
Ronald Reagan	Republican	1980	1981–9
		1984	
George H. W. Bush	Republican	1988	1989–93
William J. Clinton	Democrat	1992	1993–2001
		1996	
George W. Bush	Republican	2000	2001–

Alongside the changing character of the national government, there have been other long-term shifts. In particular, the powers of the executive branch have grown since the Constitution was written. Indeed, in a celebrated phrase, Arthur Schlesinger Jr referred, in the early 1970s, to the 'imperial presidency'. He was suggesting that the contemporary president (and he had Richard Nixon in his sights), commanded powers comparable with an emperor. Although presidential power has fluctuated since the 1970s, some have described George W. Bush's presidency – in the period following the attacks of 11 September 2001 – in similar terms.

There are seven principal reasons for the growth in presidential power.

1 Particular presidential styles or decisions by individual presidents set precedents that would be followed by their successors. Their actions enlarged the scope of the office and changed expectations about its nature.

2 Congress is a slow and bureaucratic institution. As Clinton Rossiter asserted in a celebrated phrase: 'secrecy, dispatch, unity, continuity, and access to information – the ingredients of successful diplomacy – are properties of his office, and Congress . . . possesses none of them' (1963: 26). Furthermore, although there were significant divisions after the First World War and during the Vietnam era, there was – for much of the twentieth century – a broad consensus about the character of US foreign policy. Following the Japanese

attacks on Pearl Harbor, Congress unanimously backed
a declaration of war. Faced by Soviet communism, few
dissented from the Cold War goal of *containment*.
Congress therefore held back and acquiesced in
administration decisions.

3   At times, the Supreme Court has also played a role in
bolstering presidential authority. In 1936, in the case of
US v. *Curtiss-Wright Export Corporation*, the Court
upheld a 1934 Act permitting the president to embargo
arms shipments to foreign combatants in a south
American war.

4   Although the Constitution stipulates that treaties
require the 'advice and consent' of the Senate,
successive presidents have circumvented this by drawing
up executive agreements with the heads of foreign
governments:
(a) In 1940, President Franklin Roosevelt used an
executive agreement to 'swap' fifty destroyers for air
bases in the British Empire.
(b) In 1973 an executive agreement signed between
President Richard Nixon and South Vietnam promised
that the US would 'respond with full force' to North
Vietnamese violations of the Paris peace agreement that
had ended American military intervention in Vietnam.

5   Most importantly of all, the president's constitutional
power as commander-in-chief allowed him to deploy
troops and undertake military initiatives that had far-
reaching strategic importance:
(a) In October 1983, US marines occupied Grenada
and removed the radical New Jewel movement from
power. Congress played a negligible role in this.
(b) In April 1986, the Reagan administration ordered
American air attacks on Tripoli and other targets in
Libya. President Reagan argued that the action had
been self-defence, and fell within his responsibilities as
commander-in-chief.
(c) The Reagan administration also fought a covert and
– critics asserted, illegal – war in Nicaragua by backing

the rebel Contras during the mid-1980s.

(d) In December 1989, President Bush sent US troops into Panama, arresting the country's military ruler, General Manuel Noriega, who had been accused of involvement in the international drug trade.

(e) President Clinton deployed troops or took other forms of military action in a number of countries including the former Yugoslavia, Haiti, Iraq and the Sudan.

6 The president has the constitutional right to veto legislation passed by Congress (see Table 2.7). If he wishes to do this, Article I specifies that he must send a statement to Congress within ten days of a bill being passed, setting out his reasons for refusing to sign it. A presidential veto can only be overridden by a two-thirds majority in both houses, which is difficult to muster. The president can also employ the *pocket veto*. If the president does not sign a bill within a ten-day period, and Congress has, by this time, adjourned, the bill does not pass into law.[1]

Table 2.7 Presidential vetoes

The Constitution allows the president the power to veto legislation passed by Congress. If he does this, the bill falls unless his veto is overridden by a two-thirds majority in both chambers. This is very difficult to muster.

Years in office	President	Regular vetoes	Vetoes overridden	Pocket vetoes
1953–61	Eisenhower	73	2	108
1961–3	Kennedy	12	0	9
1963–9	Johnson	16	0	14
1969–74	Nixon	26	7	17
1974–7	Ford	48	12	18
1977–81	Carter	13	2	18
1981–9	Reagan	39	9	39
1989–93	Bush	29	1	17
1993–2001	Clinton	36	2	1
2001–	Bush	—	—	—

Note: These figures do not include the line-item veto that was to be declared unconstitutional. There have been disputes about the use of the pocket veto and the circumstances in which it can be deployed.

Sources: adapted from H. W. Stanley and R. G. Niemi (2000), *Vital Statistics on American Politics 1999–2000*, Washington DC, CQ Press, p. 256, and N. J. Ornstein, T. E. Mann and M. J. Malbin (2002), *Vital Statistics on Congress 2001–2002*, Washington DC, The AEI Press, p. 151.

7 The president can issue executive orders. The authority for these stems from the powers assigned to the president under the Constitution, legislation already passed by Congress, or from his role in heading the executive branch.

The overall picture is not, however, one-sided. Alongside his powers, the president is also subject to limits and constraints.

- The Senate can exercise its constitutional prerogatives. In 1919–20 when President Woodrow Wilson submitted the Treaty of Versailles, it was rejected.

- The 1973 War Powers Resolution asserted that – unless Congress had declared war – it could require the president to withdraw US forces involved in overseas hostilities within a period of sixty days. A further thirty days was permitted if the president certified that further military action was necessary to disengage US military personnel from a conflict safely. The Resolution also called upon the president to consult with Congress 'in every possible instance' before deploying troops.

- In 1980, President Jimmy Carter withdrew SALT-II – the Strategic Arms Limitation Treaty – that he had concluded with the USSR, once it had become clear that, in the aftermath of the Soviet invasion of Afghanistan, the Treaty would be rejected by the Senate.

- Congress has also used its 'power of the purse'. In December 1970 it prohibited funding for combat troops in Cambodia and in June 1973, this was extended to the remainder of south-east Asia.

- Presidents have, in practice, paid heed to Congressional sentiment. President George Bush sought – and gained – Congressional backing before hostilities began in the 1991 Gulf War.

- In 1996, Congress played a part in the active shaping of US foreign policy by passing the Cuban Liberty and Democratic Solidarity Act, also known – after the names of its initial sponsors – as Helms-Burton. The Act strengthened the economic embargo on Cuba, ruled out negotiations with the Castro government, and imposed penalties on foreign companies investing in Cuba (Dumbrell 2000: 92).

- In the wake of September 11th, President George W. Bush felt obliged to seek Congressional backing for retaliatory and preventative action against the terrorists and their backers. In October 2002, the House of Representatives agreed to the use of force against Iraq by 296–133. The Senate vote was 77–23.

Table 2.8 Supreme Court Chief Justices, 1946–present

Period of Office	Chief Justice
1946–53	Fred M. Vinson
1953–69	Earl Warren
1969–86	Warren E. Burger
1986–	William H. Rehnquist

Source: adapted from H. W. Stanley and R. G. Niemi (1998), *Vital Statistics on American Politics, 1997–1998*, Washington DC, Congressional Quarterly, pp. 268–9.

THE US SUPREME COURT

The role of the Supreme Court was not specified in the Constitution but progressively evolved. It undertakes *judicial review*. The Court which has – since 1869 – consisted of nine judges, interprets the Constitution by ruling upon the constitutionality of laws or the actions of government officials in cases brought forward to them. If a federal or state law is deemed unconstitutional, it is struck down. The power of judicial review – and the growing emphasis on the implied rights that were discerned in the Constitution – placed the Supreme Court at the heart of political decision-making.

- In 1954 – in *Brown* v. *Board of Education* (Topeka, Kansas) – the Court ruled that segregation in the public (or taxpayer-funded) schools was unconstitutional. By consigning African-American children to separate neighbourhood schools, they were not being accorded the 'equal protection of laws' guaranteed in Amendment XIV.

- In 1973 – in *Roe* v. *Wade* – the Court built upon an implied 'right to privacy' that had been established earlier and asserted that women had a right to an abortion. The ruling provoked bitter controversy. Its critics included evangelical Christians who opposed abortion on moral grounds and those who believed that the Constitution should be interpreted in more literal terms. It contributed to the growth of the Christian right, who subsequently became a potent force within the conservative movement and the Republican Party.

- In 2003, in *Lawrence et al.* v. *Texas*, the Court ruled that the right to privacy extended to homosexuality. A Texas law – which had outlawed gay sex – was thereby struck down. As Justice Anthony Kennedy argued: 'The petitioners are entitled to respect for their private lives. The State cannot demean their existence or control their destiny by making their private sexual conduct a crime' (Pianin 2003).

Nonetheless, there are constraints on the Court. In contrast with a legislature, it follows legal procedures. Although earlier rulings are sometimes overturned, there is a degree of respect for precedent. The judges cannot decide issues on the basis of their personal preferences but must instead be guided by a reading of the Constitution. The Court does not, furthermore, have enforcement powers. The process of desegregation in schools – ordered by the Brown ruling but resisted by many white southerners – depended upon the executive branch.

Federalism

The US Constitution also rests on federalism. Power is shared between the federal – or national – government and the individual states. This goes beyond devolution insofar as the states have entrenched powers that are drawn from the Constitution.

Article II assigned a formal role – through the Electoral College – to the states in the choosing of a president. In Article IV, the states are assured that their boundaries will not be changed without their consent and they will be given equal representation in the US Senate. Article V specifies that the Constitution can only be amended with the assent of three-quarters of the states.

Amendment X, which formed part of the Bill of Rights, and was added in 1791, was intended to ensure that these states were not subsumed by the national authorities. It states that 'the powers not delegated to the United States by the Constitution, nor prohibited by it to the States, are reserved to the States respectively, or to the people'. In other words, those decision-making powers not specifically assigned to the federal govern-ment are the prerogative of the individual states. The states can make their own laws on these matters. As a consequence, there are significant differences between the states.

- Health-care provision varies considerably.

- Vermont allows same-sex couples to enter into 'civil unions' that have some of the attributes of marriage. Restrictions on gambling and alcohol depend upon state law.

- While twelve states have abolished capital punishment, the majority have the death penalty on their statute books.

However, since the writing of the Constitution, the power of the national government has grown and the states have lost much fo their former autonomy. This can be attributed to three principal developments. The Civil War (1861–5) established that the US was not a mere association between the states but a unified country. Constitutional amendments and Supreme Court rulings eventually created national rights that the states could not deny to their citizens. The authority of the national government was also bolstered by the growing importance of its role in managing the economy. These developments have led some commentators to suggest that the US is now, to all intents and purposes, a unitary state in which power is centralised.

The Reagan administration was committed to reversing what it portrayed as the usurpation of state powers by the federal government. It offered *New Federalism*. However, although grants-in-aid from the national government to the states were rationalised and reduced, few other measures were implemented.

However, some laws – most notably the 1996 Personal Responsibility and Work Opportunity Act (welfare reform) – and a number of US Supreme Court rulings have extended 'states' rights:

- In 1995, in *United States* v. *Lopez*, the Court restricted the interpretation of the interstate commerce clause of the Constitution. It said that it could not be used – as it was in the 1990 Gun Free School Zones Act – to prohibit the possession of a gun within 1,000 feet of a school. By reading the clause narrowly, the Court limited the powers constitutionally assigned to the federal government. The circumscription of the interstate commerce clause was extended still further in *United States* v. *Morrison* (2000) which struck down a core provision of the 1994 Violence against Women Act.

- *Kimel* v. *Florida Board of Regents* (2000) established that states have sovereign immunity and are protected from some lawsuits. The judgement struck down the Age Discrimination in Employment Act.

The states responded to the changing political environment by becoming more assertive, imaginative and innovative. They began to promote their own interests more forcefully through organisations such as the National Governors' Association, the US Conference of Mayors, the National League of Cities and the National Council of State Legislatures. Furthermore, a *culture of innovation* emerged at state level. The states pioneered radical tax cutting, school choice and law enforcement.

However, the states encountered difficulties in 2000–2. Tax revenue fell as a consequence of economic downturn. There were also more 'unfunded mandates'. These included the measures that the states had to adopt in extending 'homeland security'.

Elections

US presidents are elected every four years. If, however, the president dies in office or resigns, the vice-president takes his place. There is a two-and-a-half month transition period between the election (which is held on the first Tuesday after the first Monday in November) and inauguration day (20 January).

The US Constitution established an indirect system of election for the presidency. Each state is assigned a number of Electors based upon its representation in Congress (which is, in turn, based upon its population). There is a process of reapportionment every ten years to account for population shifts. The Electors – who are selected on the basis of the vote among the people in each state – constitute a 'College' that formally chooses the president. Although the system is widely regarded as an anachronism, it generally attracted little attention because it almost always gave the presidency to the candidate who had won a majority of the popular vote across the country. However, in 2000, a majority of those who voted backed Al Gore, the Democratic candidate. Following a protracted and bitter dispute about the winner of the vote in Florida, its Electoral College Vote was assigned to George W. Bush. He thereby gained the presidency, albeit by the narrowest of margins.

US elections have long been characterised by low levels of turnout. In 2000, just 51.2 per cent of the voting-age population cast a ballot.

Election campaigns, the mood of the nation, and the ways in which issues are presented can pull voters towards a particular candidate. In Congressional contests, the incumbent is almost always re-elected. However, election outcomes are also shaped by long-term structural variables. The major parties represent distinct social blocs. The Democrats draw much of their support from the minorities, women (particularly single women), lower income groupings, and the larger cities that serve as immigrant 'gateways'. The Republicans attract disproportionate numbers of votes from among whites (particularly men) and the more rural 'heartland' states.

Political parties

Since its early years, the US has always had a two-party system. Since the 1850s, the Democrats and the Republicans (or GOP – Grand Old Party) have been dominant. Although there are minor parties such as the Greens, the Reform Party and the Libertarian Party, they are either peripheral or have been short-lived. In the 2000 presidential election, for example, they attracted less than 4 per cent of the vote (see Table 2.9).

Why have minor parties failed to make an electoral breakthrough? There are seven principal reasons:

1. Many of the attempts to build alternatives to the Republicans and Democrats have been made by groupings associated with the political fringes. Their thinking is far removed from the mainstream.
2. Many minor parties have been ridden by factional rivalries and internal tensions.

3. There are administrative and legal obstacles. Many states require that candidates gain a certain number of signatures before their names can be placed on the ballot. The principal parties need only submit a limited number.

4. Congressmen represent single-member districts. There is a simple plurality – or 'first-the-the-post' – electoral system, and few people will vote for a small party that they believe has no realistic prospect of success.

5. There are also financial difficulties. Modern election campaigns depend upon television commercials and direct mail. They are therefore capital-intensive.

6. For many individuals and campaigns, interest-group activity offers a more effective avenue of influence than the formation of a party.

7. Minor party votes are often a function of voter-discontent. At times of relative prosperity and in periods of social cohesion, there is little to sustain their protests against 'establishment' politicians.

Table 2.9 The 2000 presidential election – minor party candidates

Candidate (Party)	Number of votes	Percentage of the vote
Ralph Nader (Green)	2,882,955	2.74
Patrick J. Buchanan (Reform)	448,895	0.42
Harry Browne (Libertarian)	384,431	0.36
Howard Phillips (Constitution)	98,020	0.09
John S. Hagelin (Natural Law)	83,714	0.08
James E. Harris, Jr (Socialist Workers)	7,378	0.01
L. Neil Smith (Libertarian)	5,775	0
David McReynolds (Socialist)	5,602	0

Note: Only those gaining over 5,000 votes have been included. Six further candidates – whose votes ranged between 161 and 4,795 – have been excluded from the table.
  Source: adapted from Federal Election Commission (2001), *2000 Presidential Popular Vote Summary for all candidates listed on at least one state ballot*, www.fec.gov/pubrec/fe2000/prespop.htm

Although the Democrats and Republicans dominate the American political process, influential commentators suggest that they are in decline:

'The two parties are in full retreat in all the areas that they have traditionally dominated. No matter whether it is selecting candidates, fundraising, running campaigns, mobilising voters, or co-ordinating government, the argument is that the parties have become less and less relevant. In short, the parties are no longer doing the things which parties are even minimally expected to do. (Bailey 1990: 12)

According to those who talk in these terms, the process of party decline has had significant consequences. It has contributed to low levels of turnout in elections and the *individualisation* of politics. There is little voting discipline among members of Congress and the state legislatures. This impedes decision-making and the passage of legislation.

The party decline model has, however, been challenged.

- Although the proportion of voters regarding themselves as 'independents' rather than party identifiers has grown, there are – in practice – relatively few 'pure' independents. Instead, most 'lean' towards either the Democrats or Republicans.

- The parties have also made sustained attempts to recapture the nomination process. Within both, the individual backed by the party 'establishment' has become the presidential candidate.

- The parties began to establish more pro-active forms of national leadership during the 1970s. They established permanent headquarters, comprehensive databases of supporters and websites. They also became much more involved in fund-raising activities.

Pressure groups

Pressure groups and lobbying activities are a particularly important feature of the American political process. They direct their efforts towards all three branches of the federal government, state authorities and local forms of government.

As well as lobbying decision-makers and issuing advertisements, pressure groups also intervene in elections. Political action committees – which are established by groups and companies – contribute to candidates' campaign funds. Furthermore, some organisations produce 'voter guides' during pre-election periods. Although they do not explicitly call for a vote for or against a particular candidate, their preferred choice is often readily evident. In the run-up to the November 2000 elections, the Christian Coalition of America distributed 70 million voter guides throughout all fifty states.

Groups can also submit amicus curiae briefs when a case is under consideration by the courts. In some celebrated cases, groups have 'sponsored' a litigant by providing funding and the services of lawyers. In 1954, the National Association for the Advancement of Colored People 'sponsored' a number of school desegegration cases.

In a federal system of government, many decisions are made at a state rather than a national level. Interest groups, companies and the lobbyists who act on their behalf, therefore have a presence in the different state capitals as well as Washington DC. Indeed, a 2003 study of thirty-nine states suggested that $715 million was spent by lobbyists in the different state capitals during the course of 2002. As the Center for Public Integrity, which conducted the survey, recorded: 'More than 34,000 of those interests – companies, issue organizations, labor unions and others – hired a whopping 42,000 individuals to do just that, averaging almost 6 lobbyists – and almost $130,000 – per legislator' (Center for Public Integrity 2003).

A 2001 study by *Fortune*, a business magazine, offered a picture of the degree of influence that particular groups had gained (see Table 2.10). It asked Washington 'insiders' to rate key pressure groups.

Table 2.10 Washington's 'power 25', 2001

Group	Overall Rank	Previous Rank	Democratic Rank	GOP Rank
National Rifle Association of America	1	2	2	1
American Association of Retired Persons	2	1	1	3
National Federation of Independent Business	3	2	6	2
American Israel Public Affairs Committee	4	4	3	4
Association of Trial Lawyers of America	5	6	5	7
American Federation of Labor-Congress of Industrial Organizations	6	5	4	12
Chamber of Commerce of the United States of America	7	7	9	5
National Beer Wholesalers Association	8	19	28	6
National Association of Realtors	9	15	24	8
National Association of Manufacturers	10	14	26	9
National Association of Home Builders of the United States	11	16	17	15
American Medical Association	12	13	12	18
American Hospital Association	13	31	15	17
National Education Association of the United States	14	9	7	34
American Farm Bureau Federation	15	21	29	11
Motion Picture Association of America	16	17	8	23
National Association of Broadcasters	17	20	13	19
National Right to Life Committee	18	8	31	10
Health Insurance Association of America	19	25	14	22
National Restaurant Association	20	10	34	13
National Governors Association	21	12	25	20
Recording Industry Association of America	22	40	16	28
American Bankers Association	23	11	23	27
Pharmaceutical Research & Manufacturers of America	24	28	27	29
International Brotherhood of Teamsters	25	23	11	41

Source: adapted from Fortune.com (2001), *The Power 25: Top Lobbying Groups*, May 28, www.fortune.com/fortune/power25 and J. H. Birnbaum (2001), *Power, 25 2001: Whose Party Is It?*, 2 August, www.fortune.com/fortune/washington/0,15704,373095,00.html

THE US AND THE WORLD (FOREIGN POLICY AND INTERNATIONAL RELATIONS)

What considerations determine, shape and guide US foreign and defence policy? There are different answers to this question.

Some theorists adopt a *realist* approach. Countries, they assert, pursue their own national interest and are engaged in a struggle for power. In other words, whatever rhetoric is employed, countries do not act on the basis of moral concerns or ideological principles. Instead, they are simply seeking to gain advantages for themselves. Through much of history, international peace and stability depended upon a balance of power between more or less equally matched nations.

From a realist perspective, the US is – like other countries – pursuing its own national interest. It is guided by notions of 'homeland security' and the need to advance its own strategic, political and economic interests. It has therefore maintained relative friendly relations with some countries – such as China – that deny democracy but taken military action against others – most notably Iraq.

Others see the making of policy in more idealist terms. Foreign policy, they argue, is shaped by attempts to realise particular ideals. For some countries, these ideals may rest upon the enslavement of other countries. However, the US has always been committed to internationalist principles. As Irving Kristol – an influential neo-conservative – suggests, the US differs markedly from other nations:

> The American people see their nation as being an exceptional one, with a very special mission in the world. This mission has an ineradicable moral component – our foreign policy is supposed to make the world a better place for humanity to inhabit. There is consensus on this. (Kristol 1996)

There is, however, as Kristol notes, much less consensus about the methods that should be employed in pursuit of a better world. For some, the US should avoid foreign 'entanglements' and serve as an example of democracy and liberty to others across the globe. In other accounts, the US should play a more pro-active role through the 'export' of democratic values and nation-building abroad. In practice, observers suggest, US policy-making has shifted backwards and forwards between these ways of thinking.

There are also some observers drawn principally – but not exclusively – from the radical left who describe US foreign and defence policy in terms of imperialism. The concept of imperialism is tied to Marxist thinking. It was developed, in particular, by Vladimir Lenin, the architect of the 1917 Russian revolution, who represented it as the 'highest stage of capitalism'. From this perspective, large-scale companies and 'finance capital' are engaged in a desperate search for markets and resources. In all of the most economically advanced countries, the government apparatus and the armed forces act on their behalf. From the late nineteenth century onwards, there was a scramble to occupy and hold territory. Although most colonies gained their independence in the mid-twentieth century, they remained subject to the economic might of the imperialist powers. Marxist theorists talk of *neo-colonialism*. From this perspective, US policy has been driven – particularly in regions such as the Middle East – by a search to ensure access to resources such as oil. Furthermore, they suggest, US policymakers have sought to destabilise governments that have obstructed or challenged American economic hegemony. They point to the role of US agencies in orchestrating the 1973 coup d'état that removed the leftist government of Salvador Allende in Chile.

Both the long-term processes and the key events of the twentieth century are seen through these different perspectives.

At times, the US has sought to reshape the world. In the closing stages of the First World War, President Woodrow Wilson put forward fourteen points based upon the principles of liberal internationalism. The points included an end to secret diplomatic understandings, arms reductions, open access to the seas and the formation of a 'general association of nations'.

However, Wilson's efforts were rebuffed by American opinion. The US Senate rejected the Treaty of Versailles which had brought the First World War to a close. The US did not join the newly formed League of Nations and isolationist thinking held sway. The US only entered the Second World War when Japanese forces attacked the US naval base at Pearl Harbor in December 1941.

The US emerged from the Second World War as a 'superpower'. Although some isolationist voices were also heard after 1945, the threat posed by the USSR and expansion of the communist bloc across both eastern Europe and Asia led the US to assume leadership of the 'free world'. For Cold War 'hawks', the US nuclear arsenal and NATO offered an assurance that the west would not be engulfed by the Soviet Union. The US thereby became the guarantor of western security.

The fear of communist expansionism also led to US military intervention in Korea (1950–3) and Vietnam. However, Vietnam represented a significant military and political defeat for the US. American forces were sent to support South Vietnam's struggle against the Vietcong's guerilla insurgents and North Vietnamese troops. In the face of domestic opposition to the war and its intractability, US combat troops withdrew in 1973 and – two years later – the south surrendered. Vietnam was reunited under communist rule. About 58,000 American soldiers were killed. The 'ghost' of Vietnam haunted US decision-makers in subsequent decades. There were repeated fears that the US would again be dragged into a military quagmire.

Once the Cold War came to a close, the US emerged as the world's one 'hyperpower'. It was unchallenged for global dominance. However, the demise of the Soviet Union and the military threat that it posed also left the US unsure of its role. This uncertainty lasted throughout the 1990s. There was intervention abroad – for example, in the former Yugoslavia – but it was limited in scope and scale. Military action was taken against Iraq in the Gulf War of 1991. However, it did not go beyond the eviction of Iraqi forces from Kuwait.

The Bush administration – which assumed office in January 2001 – began with a different agenda. Its strategists scorned earlier attempts at 'nation-building' in countries such as Bosnia. There seemed to be a spirit of both unilateralism – whereby the US paid less heed to other nations – and disengagement.

This changed following September 11th. In place of disengagement, the US committed itself to the 'war on terrorism'. In Afghanistan, the Taliban regime – which had sheltered Al-Qaeda – was swiftly driven from power. Bush then identified a broader 'axis of evil' involving Iraq, North Korea and Iran.

CULTURAL STUDIES

Accounts and surveys of American society have increasingly drawn on cultural studies. It is a component in almost all American Studies courses and it is the dominant strand within a number of them.

The notion of cultural studies requires some explanation. The term 'culture' is defined in different ways. It is popularly used to refer to 'highbrow' pursuits such as fine art and the opera. It is employed by some anthropologists as a description of collective behaviour. However, in most of the social sciences and the arts, the concept has a broader meaning. It embraces ideas, relationships and institutions.

In contemporary cultural studies, there has been a particular emphasis on themes and topics associated with popular culture. There has been a focus on, for example, criminality, the media, subcultures, gender and sexuality.

Cultural studies has – as a subject – further characteristics:

- There is a stress on the power relationships underpinning particular cultural phenomena. What, for example, does gangsta rap – which has often used lyrics that many regard as degrading to women – say about contemporary race and gender relationships? This focus on power has led many practitioners of the subject towards an emphasis on inequalities of power and the character of oppression. In many accounts, there is a sense of identity with those who are oppressed and the patterns of resistance that have emerged among them. There are ties and associations with radical theories that seek a fundamental restructuring of society.

- Cultural studies has, at the same time, drawn upon and incorporated concepts, theories and methodologies from other disciplines. It owes a particular debt to semiotics, the study of signs. Language, it is said, is structured around clusters of signs – or codes – that convey both explicit and implicit meanings. It reflects the power struggles between dominant and subordinate groupings.

- Although cultural studies offers a radical critique of society, there has been, as Chapter 1 noted, a pulling away from 'grand narratives' – such as Marxism – that seek to offer an overall and, in effect, complete theory of society, politics and history. In place of this, cultural studies has a more modest vision and generally considers small-scale processes. It emphasises the ways in which these are represented and 'manufactured'.

LITERATURE AND DRAMA

'American literature may be said to begin with the chants and spoken tales of Native Americans. As English speaking settlers overcame those having Dutch, Spanish or French as their native tongues, English became the language in which American literature was written.' (University of Hull)

During the years preceding the revolution and for decades afterwards, American literature often tended to be imitative of British forms of writing. However, in the period preceding the Civil War (1861–5), distinctive American concerns began to emerge. James Fenimore Cooper (1789–1851) evoked the different vistas associated with the frontier and notions of a wilderness lying beyond the territory that had been settled by European-Americans. As Stephen Matterson records:

> These themes included the legacy of American history, a confrontation with the American landscape, the frontier, the nature of democracy, and a fresh awareness of America's place in the world. A more confident use of American idiom and language was also characteristic of the period. (Matterson 2003: 11)

Transcendentalism emerged against this background. It was a literary movement, but it had religious and philosophical associations. Informing writers such as Ralph Waldo Emerson (1803–82) and Henry David Thoreau (1817–62), transcendentalism stressed the abilities of the self-reliant individual as well as the ties between each human and God.

Later writers built upon this. Walt Whitman (1819–92) was one of the US's most influential and celebrated of poets. Breaking with convention, *Leaves of Grass* was in free verse, drawing upon slang and incorporating sexual references.

By the beginning of the twentieth century, the process that had begun decades earlier had run its course and American literature had established a firmly independent character. Indeed, it offered a style and a vision that was increasingly emulated in other countries. As Malcolm Bradbury and David Corker have noted:

> By the end of the 1920s you could no longer think of American writing as a provincial literature, a branch of the English tree. Culturally as economically, the United States shifted, around the wartime years, from being a debtor to a creditor nation. (Bradbury and Corker 1975: 41)

Twentieth-century literature, poetry and theatre drew on the diversity and heterogeneity of American society. Formerly silent voices – such as those of women and the minorities – were increasingly heard, although they too continued to reflect, reproduce and address established American themes.

Baldwin, James (1924–87)

James Baldwin was born in Harlem, New York City. In 1948, he left for Paris, hoping that the distance that this placed between him and the US would enable him to write about American society. *Go Tell It On The Mountain* (1953) was an autobiographical work about growing up in Harlem. The depth and passion of his work and, in particular, the descriptions of black American life made him a voice for civil rights. However, his openly gay lifestyle, and the way in which he addressed profoundly controversial themes – most notably homosexuality and interracial relationships – tended to isolate him among blacks as well as whites.

Faulkner, William (1897–1962)

Faulkner is one of the most significant figures in the history of southern literature. Much of his work was set in 'Yoknapatawpha County', a fictional county set in Mississippi, and addresses many of the tensions and strains facing the south as it edged towards modernity. In 1949 Faulkner received the Nobel prize for literature.

Fitzgerald, F. Scott (1896–1940)

Fitzgerald is known principally for *The Great Gatsby* (1925). To a greater extent than perhaps any other book, *The Great Gatsby* addressed the American dream and the belief that the US is an open society offering opportunity and the possibility of re-emergence for all. Self-made millionaire Jay Gatsby embodies the casting off of the past and the pursuit of ambition, greed and accumulated wealth. His story is a cautionary tale. Robert Redford and Mia Farrow took the leading roles in the 1974 film version.

Frost, Robert (1874–1963)

Despite many personal tragedies, Robert Frost was the foremost New England poet of his generation. His work often seemed synonymous with the Yankee vision. He recited his 1942 poem, *The Gift Outright*, at John F. Kennedy's inauguration ceremony:

> The land was ours before we were the land's.
> She was our land more than a hundred years
> Before we were her people. She was ours
> In Massachusetts, in Virginia,
> But we were England's, still colonials,
> Possessing what we still were unpossessed by,
> Possessed by what we now no more possessed.
> Something we were withholding made us weak
> Until we found out that it was ourselves
> We were withholding from our land of living,
> And forthwith found salvation in surrender.
> Such as we were we gave ourselves outright
> (The deed of gift was many deeds of war)
> To the land vaguely realizing westward,
> But still unstoried, artless, unenhanced,
> Such as she was, such as she [will] become.

James, Henry (1843–1916)

Henry James was born into a wealthy family. He travelled widely in Europe and eventually became a British citizen. Much of his work addresses the experiences of Americans living abroad. It tended not to concentrate on story or plot. Instead, there was an emphasis on character and detail. *Daisy Miller* (1879) charts the tension between the innocence and youth of an American and European sophistication. In *The Portrait of a Lady* (1881) a young American woman is the victim of her provincial attitudes while visiting Europe. A number of his novels – including *The Portrait of a Lady* and *Wings of a Dove* - have been made into films.

Kerouac, Jack (1922–69)

Kerouac won acclaim as a member – along with other writers such as Allen Ginsberg and William S. Burroughs – of the *Beat* generation, and for his 1957 book *On the Road*, which tells of four journeys across the US.

Mailer, Norman (1923–)

Mailer's work includes *The Naked and the Dead* (1948). The book drew upon his personal experiences in the Second World War. *The Executioner's Song* (1979) was based on the story of Gary Gilmore, a convicted murderer, and the re-imposition of capital punishment in the US. Mailer was for a long period been associated with radical politics. He co-founded the *Village Voice*, a New York paper, and was imprisoned in 1967 for his role in demonstrations against the Vietnam War. Nonetheless, his mocking hostility towards the women's movement led him to take part in a public debate with leading feminists such as Germaine Greer, which was charted in the 1971 documentary, *Town Bloody Hall*.

Miller, Arthur (1915–)

Miller is an influential playwright who was married to Marilyn Monroe for four years.

His first success came in 1947 with *All My Sons*. It told of a factory owner who sold defective parts to the US government during the First World War thereby causing the deaths of American pilots. These themes – dishonesty and guilt – were built upon in later, more well-known plays, most notably *Death of a Salesman* (1949), *The Crucible* (1953) and *A View from the Bridge* (1954). *The Crucible* – which tells of the witch trials in the early New England settlements – has been widely seen as an allegorical account of McCarthyism and the public naming of communist sympathisers.

The 1996 film of *The Crucible* featured Daniel Day-Lewis and Winona Ryder.

Morrison, Toni (1931–)

Beloved (1987), Morrison's best-known novel, draws upon the African-American experience and addresses the brutal legacy of slavery. It is the story of a former slave, Sethe, who is haunted by the ghost of her murdered daughter and is visited by both poltergeists and a strange, beautiful young woman calling herself Beloved. *Jazz* (1992) is a tale of love and murder set in Harlem in the 1920s. *Beloved* (1998) has been made into a film. Directed by Jonathan Demme, it starred Oprah Winfrey and Danny Glover.

O'Neill, Eugene (1888–1953)

O'Neill was one of the most influential playwrights. His plays – such as *The Iceman Cometh* – charted and explored personal tragedies. Set in the north-east, they were innovative in terms of both content and production techniques.

Poe, Edgar Allan (1809–49)

Poe is best known for his tales of mystery, the supernatural and horror. He pioneered detective fiction. However, alongside the short story, Poe was also a poet and the author of highly influential literary criticism. His work includes 'The Black Cat', 'The Pit and the Pendulium', 'The Murders in the Rue Morgue', 'The Raven' and 'The Fall of the House of Usher'.

Steinbeck, John (1902–68)

Steinbeck is best known for *Of Mice and Men* (1937), *The Grapes of Wrath* (1939) and *Cannery Row* (1945). Much of his work was shaped by – and charted – the depression years of the 1930s. *The Grapes of Wrath* sought to record the westward migration of the Oklahoma poor ('Okies') who sought to escape the poverty of the Dust Bowl by heading towards California. Although the book ends on a note of hope, the figure of Tom Joad came to symbolise the desperate plight of the farming communities and the obstacles placed in the way of those who sought to maintain the American dream. The 1940 film of *The Grapes of Wrath* starred Henry Fonda and Jane Darwell.

Twain, Mark (1835–1910)

Samuel Langhorne Clemens, who wrote under the name of Mark Twain, is one of the US's most acclaimed writers. He is remembered for *The Adventures of Huckleberry Finn* (1885), *The Adventures of Tom Sawyer* (1876), *A Connecticut Yankee in King Arthur's Court* (1889), along with numerous stories, essays and articles. As has been noted:

> At the heart of Twain's achievement is his creation of Tom Sawyer and Huck Finn, who embody that mythic America midway between the frontier American wilderness that produced so much of the national mythology and the emerging urban, industrial giant of the twentieth century. (Roth 1995: 682)

Williams, Tennessee (1911–83)

Williams is a celebrated dramatist. His plays include *The Glass Menagerie* (1944), *A Streetcar Named Desire* (1947) and *Can on a Hot Tin Roof* (1955). Set against a southern background – which has a surface gentility – they chart the torment and pain of many human relationships.

INTERDISCIPLINARY APPROACHES

Although all American Studies courses have a multidisciplinary structure, a number also have an *interdisciplinary* dimension insofar as they seek to cross the boundaries between the different academic disciplines. An interdisciplinary programme of study focuses on a topic, historical period or culture and considers it from two or more disciplinary perspectives. Some interdisciplinary themes have attracted particular attention from lecturers, researchers and students. These include the concept of the 'frontier', notions of national identity and representations of the American south.

The 'frontier'

American Studies – particularly in its early days as a discipline – sought to understand American identity. What, observers asked, does it mean to be an American? How does 'being American' differ from other nationalities, particularly those in Europe?

In recent years, questions such as these are regarded with greater caution than in the past. There has been a retreat from attempts to make broad generalisations about the character of the American people. Indeed, the concept of 'national character' has been increasingly regarded as inherently problematical. There are profound dangers, it is said, in asserting that the people of a particular country shared common characteristics. In particular, the idea of a 'national character' neglects the many differences between social groupings. Men, women, whites, blacks, Latinos, and Asian-Americans are aggregated together and treated as a homogenous bloc. The separate and distinct experience of the different minorities is neglected. As Neil Campbell and Alasdair Kean note, the search for an American national character rests upon:

> the tendency to reduce questions of national identity to some essential singularity and in doing so give undue weight to the experience of specific groups and traditions in explaining America, at the expense of other groups whose experience is, as a result forgotten or marginalised. (Campbell and Kean 1997: 2)

The picture that emerged from these accounts 'privileged', in particular, the experience of white Anglo-Saxon Protestant – or WASP – men. The 'forgotten' or 'marginalised' groupings included women, African-Americans, Latinos and the native-American tribes. In recent decades, many of those engaged in American Studies have sought to recover their perceptions and understandings.

Nonetheless, some tentative conclusions can still be drawn about the 'American character' and its defining features. Some early commentaries are still regarded as instructive. The work of Frederick Jackson Turner (1863–1932), a history professor at the University of Wisconsin, is often cited. He argued that the frontier marking the settlers' shift westwards across the continent, or, as Turner put it, 'the meeting point between savagery and civilization', had imbued American society with its defining characteristics. The task of taming the environment required the abandonment of European culture and thought. Immigrants from different European countries were compelled to live, work and trade together. Frontier life bred self-reliant individualism. It laid the basis for a restless impatience with accumulated experience, a firm conviction that barriers and setbacks could always be transcended, and a pronounced hostility to government officialdom:

That courseness and strength combined with acuteness and inquisitiveness; that practical, inventive turn of mind, quick to find expedients; that masterful grasp of material things, lacking in the artistic but powerful to effect great ends; that restless, nervous energy; that dominant individualism, working for good and for evil, and withal that buoyancy and exuberance which comes with freedom – these are traits of the frontier, or traits called out elsewhere because of the existence of the frontier. (Quoted in Etulain 1999: 37)

Although subject to far-reaching criticism, Turner's emphasis on the role of the frontier has been very influential. Many accounts have suggested that American consciousness is still haunted by notions of a wilderness lying beyond the western 'frontier' and the challenges of taming it. It has been represented in different ways. At times, the untamed west is a source of danger and threat. It is a wilderness defined by savagery and temptation. It threatens to undermine the authority and integrity of the community. In other representations, it is a new Garden of Eden that could flourish with proper cultivation.

These notions cannot be understood from history and politics alone. Some important schools of American art have depicted the tensions between these different perceptions of wilderness. Joshua Johns suggests that the 1836 Thomas Cole painting *The Oxbow (The Connecticut River near Northampton)*, captures this. The picture conveys:

the tension between wilderness and garden, savagery and civilization . . . European conventions of landscape painting are employed to comment on the state of the physical place of America. The savagery of the storm clouds over the wilderness retreats from the advancing cultivated landscape of civilization. (Johns 1996)

The 'frontier' is tied to images of the 'wild west'. Realities became intertwined with myths, particularly during the period after the 'frontier' was 'closed' and the entire US was permanently settled. There were stories of cowboys and 'Indians'. There were tales of pioneers trekking across the Rockies. Today, 'Marlboro Country' evokes particular images. The west is a place where individuals can 'find' and test themselves. Representations have informed countless works of fiction and films from *The Searchers* (1956) to *Thelma and Louise* (1991).

The 'melting pot' and American identity

Some studies acknowledge the role of the 'frontier', but instead stress the role of mass immigration in shaping American identity. In the US, different nationalities were brought together so as to forge what Hector St John de Crevecoeur termed a 'new man'. Writing in 1782, he argued that American character rested on:

> that strange mixture of blood, which you will find in no other country. I could point out to you a family whose grandfather was an Englishman, whose wife was Dutch, whose son married a French woman, and whose present four sons have now four wives of different nations. He is an American, who, leaving behind him all his ancient prejudices and manners, receives new ones from the new mode of life he has embraced, the new government he obeys, and the new rank he holds . . . Here individuals are melted into a great new race of men, whose labours and posterity will one day cause great changes in the world. (Quoted in Gleason 1980: 31)

Such sentiments were built upon in the early twentieth century as the notion of America as a *melting pot* – which created a composite nationality through the blending together of immigrants from different backgrounds – gained currency.

Other accounts have a different emphasis. American identity is, they assert, *ideational*. In contrast with the nations of Europe and Asia, 'being American' rests upon shared ideas, beliefs and principles rather than having family connections with a country that go back over many generations. Some observers describe the ideas and principles that form a basis for US identity as the 'American creed'. They include a commitment to personal rights and liberties, limited government and a faith in the ability of individuals to climb the economic ladder through their own effort. This is sometimes dubbed the 'American dream'. During the McCarthy era – when the Cold War was at its height and there were fears of an attack by the Soviet Union – those who were suspected of not subscribing to these ideas were deemed 'unAmerican'.

Some studies go further and point to the sense of a national mission that, they suggest, informs American thinking. They point to the seventeenth-century origins of the country. The pilgrims who founded the early New England colonies were committed to the purification of the Christian church so that it accorded more closely with God's will. The early settlements feared both God's wrath and the Devil's work. Their faith imposed a strict sense of self-discipline on the communities. The persecution of alleged witches ensured that they remained tightly bound, despite the fragmenting effects of frontier life and trading relationships.

These settlements bequeathed the notion that the US has a significant role to play in the regeneration of humanity. Although, in some accounts, this leads to assertions that it should do this through the force of example by isolating itself from the corruption of other countries, it has also contributed to the belief that the US should bring principles such as freedom and democracy to an oppressive, corrupt and unenlightened world. As Loren Baritz put it at the time of the Vietnam War:

> In countless ways Americans know in their gut . . . that we have been Chosen to lead the world in public morality and to instruct it in political virtue. We believe that our own domestic goodness results in strength adequate to destroy our opponents who, by definition, are enemies of virtue, freedom, and God. (Baritz 1985: 11)

While defeat in Vietnam chastened US foreign-policy ambitions, there are suggestions that the 'war on terrorism' that has been pursued since the September 11th attacks has resurrected these earlier notions. The Bush administration has talked of bringing liberty and democracy to the Middle East through the 2003 war in Iraq.

The American south

The American south – a term generally understood to describe south-eastern states such as Virginia, the Carolinas, Georgia, Florida, Alabama, Mississippi, and Louisiana – has been the subject of extensive study.

Most of these accounts stress the ways in which its defining characteristics differ from those that mark out the remainder of the country. Indeed, some observers have talked of 'southern exceptionalism'. While the northern states ended slavery in the early nineteenth century, the slave system remained integral to the south's agrarian economy. Fearing northern domination, and the abolition of slavery, the south broke away – or *seceded* – from the US in 1861 and established itself as a separate country: the Confederate States of America, or Confederacy. Southern secession provoked the Civil War (or 'war between the states' as it still dubbed in the south) that culminated, after four years, in northern victory. The defeat of the Confederacy enabled the US to remain united as one country.

However, although slavery was abolished following the passage of Amendment XIII to the Constitution at the end of the Civil War and the imposition of northern military rule, the Jim Crow laws – which were introduced from the 1880s onwards – led to the imposition of *segregation* across the southern states. For the eighty years that followed, blacks were confined – by law – to separate and invariably unequal facilities. The legal institutionalisation of white supremacy was backed by organisations such as the Ku Klux Klan and more informal expressions of racism. There were an estimated

4,753 lynchings between 1882 and 1968. The Jim Crow laws were only ended when the 1964 Civil Rights Act, which outlawed segregation, and the 1965 Voting Rights Act, which ensured that African-Americans could freely participate in elections, were passed.

Many observers talk today about the decline of southern distinctiveness. They point to increased levels of geographical mobility between the regions and the emergence of a quasi-national media. However, to a degree, the south still has a separate identity.

- The south remains the poorest of the regions. In 2000, the median household income level was $38,410 compared with $42,148 for the US as a whole (US Census Bureau 2001).

- Crime rates are significantly higher in the south. The law is also enforced with greater severity. The death penalty is, for example, more widely applied.

- There are higher levels of religious commitment in the south. In particular, there are greater numbers of evangelical 'born-again' Christians, for whom conversion is a profound personal experience. Many understand the Bible as a literal account of human history.

- Political and cultural attitudes are more conservative in the south. Although white southerners were – until the 1960s – the Democrats' most loyal voting bloc, they are now tied to the Republicans.

Arguably, however, southern distinctiveness goes beyond these factors. It extends to the everyday *folkways* that collectively form a culture. As John Shelton Reed has observed:

These days southern identification is not so much a matter of shared history as a shared cultural style – some cultural conservatism, religiosity, manners, speech, humor, music, that sort of thing. (Shelton Reed quoted in Fox-Genovese and Genovese 2001)

Some of these folkways have been mocked. *The Dukes of Hazzard*, a 1970s television series, gently teased rural southern life and used cultural stereotypes to construct characters such as 'Boss Hogg'. *My Cousin Vinny* (1992) is a celebrated and rewarding comedy film that explores some of the perceived differences between northern city life and the south.

Many courses and research essays within American Studies consider all the forms of cultural expression that define the south. They attempt to understand the character of the region through its history and politics but also through literature, drama, film and music.

- The writings of William Faulkner charted the dilemmas – many of which were derived from the tension between the past and present – facing the deep south.

- Tenessee Williams's plays – such as *Cat on a Hot Tin Roof* (1955) and *A Streetcar Named Desire* (1947) – explored the contrasts between romanticised representations of the south and the more brutal realities of daily life in the region.

- One of the earliest motion pictures, D. W. Griffith's *The Birth of a Nation* (1915), charts the history of the south. It depicts the Civil War era and the racial politics of the Reconstruction period that followed. It is a celebration of the Old Plantation South and an indictment of black empowerment and interracial sex. The Ku Klux Klan appear as the heroic guardians of the white race and civilisation. Two decades later, *Gone with the Wind* (1939) also idealised the 'old south' but in much more restrained and less propagandistic terms. It was represented as an era of order and hierarchy. African-Americans 'knew their place'. As the foreword to the film explains:

There was a land of Cavaliers and Cotton Fields called the Old South. Here in this pretty world, Gallantry took its last bow. Here was the last ever to be seen of Knights and their Ladies Fair, of Master and of Slave. Look for it only in books, for it is no more than a dream remembered, a Civilization gone with the wind . . . *(Gone with the Wind)*

- The south gave rise to a number of different musical forms. The blues first emerged among the black cotton-pickers in the Mississippi Delta and have a primitive, emotive style that reflects the hardships of life. The south is also, however, associated with jazz, gospel, cajun, country and bluegrass. Each has a distinct style that says much about the different communities and cultures that gave rise to them.

3   AMERICAN STUDIES AT UNIVERSITY

This section of the book looks at the different degree courses that are offered in the UK. It outlines the themes that are considered in first-year courses, second- and third-year options, the period of study that may be available at a US university, and the methods of assessment.

'People often ask, "why do you want to study America?" I chose American Studies because I had – by taking Government and Politics at GCSE and A-level – already studied the country. These courses had gone pretty well. I also wanted to study the variety of subjects that American Studies offers. I was also persuaded by the opportunity to spend a year at an American university.

'The American Studies course that I took covered a wide range of themes and topics. These included the History of Native American Art and the Geography of Chicago City. Courses were based around presentations, coursework and exams.

'Throughout the first year, I was taught the basics: the history of America, the country's politics and literature. Other modules concentrated on specific geographical areas of the US such as the 'wild west' and the south.

'The second year concentrated on particular aspects of American culture such as African-American history and literature, social and economic history, and the growth of the American city. During your second year, you need to start to think about your dissertation. However, because

American Studies is such a varied topic, it can be on just about anything!

'The third year gives you two options: to study at an American University for a year or complete your degree in the UK in three years. If you choose to study in the US, you come back and complete a fourth year. I chose to stay in the UK to finish my degree in three years. (I had been to the States every summer on a working visa programme.)

'The third year was by far and away my most enjoyable year because you have the opportunity to choose which modules you want to study (the first and second year teach core subjects). In my final year I studied the History of the US through film, America's involvement in Vietnam, American Presidents and Women's History. Since you choose the subject, you have far more interest and will probably get better results.

'The dissertation is completed during the third year. I researched and wrote a 10,000 word dissertation entitled: "Alcatraz: Rehabilitation or Trash Can". The project argued that the prison was used as a media stunt by the FBI and eventually became a warehouse harbouring criminals who committed minor offences.

'Like so many non-vocational degrees, students often wonder what they will do once they have graduated from university. Employers are becoming increasingly aware that more and more students are coming from university with a variety of degrees.

'There are a number of opportunities once you have graduated in American Studies. First, you can go on to postgraduate studies. Many universities are offering American Studies at MA level. Second, there are job opportunities in, for example, journalism, teaching or the civil service. I am planning to return to University in September 2003 to study a Post Graduate Certificate in Education, and hope to teach in Texas within the next two years.'

Kelly Arland, September 2003, American Studies student at the University of Leicester, 1999–2002.

American Studies is offered as either a single honours course, or a component of a broader degree programme at forty-four universities and colleges (December 2002):

University of Birmingham
Brunel University
Canterbury Christ Church University College
University of Central Lancashire
De Montfort University
University of Derby
University of Dundee
University of East Anglia
University of Edinburgh
University of Essex
University of Glamorgan
University of Gloucestershire
Goldsmiths College
University of Hull
University of Keele
University of Kent at Canterbury
King Alfred's College of Higher Education
King's College London
University of Lancaster
University of Leicester
Liverpool Hope University College
Liverpool John Moores University
Liverpool University
London Metropolitan University
University of Manchester
Manchester Metropolitan University – All Saints
Manchester Metropolitan University – Crewe and
    Alsager Faculty
Middlesex University
University College Northampton
University of Northumbria at Newcastle
University of Nottingham
University of Plymouth
Queen's University Belfast

University of Reading
College of Ripon and York St John
University of Sheffield
University of Sunderland
University of Sussex
University of Ulster at Jordanstown
University of Wales Aberystwyth
University of Wales Lampeter
University of Wales Swansea
University of Warwick
University of Wolverhampton

Source: ARNet – Online Resources for American Studies (2002), *American Studies In The United Kingdom: Under-graduate and Postgraduate Courses*, www.americansc.org.uk/Eccles/Index.htm

Almost all American Studies courses allow students to specialise in one or two areas during their second and third years after following more broadly based introductory courses. There are, however, differences between courses that should be considered by applicants.

- Although all are multidisciplinary in character, some attach particular weight to certain disciplines – such as literature or cultural studies – within their overall programme of study. Indeed, courses are based in different departments or faculties. At some universities, American Studies courses have a 'home' within History. At others, it is English, Politics, or Cultural Studies.

- Some courses will emphasise the interdisciplinary nature of their courses to a greater extent than others.

- Some courses allow students to take American Studies together with either an unrelated or an allied subject – such as Canadian or Latin American Studies – while others are more restrictive in character.

- Study at a university in the US for a semester or year will be a core component of the course. For this reason, many – but not all – American Studies programmes are four rather than three years in length. The period abroad can be challenging but will also be rewarding. It can pose difficulties for students with childcare or household responsibilities. Furthermore, although there is local authority assistance and the opportunity to work in the US, sources of finance will require consideration.

University courses are liable to change and revision. Furthermore, this section of the book can only offer extracts from course programmes. Applicants should gain a full picture by consulting university prospectuses and the leaflets or booklets that may be issued by particular departments. The Eccles Centre for American Studies at the British Library issues an annual listing of American Studies courses offered across the UK. The American Studies Resources Centre publishes an online edition:

American Studies Resources Centre
Aldham Robarts Centre
Liverpool John Moores University
Mount Pleasant
Liverpool L3 5UZ
Tel and fax: 0151 231 3241
Website: www.americansc.org.uk
E-mail: info@americansc.org.uk

A 'hard copy' version can be obtained from the Eccles Centre:

The Eccles Centre for American Studies
The British Library
96 Euston Road
London NW1 2DB
Tel: 020 7412 7551 or 7757
Fax: 020 7412 7792
Website:
    www.bl.uk/services/information/american.html#4

What themes and topics will be studied at in the first semester and subsequent years at university?

. . . this four-year, multidisciplinary programme explores the culture of the United States within the broad context of history, literature and society. The core of the programme is American history and literature, branching out into politics and cultural studies and taking in Canadian studies. Each element combines with all the others to give you an integrated understanding and appreciation of North American life. (University of Birmingham: www.bham.ac.uk/uscanada/)

The American Studies programme at the University of Central Lancashire is designed for students with interests in the cultural expressions of American society – whether in writing, music, film, speech or style – and who want to learn ways of critically examining what these forms say about American life and culture. American Studies provides a firm grounding for students to develop skills and knowledge in cultural studies and apply them to the study of one of the world's most dynamic societies; to prepare themselves for a possible career in journalism, the media, education, international or cultural affairs; and to carry on to study at postgraduate level.

The emphasis here is on the various cultural practices of American society. Students in other universities may well make the choice to study, say, American history or politics or literature exclusively, with little attention to the many interlocking ways in which the nation's people express themselves culturally. But that is in fact our unique focus. (University of Central Lancashire: www.uclan.ac.uk)

Throughout the programme the emphasis is on interdisciplinary work which actively encourages students to see the connections and relationships among several disciplines or areas of study (literature, history, popular culture, politics, the visual arts, music and cultural studies). Students spend one semester studying at one of our partner institutions in Alabama, Arkansas, Indiana, New Hampshire, Tennessee, Utah and Virginia. (University of Derby: www.derby.ac.uk/)

The American Studies department views the first year as a foundation year. Hence, while later years allow students to pursue their own choices of modules, the first year consists of a series of required modules. All students in the Single Honours programme take the following modules: American History I: Themes and Issues to 1880; American Literature Survey to World War I; Topics in American Culture and History (Semester 1); American History II: Themes and Issues Since 1880; 20th Century American Literature Survey; Topics in American Culture and History (Semester 2). Joint Honours students take the first two modules of each semester. (University of Hull: www.hull.ac.uk/)

At Keele University American Studies is taken in combination with another subject as part of the Dual Honours degree programme. The American Studies programme aims to introduce students to a diverse range of themes and approaches relating to the history, culture and contemporary character of the United States. The programme is both multi- and interdisciplinary in its intent. All students have the opportunity to pursue their disciplinary interests – in history, literature, politics, geography, and popular culture – whilst at the same time being encouraged to explore the intellectual links between them . . . In the first year all students take a common introductory course, which consists of the following: Introduction to American Studies I and II, which provide a basic grounding in American historical development from the colonial period to the present day; American Literature, which introduces students both to key authors, from Nathaniel Hawthorne to Toni Morrison, and to some of the recurrent issues of America's literary culture; and American Government and

Politics, which examines the political system and includes study of institutions such as the Presidency, Congress and the Supreme Court. (University of Keele: www.keele. ac.uk/depts/as/ashomepage.html)

The University of Kent at Canterbury offers three BA (Hons) degrees in American Studies. Each allows some concentration in a particular discipline; all offer the chance for interdisciplinary study of the United States. All students spend their third year at a university in the United States. The exchange institutions include University of Massachusetts (Amherst), University of Indiana (Bloomington), University of California (Santa Barbara, San Diego, Berkeley), University of Maryland. In addition to the American Studies programmes the University also offers three 3-year degrees specialising in American Literature. (University of Kent at Canterbury: www.ukc.ac.uk/)

American Studies at Lancaster University focuses on the culture, history and politics of the United States of America. Its central assumption is that this is best achieved through the rigorous engagement with disciplines across the humanities and social sciences. In other words, American Studies is understood to be a fundamentally interdisciplinary subject. Moreover, because the subject involves the study of another nation, students are required to spend a year at a North American university. Since Lancaster University has a long experience of student exchanges between its constitutive departments and North American universities, this year abroad is an integral part of the course. Thus, unlike courses in American Studies at most other British universities, American Studies at Lancaster University is a three rather than a four-year degree course. (University of Lancaster: www.lancs.ac.uk/depts/history/histwebsite/homepage.htm)

The School of Comparative American Studies (CAS) offers a degree programme which examines the whole of the Americas – Canada, the United States, Latin America and the Caribbean – through interdisciplinary study of the history, culture and literature of the Americas. It is an unusual programme. While most other American Studies degrees in Britain tend to restrict themselves to the United States, Warwick takes the pan-American experience as its subject and aims at a wider vision in which students will come to recognise the transatlantic experience as a whole with and without its patterns of political frontiers and larger divisions based on language, religion or industrial development.

CAS is a four-year degree, starting with introductory core courses in the first year, and then offering a wide range of options in different disciplines. It is a multi-disciplinary degree, examining the Americas from several perspectives. The course incorporates Spanish language teaching for three years, and has an integral year abroad. (University of Warwick: www.csv.warwick.ac.uk/undergrad/arts/cas/)

SECOND- AND FINAL-YEAR OPTIONS

While most first-year courses have a broad character, this is narrowed down in subsequent years. Many second-year courses build upon the first-year programme by introducing students to politics, history and literature in greater depth. In the final years, there is the opportunity to study specialist modules. In some cases, these will be drawn from a particular discipline. In other instances, they will be interdisciplinary in character. In recent years, final-year options in American Studies have included:

Native-American history and culture
Slavery and Race in the Americas
Slavery and Slave Life in the American South
Sexuality and Marriage in the Americas
From McCarthy to Elvis: America in the Fifties
Gender and Recent American Writing
Political Protest in North America

Culture and Consumption in the USA 1920–60
Abraham Lincoln and the Crisis of Union
The Man Who Knew Too Much: Hitchcock's Films
AIDS Cultures
Immigrants in American Society, 1815–1945
Twentieth-Century North-American Short Story
The American Presidency: Truman to Clinton
Environmental History
Anglo-American Special Relationship
American Humour
American Popular Culture
Foreign Policy of the USA
Latin America and the United States
New American Cinema
The Decision to Use the Atom Bomb

STUDY ABROAD

'Living in the country teaches you more about American culture and the American way of life than any textbook ever could.' University of Hull graduate, (www.hull. ac.uk/courses/ug/americanstudies.html)

Many American Studies degree programmes include a period of study at a university in the United States. The amount of time that students spend abroad varies between courses and universities. It may be a month during the summer holidays, a semester, or an entire academic year. It will usually be taken after completion of the second year.

- The study period is a crucial component of the overall degree programme. A proper understanding of another society requires first-hand experience.

- Students do not have to pay the tuition fees charged by the US university. In most cases, basic living expenses and the cost of one return flight are paid by a student's local education authority.

- There may be an opportunity to take paid employment on campus, in libraries, administration or campus shops and food outlets.

- The study period in the US counts towards the overall degree. Students will be able to transfer credits from the courses that they take in the US.

- Most US universities are much larger than a British university. They can therefore offer a very broad range of courses, programmes and options. The scale of choice open to students and the specialist expertise of the teaching staff ensure that British students gain much from the experience.

- Students almost always have a choice of US universities. In 2003, the University of Wales Swansea offered – among others – the opportunity to study at the following institutions:
    University of Massachusetts
    Louisiana State University
    University of Illinois
    University of Tennessee
    University of Southern Mississippi
    University of Wisconsin
    Washington State University
    University of Ohio
    University of Northern Arizona
    University of New York
    University of Wyoming
    Source: adapted from University of Wales Swansea (2003), *American Studies Schemes of Study*, www2.swan.ac.uk/courses/american_studies/schemes.htm

What courses do British students take in the US? The guidance given by the University of Reading is broadly representative:

During the term abroad students are required to sign up for four 'classes' (the equivalent of modules at Reading). All classes are selected from the range of options offered by the host institution, and must be approved by the Director. However, we are not over-prescriptive about what classes are undertaken, provided that they have some reasonable bearing on the American Studies degree programme. Generally we advise students to opt for topics within the component disciplines of American Studies at Reading – that is, in literature, history, politics or film. However, it may also be worth considering courses in other areas such as popular culture or ethnic studies, so as to take advantage of opportunities not available at Reading.

The work done during the Study Visit, and the grades awarded on the basis of written assignments, quizzes, class attendance, and end-of-term examinations, contribute to Finals assessment at the University of Reading. It is therefore vital that students satisfy all the formal requirements of each course taken at the host institution. Failure to do so will affect their overall degree classification.

Source: adapted from University of Reading (2003), *Study Visit to the United States*, www.rdg.ac.uk/Acadepts/lu/Exchange/Xhome.html

Inevitably, students have had varied experiences. Even a short period abroad requires extensive financial and logistical planning. There are inescapable uncertainties. Nonetheless, most talk in very positive terms. Kate Lefley, who took American Studies at the University of Leicester, spent a year (2001–2) at the University of Texas at Austin:

Living in Austin allowed me to travel all over Texas. I went to Dallas to see where JFK was shot, I visited San Antonio (to see the Alamo) as well as other cultural sites in Fredericksburg, El Paso, Corpus Christi and Nuevo Laredo. During my year in the US, I also went to New York City, New Orleans, Albuquerque, the Grand Canyon, Los Angeles, San Francisco and Las Vegas. Most of these places were visited on road trips and these journeys gave me a thorough understanding and love for the expanse of emptiness that makes up much of America.

I now understand why Americans feel such a passion for a country that is still largely untouched and untamed.

It was important for me to become part of a community during my stay. I now have a greater awareness and respect for those who put religion at the forefront of their lives. And being a part of a 50,000-strong student body was also an experience that cannot be rivalled by any other. I particularly remember the atmosphere of the gigantic football stadium (and the passion of the Longhorn fans), the pro-choice/pro-life debates that fill campus campaign sites for a week each year, the sororities that asked me to join and the fraternity parties that often lived up to their reputations. Austin is a fantastic city for young people and young families with its liberal attitude combined with Texan pride and various sites of natural beauty. I was also lucky enough to live in a co-operative house that summed up much of Austin's charm with its hippie attitudes to communal living.

The classes that I took at the University of Texas were an event in themselves. We were graded on class participation and downgraded if we didn't attend a sufficient number of classes. Most of my classes, rather than lectures, were in a classroom setting with fifteen to twenty-five students. It was totally different to British universities and much more like A-level studies, where there is neither a lecture nor seminar but, instead, a class discussion. Being in this environment made all of my fellow Brits much more vocal in classroom discussions and the returning exchange students to Britain seemed to contribute more willingly than third-year American Studies students. The workload was greater at times than in England but the level was lower and high grades were often achievable if you could just keep up. There was also constant assessment with midterms and pop quizzes. It was not therefore just a matter of cramming and revising at the end of each semester.

The most important part of my trip was undoubtedly the experience of 9/11. Despite all the arrogance and ignorance that, I feel, America can force on the world, seeing Americans live through a terrorist attack allowed me to see how the domestic security that they had enjoyed could be shattered in just one day. Many people were incredibly angry. Some directed this at Al-Qaeda but many in Austin also directed it to their own government.

ASSESSMENT

Assessment on American Studies and almost all other undergraduate courses depends upon a combination of continuous assessment and examination papers. In many universities, a proportion of the overall mark depends upon attendance and participation in classes. The approach adopted at the University of Kent at Canterbury (UKC) is representative.

Level 1: 100% coursework (essays, class participation) in the first half of the year, 50:50 combination of coursework and examination in the second half of the year.
Level 2/3: depending on the modules you select, assessment varies from 100% coursework (extended essays or dissertation), to a combination of examination and coursework, usually in the ratio 50:50, 60:40 or 80:20.

For its part, the University of Wolverhampton notes:

. . . you will be taught using a mixture of lectures, seminars, tutorials and group presentations. Each module is assessed differently and you will encounter a wide range of methods including any combination of essays, individual and group presentations, seen and unseen exams, individual projects, reports, practical exercises, coursework portfolios and classroom-based tests.

AMERICAN STUDIES AND JOBS

American Studies is – like many other university disciplines – a non-vocational subject. It does not lead directly to a particular occupation or form of employment. Nonetheless, American Studies courses seek to ensure that their students have a firm grasp of current affairs and an understanding of the dynamics shaping the contemporary world. Graduates will be well used to assessing different and competing arguments. They can draw on a range of disciplines and methodologies. They will also have horizons that go beyond their own society and background. Therefore, although American Studies graduates have gone to find employment in a very broad range of careers and occupations, they are particularly well equipped for work in the media and posts with an international dimension. Students will also acquire and develop more generalised or 'transferable' skills. These include the ability to:

- draw together and integrate ideas from a range of sources;

- assess ideas and arguments in a critical and analytical way;

- work with and apply concepts, models and theories;

- construct essays and other forms of extended writing;

- present ideas in a coherent and appropriate form to different groups and audiences.

At the same time, university students also become independent learners. They should gain self-motivation and time-management skills. They can work under pressure and meet deadlines. They will also be well used to working with others as part of a group. Many will be well-rounded individuals who have taken an active part in at least one of the sporting, social or intellectual activities offered by university societies and clubs. All of this has a direct or indirect value in the job market:

American Studies will facilitate numerous skills including spoken and written communication, the ability to construct an argument, teamwork and autonomous learning. Moreover, employers often believe British graduates are too narrowly focused in the work. As a multi- and interdisciplinary subject, American Studies inculcates the breadth of study that employers seek. (Liverpool Hope University College)

CHOOSING UNIVERSITIES – QAA REPORTS

Student choices are inevitably based on a considerable number of variables. These include the courses that are offered, financial considerations, accommodation, the character of the city in which the university is located and varied personal circumstances.

However, the character of the university and the course will also be important. Some of the differences between American Studies courses have already been highlighted. In particular, there are different emphases in terms of the disciplines that comprise the subject.

How can you find out more? The university prospectus and the course booklets that may be available will give you guidance. There may be additional information on the university website. However, you can go further. The Quality Assurance Agency for Higher Education (QAA) offers assessment reports on the teaching of subjects. Their coverage includes curriculum design, teaching, learning and assessment, student support and guidance, and learning resources. Courses are graded on the basis of six factors. The reports are published on the QAA website and the American Studies reports can be found at:

www.qaa.ac.uk/revreps/subjrev/American%20Studies/americanstudiesindex.htm.

The QAA's head office is:
Southgate House
Southgate Street
Gloucester GL1 1UB
Tel: 01452 557000
Fax: 01452 557070
E-mail: comms@qaa.ac.uk

4   KEY TERMS

This section introduces and explains some of the key
terms and core concepts that may be encountered on
American Studies courses. (Cross-references to these
key terms and concepts are in bold type.)

abortion
The morality of abortion has been a core issue in US politics for at
least three decades. In 1973, in *Roe* v. *Wade*, the Supreme Court
asserted that abortion was a constitutional right. The ruling was
derived from a 'right to privacy' that – although not specified in
the Constitution – was said to be implied in its words and phrases.
The *Roe* judgment contributed to the political mobilisation of
many evangelical Christian voters – who were deeply opposed to
abortion – and the emergence of the **religious right**.

abstract expressionism
The term refers to a movement of American artists who were
influential from the late 1950s onwards. Their ranks included
Jackson Pollock and Mark Rothko.

affirmative action
Affirmative-action programmes have been pursued in education, government and companies since the early 1970s. They
seek to ensure that minorities and women are much more fully
represented at the highest levels of business and government.
In their 'hardest' form, they can involve quotas so that those
from groupings who have traditionally been disadvantaged
are given preference over white men when hiring decisions are

made. Affirmative action has been deeply controversial. It has, however, been upheld – at least in a diluted form – by the US Supreme Court.

Alger, Horatio (1832–99)
The work of Horatio Alger, an influential novelist, who wrote *Ragged Dick, or Street Life in New York with the Bootblacks* (1867–8) and countless other stories in which the hero escapes poverty, gave expression to notions of the American dream.

American dream
The 'American dream' is the long-established belief that US society permits upward mobility. Individuals can – with sufficient labour, application and imagination – become prosperous and accumulate wealth.

American Federation of Labor – Congress of Industrial Organizations (AFL-CIO)
The AFL-CIO brings together the US trades – or labour – unions. Traditionally rooted in the traditional, capital-intensive industries, union membership fell from 25.4 per cent of the total workforce in 1954 to under 14 per cent at the end of the 1990s.

American revolution *see* **war of independence**

Appomattox
Although there was no formal end to the Civil War, the surrender of General Robert E. Lee at the Appomattox Courthouse (Virginia) in April 1865 marked the defeat of the southern Confederacy.

Articles of Confederation
A year after the adoption of the **Declaration of Independence**, the Continental Congress – which represented the colonists – adopted a constitution, the Articles of Confederation. They were not, however, ratified by all of the thirteen former colonies – which had become states – until 1781. The Articles rested upon a loose and decentralised system of government. Decision-making

was inevitably a slow, cumbersome and uncertain process. The political weaknesses of the Articles, and fears that the newly created nation might fragment, led to the calling of a constitutional convention in 1787 and the writing of the US Constitution.

axis of evil
In the 2002 State of the Union Address, President George W. Bush identified three countries or 'rogue states' – Iran, Iraq and North Korea – as members of an 'axis of evil'. Although the speech provoked fears that the US would be embroiled in war and criticisms that these nations had been picked rather arbitrarily, Bush spoke in assertive terms:

> By seeking weapons of mass destruction, these regimes pose a grave and growing danger. They could provide these arms to terrorists, giving them the means to match their hatred. They could attack our allies or attempt to blackmail the United States. In any of these cases, the price of indifference would be catastrophic.

Balkanisation
Some commentators suggest that immigration – and the growth of the Latino population – are leading to the break-up of the US. The term 'Balkanisation' suggests that a comparison can be drawn with the fate of the former Yugoslavia.

Bay of Pigs
In April 1961, Cuban exiles trained by the **Central Intelligence Agency** landed on the Cuban shore. They were, however, speedily defeated and hopes that the invasion would ignite a popular rebellion that would lead to the overthrow of Fidel Castro's regime were quickly abandoned.

Beats
The Beats were a literary grouping that emerged in both San Francisco and New York during the mid-1950s. They adopted an aggressively non-conformist style, consciously challenging cultural and social orthodoxies. They included Allen Gins-

berg, William Burroughs and, most notably, Jack Kerouac, author of *On the Road* (1957).

Bill of Rights
The Bill of Rights – the first ten amendments to the US Constitution – defines the rights and liberties of both the people and the individual states. It thereby places constraints upon the powers of government. The provisions of the Bill of Rights include freedom of speech, constraints upon the searching of homes, and the right to 'a speedy and public trial'. These amendments were ratified in 1791.

Black Panthers
The civil rights movement spawned other groups and organisations. Some had a radical character. Whereas the civil rights movement stressed non-violence and the importance of blacks and whites working together in pursuit of legal equality, the Black Panther Party – which was formed by Huey Percy Newton and Bobby Seale in 1966 – emphasised the need for armed actions, revolution and autonomous forms of black organisation.

Blues
The blues were originally an African-American musical form based upon relatively simple structures and a degree of emotional intensity. The precise character of the blues was shaped by its social setting. (Mississippi) Delta or rural blues was guitar-based from the later decades of the nineteenth century. Rhythm and blues (R&B) emerged in the bigger cities of the north during the 1940s. It incorporated the saxophone and had a marked swing. From the 1950s onwards, blues influenced white musicians and informed the evolution of rock music.

Boston Tea Party
The Boston Tea Party is widely celebrated as a defining moment that led the American colonies towards the **war of independence**. Many Americans had been boycotting English tea because of the taxes placed upon it by the British authorities. The British then attempted to break the boycott by

offering financial aid to the East India Company, allowing it sell tea cheaply. In December 1773, about fifty members of a radical Patriot organisation boarded three ships in Boston harbour and threw the chests of tea overboard. The coercive measures adopted by the British in the wake of the Tea Party further fuelled the anger of many colonists.

Brown v. *Board of Education* (Topeka, Kansas) (1954)

In the *Brown* ruling, the US Supreme Court struck down laws that segregated schooling. The case was brought by Oliver Brown, who had sought to enrol his daughter in his neighbourhood's white elementary school and was backed by the most long-established of the civil rights organisations, the

National Association for the Advancement of Colored People (NAACP). The Court – headed by Chief Justice Earl Warren – unanimously concluded that the segregation of schools inevitably relegated black children to a subordinate status and therefore deprived them of the equal protection of the law assured by Amendment XIV. The *Brown* decision was limited to education and was only partially implemented. Nonetheless, it provoked intense hostility from the white south. It also provided a basis upon which the civil rights movement of the 1950s and 1960s could build.

Bush, George H. W. (1924–)

After eight years as Ronald Reagan's vice-president, Bush was elected to the presidency in 1988. Although he appeared to break a key election pledge by agreeing to tax increases in 1990, his re-election seemed an inevitability after the US and allied victory in the 1991 Gulf War. However, a recession and an imaginative campaign by the Democratic challenger, Bill Clinton, led to his defeat in 1992.

Bush, George W. (1946–)

George W. Bush stood for the presidency in 2000, having served as Governor of Texas. The mathematics of the Electoral College allowed him to secure the presidency although he gained fewer popular votes than his Democratic opponent, Al

Gore. His presidency was invigorated, however, by the terrorist attacks on 11 September 2001. His approval ratings soared to record levels and, for a period, his personality seemed to accord with the public mood. However, a faltering economy and the uncertainties associated with the aftermath of the Iraq war took their toll on his popularity.

Central Intelligence Agency (CIA)

Popularly known as 'spooks', the CIA is the US government agency responsible for espionage and intelligence-gathering operations abroad. The agency has been criticised by some liberals and radicals for its alleged interference in other nations. It was, for example, accused of being implicated in the military overthrow of the leftist president of Chile, Salvador Allende, in September 1973.

checks and balances

Checks and balances are limits – or constraints – that are placed upon the different branches of government. Congress can, for example, check the powers of the president by refusing to confirm a nomination that he puts forward or by failing to ratify a treaty that he has concluded with another nation. Checks and balances ensure limited government although it can also be argued that they prevent effective decision-making and contribute to **gridlock**.

'City upon a hill'

The **Puritans** – who established the first New England settlements – believed that their communities would serve as a beacon to others across the world. Their commitment to Christianity would offer hope and inspiration. These notions were expressed in their clearest form by John Winthrop, who became the first governor of Massachusetts Bay Colony. As he sailed towards the new world in the spring of 1630, he spoke to the other colonists, telling them that their destiny was to build 'a City upon a hill' in New England. The idea that the US should be an exemplar nation that others could join and follow has an important place in American thought. Indeed,

350 years later, Winthrop's words were echoed by President Ronald Reagan:

> I've spoken of the shining city all my political life . . . in my mind it was a tall, proud city built on rocks stronger than oceans, windswept, God-blessed, and teeming with people of all kinds living in harmony and peace . . . And if there had to be city walls, the walls had doors and the doors were open to anyone with the will and the heart to get here. That's how I saw it, and see it still.

Civil Rights Act (1964)

The Civil Rights Act brought the segregationist era to a close by prohibiting discrimination in the provision of public facilities such as cinemas, restaurants and transportation.

civil rights movement

The civil rights movement brought together organisations such as the Congress of Racial Equality (CORE), the Southern Christian Leadership Conference (SCLC) and the Student Non-Violent Co-ordinating Committee (SNCC). It campaigned against segregation in the southern states in the 1950s and 1960s through the use of direct action. Its tactics included sit-ins, boycotts and marches. Martin Luther King, a Baptist minister from Montgomery, Alabama, came to the fore as a leading figure. His words – spoken at the Lincoln Memorial, Washington DC, on 28 August 1963 – have come to symbolise the movement:

> I have a dream that one day this nation will rise up and live out the true meaning of its creed: 'We hold these truths to be self-evident: that all men are created equal.' I have a dream that one day on the red hills of Georgia the sons of former slaves and the sons of former slaveowners will be able to sit down together at a table of brotherhood . . . I have a dream that my four children will one day live in a nation where they will not be judged by the color of their skin but by the content of their character. I have a dream today.

Civil War (1861–5)

The Civil War – or War between the States – of 1861 to 1865 was fought between the southern states – known as the Confederacy – and the north, or Union. Following the election of Abraham Lincoln as president, ie began when the south sought to secede from the Union. The defeat of the Confederacy in 1865 established that the US was a single nation offering rights to all its citizens rather than a voluntary agreement – or compact – between semi-sovereign states.

Cold War

Although many historians emphasise its earlier roots, the Cold War began in the late 1940s as the tensions between the Soviet Union and the west intensified. From a western perspective, communism had an expansionist character; between 1945 and 1949, the central European nations and China were absorbed into the communist bloc. Although there was a period of détente during the 1970s and a rapprochement between the US and China, the Cold War was characterised by military and economic rivalry. Many feared that the arms race, regional wars such as Korea and Vietnam, and periodic crises would lead to a war between the superpowers. The Cold War came to a close with the fall of the Berlin Wall in 1989 and the break-up of the Soviet Union in 1991.

colonies

A colony is a territory that is the possession of a more powerful country. The American settlers were – from the building of the Jamestown settlement in 1607 until the **war of independence** – colonists. They owed allegiance to the British monarch. Although some were corporate ventures, many of the thirteen colonies had governors appointed by the crown.

Confederacy

At the end of 1860 and at the beginning of 1861, the southern states left – or seceded from – the US. Their action came amidst growing economic differences between the north and the south and fears that slave ownership – upon which the southern economy was structured – might be restricted. It followed the election of Abraham Lincoln as US president. In the wake of secession, the southern states formed the Confederate States of America. Jefferson Davis served as its president and Richmond, Virginia, became its capital. The vice-president, Alexander H. Stephens, a former congressman from Georgia, stated that:

> Our new government is founded on the opposite idea of the equality of the races . . . Its corner stone rests upon the great truth that the Negro is not equal to the white man. This . . . government is the first in the history of the world, based on this great physical and moral truth.

Secession provoked the Civil War that ended – in 1865 – with the defeat of the Confederacy. For many years, the white south looked back nostalgically to the 'Lost Cause'.

Congress
The US Congress is the national legislature and makes federal law. It is *bicameral* and divided into two chambers: the House of Representatives and the Senate, each of which has a particular character and constitutionally specified responsibilities. Its powers were established in Article although the US Supreme Court has ruled that it also has implied powers as well as those enumerated in the Constitution. In contrast with legislatures in parliamentary systems such as Britain, the parties are relatively weak in Congress. Members of Congress often vote in a different way to other members of their own party. Those seeking the passage of a particular legislative measure are therefore compelled to build a coalition of support, often by offering political concessions.

Conservatism
Contemporary conservatism emphasises the need for limited government intervention in the economy – or *free-market economics*, individual self-reliance and law enforcement. This leads conservatives to stress the need for tax reductions and

strong policing powers. Many – but not all – conservatives also talk of moral traditionalism and the importance of the family. All conservatives emphasise the importance of national defence and endorsed an unambiguous military response to the terrorist attacks on 11 September 2001. There are, however, some tensions between those dubbed 'neo-conservatives' who are committed to the 'export' of democracy and the free market believing that it will create a more secure and less threatening global order and others who fear that such projects will embroil the US in regional conflicts and trap it in unsustainable attempts at 'nation-building' overseas.

Although it had a liberal wing for many decades, the Republican Party has had a clearly conservative character since the 1970s. There are still some conservatives in the Democrats' ranks – particularly in the south – but they are relatively few in number.

Crevecoeur, Hector St John de (1735–1813)

Crevecoeur was one of the first commentators on American life. A native of France and serving in Canada, he travelled across the north-eastern colonies. Around 1769, he settled on a farm in New York, writing *Letters from an American Farmer* (1782). Although he returned to France in 1790, he became French consul in New York City for a period after the colonies won their independence. He is remembered, in particular, for his description of the American as a 'new man'.

Crucible, The

Arthur Miller's play was first produced at the beginning of 1953. It depicted the Salem Witch Trails of 1692 – and the frenzied hysteria of a New England community gripped by the belief that many of the women in its midst are witches. In this atmosphere, accusations and confessions abound. The play is widely understood as a commentary on the times in which it was written. It was an indictment of the anti-communist mood in the US during the era of **McCarthyism**.

Cuban missile crisis

In October 1962, US spy planes found that Soviet missiles were being installed in Cuba. The Kennedy administration imposed a naval 'quarantine' on the island and – amidst widespread fears that the tensions would lead to war between the superpowers – the Soviet leader, Nikita Krushchev, ordered the dismantling of the missiles.

Declaration of Independence

The Declaration of Independence was drafted by Thomas Jefferson and is regarded as the founding document of the US. It was adopted – after some amendments were made – by the second Continental Congress on 24 July 1776. It rested on an assertion of the liberties and rights of the citizen:

> . . . all men are created equal, that they are endowed by their Creator with certain unalienable Rights, that among these are Life, Liberty and the pursuit of Happiness. That to secure these rights, Governments are instituted among Men, deriving their just powers from the consent of the governed, That whenever any Form of Government becomes destructive of these ends, it is the Right of the People to alter or to abolish it, and to institute new Government, laying its foundation on such principles and organizing its powers in such form, as to them shall seem most likely to effect their Safety and Happiness.

Du Bois, W. E. B. (1868–1961)

Du Bois was an early civil rights campaigner and a powerful intellectual voice against racism. The author of many works, most notably *The Souls of Black Folk* (1903), he played an important part in establishing the National Association for the Advancement of Colored People (NAACP). He edited the organisation's journal, *The Crisis*. Towards the end of his life, his sympathies with socialism became more pronounced and in 1961 he joined the Communist Party. He spent the last two years of his life in Ghana.

Dust Bowl

During the 1930s, the consequences of economic depression were compounded in the south-western Great Plains. Years of drought and non-sustainable farming methods turned the region into a Dust Bowl. Hundreds of thousands of people from states such as Oklahoma were forced to leave their homes. Many migrated to California. Their story – symbolised by the figure of Tom Joad – was told in John Steinbeck's novel, *The Grapes of Wrath*:

> And then the dispossessed were drawn west – from Kansas, Oklahoma, Texas, New Mexico; from Nevada and Arkansas, families, tribes, dusted out, tractored out. Carloads, caravans, homeless and hungry; twenty thousand and fifty thousand and a hundred thousand and two hundred thousand. They streamed over the mountains, hungry and restless – restless as ants, scurrying to find work to do – to lift, to push, to pull, to pick, to cut – anything, any burden to bear, for food. The kids are hungry. We got no place to live. Like ants scurrying for work, for food, and most of all for land.' (John Steinbeck, *The Grapes of Wrath*, 1939)

Dylan, Bob (1941–)

Dylan first secured public attention through his appearances in New York folk clubs. He was associated with the radicalism of the early 1960s and a number of his songs were hailed as anthems by those in the civil rights movement and peace campaigners. His embrace of the electric guitar and the adoption of a more introspective style marked the first of many shifts in his career.

emancipation proclamation

The emancipation proclamation was issued by President Abraham Lincoln. It declared that slaves held in Confederate-held territory would be free on 1 January 1863. Although it could not be enforced, it paved the way for the thirteenth amendment to the Constitution in 1865.

ethnicity

Whereas the concept of 'race' is associated with socially significant physical characteristics, an ethnicity is a grouping that shares a common ancestry, history or culture. Although often described as a race, US Latinos or Hispanics should instead be regarded as an ethnicity. The term encompasses those who are from Mexico, Puerto Rico, Cuba, or the other countries of central or south America. Many speak Spanish as either a first or a second language.

exceptionalism

The concept of American exceptionalism is used to suggest that the US has followed a radically different path to that adopted in the 'old world' countries of Europe and Asia. It is, for example, applied to describe the absence of a mass socialist party in the US.

Federal Bureau of Investigation (FBI)

The FBI was created within the Department of Justice in 1924. Headed for many decades by its legendary director, J. Edgar Hoover, the 'Feds' first established their reputation by pursuing the gangsters of the interwar years.

federalism

In a federal system of government, powers are divided between a national government and the state governments. US federalism is seen in different ways. Some have portrayed the founding of the US as a compact between the states. This implies that the states have far-reaching rights that cannot be abrogated. Others argue the American people as a whole have sovereignty. From this perspective, the rights of the states are much more limited and the constraints placed upon the states in the Constitution are of particular importance.

Federalist, The

The Federalist – generally referred to as the *Federalist Papers* – was a series of eighty-five essays. They were written by three of the **Founding Fathers** – Alexander Hamilton, John Jay and

James Madison – between October 1787 and May 1788 under the pen name 'Publius'. The essays sought to win support for the ratification of the US Constitution.

Founding Fathers

The 'Founding Fathers' or 'Framers' were the delegates from the states who attended the 1787 constitutional convention in Philadelphia. After prolonged debate, they drew up the US Constitution. Their ranks included figures such as James Madison, Benjamin Franklin, Alexander Hamilton and George Washington.

Franklin, Benjamin (1706–90)

Benjamin Franklin began his life as an apprentice printer. From these beginnings he became a publisher, newspaper owner and scientist. He is particularly known for his experiments involving electricity. After being active for at least two decades in campaigns to secure concessions for the colonies, he played a part in drafting the **Declaration of Independence** and served as a delegate at the Philadelphia convention that drafted the US Constitution.

Friedan, Betty (1921–)

Betty Friedan is best known for the book, *The Feminine Mystique* (1963). It laid the basis for contemporary feminism by arguing that, in patriarchal societies, women only found fulfilment through the achievements of their husbands and children. They were victims of false consciousness. In 1966, Friedan co-founded the National Organisation for Women (NOW), which sought equality of opportunity and campaigned unsuccessfully for ratification of the Equal Rights Amendment to the US Constitution.

frontier

Frederick Jackson Turner (1863–1932), a history professor at the University of Wisconsin, argued in a paper presented to the American Historical Association in July 1893 that the frontier marking the settlers' shift westwards across the continent or, as

Turner put it, 'the meeting point between savagery and civilization', had imbued American society with its defining characteristics. Frontier life laid the basis for a self-reliant individualism:

> That courseness and strength combined with acuteness and inquisitiveness; that practical, inventive turn of mind, quick to find expedients; that masterful grasp of material things, lacking in the artistic but powerful to effect great ends; that restless, nervous energy; that dominant individualism, working for good and for evil, and withal that buoyancy and exuberance which comes with freedom – these are traits of the frontier, or traits called out elsewhere because of the existence of the frontier.

The frontier has been a recurring theme in American discourse. In 1960, John F. Kennedy spoke of the '**new frontier**'. A celebrated description, scripted a few years afterwards, identified outer space as the 'final frontier'.

Gilded Age
During the closing decades of the nineteenth century, some family names – such as the Carnegies and the Vanderbilts – became synonymous with the accumulation of wealth through their business ventures. At the same time, there was widespread poverty and hardship.

Great Society
In 1964, President Lyndon Johnson committed himself to the abolition of racial discrimination, poverty and deprivation. There was to be a war on poverty. Government spending increased significantly and agencies proliferated. Although both the aged and the poor were offered healthcare assistance through Medicare and Medicaid respectively, the inner-cities continued to be synonymous with entrenched poverty. For conservatives, the failure of the Great Society can be attributed to the scaling back of programmes so as to pay for the **Vietnam** War. Conservatives argue that government expenditure stifled notions of self-reliance and thereby added to the numbers in poverty.

gridlock
The term 'gridlock' is employed to describe the failure of the US government to implement change or reform because of tensions between the different branches of government or, for example, between the federal government and the states.

Gulf War
The 1991 Gulf War was a response to Iraq's invasion and occupation of Kuwait. Under United Nations' auspices, a US-led alliance liberated Kuwait in 'Operation Desert Storm'. Sanctions were also imposed upon the Iraqi regime. For some, the war appeared to mark a commitment by the US to a 'new world order', a post-communist globe in which all countries would co-operate together so as to secure liberty and the rule of law.

Guthrie, Woody (1912–67)
Guthrie, a legendary folk singer, was associated with leftist politics. He is remembered for his song, 'This Land is Your Land', which offered a patriotic vision but at the same time sought to reclaim America from the wealthiest classes and the exploiters.

Hamilton, Alexander (1755–1804)
Alexander Hamilton served in the **war of independence** and after attending the **Philadelphia convention**, co-authored the *Federalist Papers*. He had a close association with **George Washington**, who had led the American armies in the war of independence and served as the first president. He became the first Secretary of the Treasury in September 1789. He subsequently led the Federalist Party, favouring relatively strong forms of central government. He died of wounds from a duel that he fought with Aaron Burr, a longtime political foe.

Hollywood
For much of the twentieth century, Hollywood, Los Angeles, was the home of the US film industry. Initially – between the 1930s and 1950s – it was dominated by the 'big five' companies, including Warner Bros and Paramount. By 1939, Hollywood

studios were producing more than 400 feature films a year. Although weakened by television and divided by the blacklisting of actors and writers who seemed to have communist sympathies, Hollywood restructured itself through mergers, television production and more adventurous forms of film making.

House of Representatives
The US House of Representatives is the lower chamber of Congress. Its 435 members (or 'congressmen') are elected every two years. The number of Congressmen from each state is dependent upon the size of its population. There is a process of reapportionment every ten years so as to take account of population shifts.

Impeachment
Federal officials – including judges and the president if accused of 'high crimes and misdemeanours – can be subject to a process of impeachment. The House of Representatives puts forward an indictment and there is a trial by the Senate. If convicted, the official is removed from office. Two presidents – Andrew Johnson (1865–9) and Bill Clinton (1993–2001) – have been impeached but both were acquitted in the Senate.

Iran–Contra scandal
The scandal became public in late 1986. A number of individuals within the White House had pursued a covert foreign policy. Arms had been sold to the Islamic government in Iran in the hope of appeasing moderates and the funds that were obtained had been transferred to the 'Contras', a right-wing rebel army fighting the leftist Sandinista government in Nicaragua. Congress had – through the Boland Amendment – specifically prohibited such aid.

isolationism
The US has, at times, pulled back and withdrawn from 'entangling alliances' with other nations. Isolationist feelings led, for example, the Senate to reject the Treaty of Versailles in 1920. However, although these sentiments have sometimes

been strongly held, particularly in the mid-western 'heartland' states, they should be set in context. From 1823 onwards, when the Monroe Doctrine was adopted, the US has sought to ensure that the countries of central and south America could not threaten its strategic interests. Furthermore, isolationist phases have often preceded and followed periods of interventionism across the globe. Versailles came after US participation in the First World War. Although there were some who called – after the end of the Cold War – for renewed isolationism, the events of September 11th ensured that those who sought the active military involvement of the US on the world stage were ascendant.

Jackson, Andrew (1767–1845)

Andrew Jackson, who grew up in the 'back country' settlements of the Carolinas, became a national hero in the Battle of New Orleans. First elected to the presidency in 1828, his period in office marked the extension of American democracy to incorporate participation by the 'common man' through the growth of mass political parties. At the same time, however, he had an autocratic style and rarely deferred to Congress.

jazz

Jazz has been described as a quintessentially American form of music. It is nonetheless difficult to define. It generally – but not always – involves a degree of improvisation. It also rests upon a sense of buoyancy or 'swing', encouraging people to move around and dance.

Jazz is said to have begun in the black neighbourhoods of New Orleans at the end of the nineteenth century. In the 1920s, it moved northwards during the 'Great Migration' of African-Americans to cities such as Chicago and New York. In the 1930s, swing bands emerged such as those led by Duke Ellington and Count Basie. In the 1960s jazz musicians began incorporating forms associated with rhythm and blues and rock into their music.

Jefferson, Thomas (1743–1826)
Thomas Jefferson was a Virginia landowner and lawyer. He largely wrote the **Declaration of Independence**. Following ratification of the US Constitution, he came to lead the Democratic-Republicans and was associated with those who opposed a strongly centralised national government. He became president in 1800 and served two terms. Under his leadership – in 1803 – the size of the US was doubled by his decision to purchase the Louisiana Territory from the French government.

Jim Crow
The term 'Jim Crow' was drawn from a minstrel show and used to refer to the **segregation** laws imposed throughout the southern states from the late nineteenth century until the 1960s.

Johnson, Lyndon B. (1908–73)
Lyndon Johnson became president on the death of **John F. Kennedy**. A former Senate Majority Leader, he was widely regarded as a conservative figure. Nonetheless, he promoted far-reaching civil rights legislation and – through the **Great Society** programmes – ensured that resources were devoted to the 'war on poverty'. In the longer term, however, his domestic policy record was overshadowed by the escalation of US intervention in **Vietnam**. Against a background of protests against the war – and growing divisions – he decided not to seek a second term as president.

Kennedy, John F. (1917–63)
Kennedy's presidency was cut brutally short by his assassination on 22 November 1963. He had held the office for less than three years. Although he committed the US to a moon landing by the end of the decade and created the Peace Corps to work in less developed countries, legislative achievements were relatively limited in character. It was not until his vice-president, **Lyndon B. Johnson**, assumed the presidency that substantial civil rights legislation was enacted. He is remembered more for his leadership during some of the most tense

moments of the Cold War. In his first inaugural address he concluded with a plea: 'Ask not what your country can do for you – ask what you can do for your country.' After the building of the Berlin Wall, he sought to associate the wider world with the city, using the celebrated words, 'Ich bin ein Berliner'. His seemingly restrained handling of the **Cuban missile crisis** won him many plaudits from historians.

King, Martin Luther, Jr (1929–68)
In 1954, Martin Luther King Jr became Pastor at the Dexter Avenue Baptist Church in Montgomery, Alabama. Within a year, a mass boycott of the buses – which by law confined black passengers to the back of the bus – had begun. The buses were eventually desegregated. It exemplified King's belief – and that of the Southern Christian Leadership Conference – that non-violent protest could bring about social change. In 1960, he moved to become an associate pastor at Ebenezer church in Atlanta. His leadership of the **civil rights movement** continued, leading to his arrest and imprisonment by state authorities in the south. After legalised – or *de jure* – discrimination was brought to an end by the 1964 **Civil Rights Act**, King turned towards poverty and disadvantage. While in Memphis Tennessee, in support of striking sanitation workers, he was assassinated.

Korean War (1950–3)
After the **Second World War,** the Korean peninsula was divided between the communist north and a southern state that was aligned with the west. In June 1950, the North Korean People's Army attacked the south capturing Seoul, the capital, three days later. Three years of war followed as US and other United Nations forces retook territory and advanced across the north towards the Chinese border. The war continued until July 1953 when an armistice was signed. It left the peninsula divided between the north and south. Since then, there have been periodic fears about North Korean intentions. In the aftermath of the September 11th attacks, the country was identified by President **George W. Bush** as part of the **'axis of evil'**.

liberalism

The meaning of the term 'liberalism' has shifted in character over the years. Traditionally, it rested upon individualism, the rights of the citizen, laissez-faire and minimal government. It preached self-reliance. Contemporary liberalism stresses personal liberty, particularly in social and cultural affairs. It is, for example, closely associated with identity politics and the black, women's and gay movements. However, it also emphasises the need for the regulation of business and the provision of government services so as to offer greater assistance to those at the lower end of the socio-economic scale. Many liberals are supporters of the Democratic Party, although some have, at times, backed more radical candidates such as the Green nominee Ralph Nader in 2000.

Lincoln, Abraham (1809–65)

Lincoln was the sixteenth president of the US. His election and fears that slavery might end provoked the secession of the southern states and led to the **Civil War**. He led the northern states throughout the war. He is remembered – in particular – for the Gettysburg Address in November 1863 where he spoke of American democracy as 'government of the people, by the people [and] for the people'. Lincoln was assassinated just days after the war had come to a close with the defeat of the south.

Madison, James (1751–1836)

James Madison, a Virginian, is among the most celebrated of the **Founding Fathers** who attended the convention at Philadelphia in 1787 and wrote the US Constitution. He ensured the ratification of the Constitution by the states through the writing – with **Alexander Hamilton** and John Jay – of the **Federalist** essays. He was the fourth president of the US, serving between 1809 and 1817.

Malcolm X (1925–65)

Malcolm X – originally Malcolm Little – came to prominence as a member of the Nation of Islam, a radical organisation that fused black nationalism, religion and authoritarianism. He took the name 'X' because, he argued, the name 'Little' had been assigned to the family by a slaveholder generations earlier. In contrast with **Martin Luther King**'s emphasis on a broad social movement that used non-violence and peaceful forms of direct action, Malcolm X rejected interracial co-operation and argued that armed action might be necessary. He is particularly remembered for the phrase that he used to summarise his strategy: 'by any means necessary'. After breaking with the Nation of Islam leader, Elijah Muhammad, in 1964, Malcolm X's thinking shifted towards both traditional Islam and notions of a revolution by the oppressed across the world. His words were also marked by less hostility to whites. He was assassinated – allegedly by Nation of Islam activists – in February 1965. His life has been depicted in Spike Lee's 1992 film, *Malcolm X* (40 Acres and a Mule Filmworks Production).

'manifest destiny'

The term 'manifest destiny' was coined in 1845 by John L. O'Sullivan, editor of the *Democratic Review*. The US, he asserted, had a purpose or mission to spread westwards from the early area of settlement along the eastern seaboard. He spoke of 'the fulfillment of our manifest destiny to overspread the Continent allotted by Providence for the free development of our yearly multiplying millions'.

Marshall, John (1755–1835)

John Marshall served as the fourth Chief Justice. During his period of office (1801–35), the Court asserted the right to declare an Act passed by Congress unconstitutional. This is known as judicial review. The landmark case was *Marbury* v. *Madison* (1803) when a section of the Judiciary Act of 1789 was struck down.

Marshall Plan

In 1947 – in the aftermath of the **Second World War** – much of Europe lay devastated. President Truman's administration adopted a plan – drawn up by General George C. Marshall, the US Secretary of State – to provide aid that would contribute to European economic recovery. The assistance would, it was hoped, lay a basis for stability and limit the appeal of the communist parties in countries such as Italy and France. By the end of 1951, $13.3 billion had been transferred to western Europe.

McCarthyism

Senator Joseph McCarthy (1908 – 57) of Wisconsin was at the forefront of efforts to identify and root out alleged communists working in government, the armed forces, or the film industry during the early 1950s. McCarthy's Senate committee compelled individuals who – like many others – had left-wing sympathies during the 1930s and 1940s to attend its hearings. It emphasised to them that the only way to demonstrate that they were loyal Americans was through the naming of others who might be Communist Party sympathisers. McCarthyism was a product of fears about Soviet expansionism and the seeming vulnerability of the west. Some observers suggest that the mood it engendered shaped films made during the period. *Invasion of the Body Snatchers* (1956) depicted the capture of a community by aliens who take human form and cannot, at first sight, be distinguished from others.

military-industrial complex

In his farewell speech as president (1961), Dwight Eisenhower warned of the dangers that he asserted were associated with the growing influence of the armed forces and the weapons industry. Although Eisenhower had conservative views, the concept of a military-industrial complex was adopted and extended by radicals so as to suggest that there was a 'hidden government' resting on elite interests. This notion informed **Oliver Stone**'s 1991 film, *JFK*.

NASA

Created in 1958, the National Aeronautics and Space Administration (NASA) – a government agency – is responsible for the US space programme. The first landing of astronauts on the moon in 1969 – just seven years after first putting a man in space – is regarded as its crowning achievement.

native Americans

Accounts suggest that the native Americans – once dubbed 'Red Indians' – settled in the American continents about two thousand years ago. They were divided on the basis of tribes such as the Cherokee, the Cheyenne, the Iroquois and the Seminole. While some were nomadic, others had a settled existence. However, as the area of European settlement shifted westwards, native Americans were forced to relinquish their former lands. Even today, although the native-American population represents less than 1 per cent of the total US population, it includes over 500 different groupings.

NATO

The North Atlantic Treaty – that created the North Atlantic Treaty Organisation (NATO) – was signed in April and ratified by the US Senate in July 1949. It was formed against a background of **Cold War** tensions and based around the principle of collective security. The alliance brought together the countries of western Europe and north America. Following the breakup of the Soviet bloc in 1989–90 and the democratisation of eastern Europe, many of these countries – which were formerly in the Warsaw Pact – sought and obtained NATO membership.

natural rights

The belief that individuals have fundamental rights imposes limits and constraints on the powers of government. The concept of natural rights underpinned the **Declaration of Independence**.

New Deal

The New Deal was a programme of economic reform established by President **Franklin D. Roosevelt** in response to the depression that had followed in the wake of the Wall Street Crash. After taking steps to rebuild confidence in the banking system, Roosevelt used the first hundred days of his presidency to initiate government programmes that would employ those without work. These projects included the Works Projects Administration (WPA) and the Civilian Conservation Corps (CCC). At the same time, the Federal Emergency Relief Administration offered assistance to those in severe need. However, despite these initiatives, the American economy only recovered slowly.

new frontier

In his address to the Democratic Party's national convention in 1960, **John F. Kennedy** talked in terms of a new frontier. It recalled earlier notions of the frontier, came to define hopes of the decade that followed, and defined Kennedy's presidency:

> We stand at the edge of a New Frontier – the frontier of unfulfilled hopes and dreams. It will deal with unsolved problems of peace and war, unconquered pockets of ignorance and prejudice, unanswered questions of poverty and surplus.

new left

Although always confined to the further fringes of the American political spectrum, the left has, at times, influenced the character of particular cultural movements. The 'new left' emerged in the 1960s. In contrast with the 'old left', which had been associated with the Soviet Union, the traditional working-class, and calls for the nationalisation of industry, it stressed participatory democracy, student rebellion and guerilla movements in the countries of south America, Africa and Asia. Through organisations such as Students for a Democratic Society (SDS), the new left merged together with the identity movements associated with feminism and black power and the anti-war movement sparked by the **Vietnam** War.

Nixon, Richard M. (1913–94)

Richard Nixon served as a congressman, senator and as Dwight Eisenhower's vice-president before winning the presidency on his second attempt in 1968. His administration is particularly remembered for the shifts in US foreign policy that took place and the circumstances in which it ended. There was a partial rapprochement with China, ending two decades of bitter hostility. In January 1973, an accord was reached with North Vietnam so as to end American intervention in south-east Asia. Although re-elected by a landslide majority in 1972, President Nixon was then embroiled in the Watergate scandal. He resigned in August 1974 and his vice-president – former House Minority Leader Gerald R. Ford – assumed the presidency.

Pearl Harbor

On 7 December 1941, against a backcloth of long-term tensions between the two nations in the Pacific region, Japanese forces mounted a surprise attack on the US naval base at Pearl Harbor on the Hawaiian island of Oahu. In two hours 18 warships, 188 aircraft and 2,403 servicemen were lost in the attack. The following day, President **Franklin D. Roosevelt** spoke to a joint session of Congress. He sought and gained and a declaration of war against Japan. This marked the entry of the US into the **Second World War**.

Pentagon

The Pentagon houses the US Department of Defense. It is in Arlington, northern Virginia.

Philadelphia convention

The Philadelphia convention was attended by delegates from the thirteen states who drafted the US Constitution and subsequently became known as the **Founding Fathers**. The constitutional convention was called because of the structural weaknesses of the forms of government established under the **Articles of Confederation**.

postmodernism

Although the concept defies agreed forms of definition, postmodernism represents a rejection of 'truth' and the large-scale structured explanations that it dubs 'grand narratives'. In place of these, it understands events and processes in terms of fragmentation and randomness. At the same time, it stresses the ways in which interpretations and understandings of events are socially constructed and reflects the position of the observer. Cultural studies has, as a discipline, been profoundly influenced and shaped by postmodernist thinking.

president
The US president is elected to serve for a four-year term and heads the executive branch of government. Despite his dominance of the world stage, the presidency is subject to checks and balances that, at times, constrain his exercise of power. Legislation, for example, is the prerogative of Congress. Furthermore, the appointment of senior officials and federal judges must be confirmed by the Senate. As Richard Neustadt, a celebrated political observer has recorded, his capabilities depend – particularly within the domestic policy sphere – upon his 'power to persuade'.

progressivism
The progressive era was at the beginning of the twentieth century. It rested upon efforts to move away from untrammelled laissez-faire and regulate the economy particularly by limiting the larger corporations and cartels. However, progressivism went beyond economics. It also sought democratic reforms so as to break the power of the political 'bosses' in the bigger cities. Some observers stress its role in imposing notions of 'efficiency' and 'Americanising' recent immigrants.

Prohibition
Amendment XVIII to the US Constitution – which prohibited the manufacture, supply and sale of alcoholic drink – came into effect at midnight on 16 January 1920. It was widely violated by ordinary individuals and bootleggers whose activities descended into violent gangsterism. Prohibition ended when Amendment XXI – which repealed Amendment XVIII – was passed in 1933. Some counties, however, continue to forbid or restrict the sale of alcohol.

Puritans
Some of the earliest European settlers on the American continent were Puritan émigrés from Britain who sought to 'purify' the Christian faith. They established communities in New England governed by strict religious principle. Their labours are celebrated annually at Thanksgiving. Although other religious traditions and cultures shaped the development of American thought, the Puritans bequeathed an emphasis on hard work, self-reliance and frugality as well as a commitment to churches that – at least in some sense – 'belonged' to their congregations. They also passed on a notion of America as a **'City upon a hill'**.

Reagan, Ronald W. (1911–)
Ronald Reagan, former Hollywood film actor and Governor of California, was the fortieth president. His period in office was closely associated with notions of a conservative 'revolution'. In 1981, he successfully persuaded Congress to cut taxation levels. At the same time, there was a significant increase in defence spending and talk of a new cold war with the USSR. The ensuing budget deficit – and the seeming lack of direction that was evident in the **Iran–Contra scandal** – tarnished memories of his presidency.

Reconstruction
In the aftermath of the **Civil War** (1861–5), southern defeat and the abolition of slavery, Congress took some steps towards the reform of southern society. Former male slaves were given the right to vote and hold public office. The Freedmen's Bureau offered practical assistance to African-Americans.

The period of Reconstruction lasted until 1877. There had been a close and disputed presidential election and the Republican candidate, Rutherford B. Hayes, only gained the presidency by agreeing to a compromise. It involved the withdrawal of northern troops from the southern states. Following this, whites progressively regained their position of political dominance. **Segregation** laws were introduced and blacks were denied the right to vote.

'religious right'

The 'religious right' refers to organisations such as the Christian Coalition and the Family Research Council. They draw much of their support from white, evangelical Christians who – in recent decades – turned towards conservatism and the Republican Party.

Roosevelt, Franklin D. (1882–1945)

Franklin Roosevelt was elected to the White House in four elections and served for a longer period than any other president. His terms of office are remembered for the construction of a broad coalition of support for the Democratic Party, the **New Deal** and wartime leadership.

Roosevelt, Theodore (1858–1919)

Theodore Roosevelt established his reputation in the 'badlands' of the west and the Spanish–American war. Becoming president following the assassination of William McKinley, his period of office had a populist twist as he challenged the powerful big business 'trusts'. In foreign policy, he asserted US interests with vigour, particularly in central and south America. In 1912, he stood for the presidency again on behalf of the progressive ticket.

Second World War (1941–5)

The US entered the Second World War in December 1941 following the Japanese attack on **Pearl Harbor**. Allied with Britain and the USSR, its forces played a pivotal role in the liberation of Europe (1944–5) and the war in the Pacific, which culminated in the Japanese surrender in August 1945.

segregation

Segregation – which is also described as **Jim Crow** – was imposed by law across the southern states from the late nineteenth century onwards. Blacks were restricted to separate – and invariably unequal – public facilities. Nearly all were denied the right to vote through the use of bogus tests that restricted the franchise.

Segregation only came to a close in the 1960s. Despite resistance to reform by significant sections of the white population – and institutionalised violence – the **civil rights movement**'s campaign of non-violent direct action led to the passage of the 1964 **Civil Rights Act** and the 1965 Voting Rights Act.

sexual revolution

The concept of a 'sexual revolution' is often invoked in discussions of the 1960s. There was – it is argued – a significant liberalisation of attitudes, particularly among young people. For many, sexual relationships outside marriage became institutionalised. Critics of the term point out, however, that attitudes towards homosexuality remained highly critical and this must, at the least, qualify the use of the phrase.

Stone, Oliver(1946–)

Oliver Stone is a radical and controversial director. His films include *Platoon, Wall Street, Born on the Fourth of July, The Doors, Natural Born Killers, JFK* and *Nixon*. Some have attracted criticism for merging fact and fiction in a way that the viewer cannot always discern and Stone's belief – most evident in both *JFK* and *Nixon* – that significant events in modern American history have been shaped by a **military-industrial complex**.

Stonewall

In 1969, the police raided the Stonewall Inn in Greenwich Village – a gay neighbourhood – in New York City. This provoked protests which some commentators described as an uprising. Stonewall has come to symbolise the birth of an assertive and politically conscious gay movement.

Supreme Court

The US Supreme Court is the third branch of government. It has the ability – if an appropriate case is brought before it – to rule on the constitutionality of laws passed by Congress or state legislatures and actions undertaken government officials including the president. The Court's power to interpret the US Constitution (termed 'judicial review') has enabled it to play a significant role in shaping American politics and society. It's brought segregation in the public schools to a close and – through *Roe* v. *Wade* (1973) – established **abortion** as a constitutional right.

Tocqueville, Alexis de (1805–59)

Tocqueville came from an aristocratic French family. His study of the early republic, *Democracy in America*, published as two volumes in 1835 and 1840, brought together a record of his travels with an incisive appraisal of life, politics and society in the US. His judgements are still widely cited.

Truman, Harry S. (1884–1972)

Harry Truman became president on **Franklin D. Roosevelt**'s death in April 1945. Although the war in Europe ended just a few weeks later, the Japanese only surrendered after atomic bombs had been dropped on the cities of Hiroshima and Nagasaki. The remainder of his presidency was dominated by the **Cold War**. In 1947, Truman offered backing to those opposing what he depicted as communist expansionism in Europe and Asia. The US – he proclaimed in what became known as the Truman Doctrine – must help 'free peoples who are resisting attempted subjugation by armed minorities or by outside pressures'. The **Marshall Plan** provided a basis for economic recovery in western Europe. When the Soviet Union blockaded the western sectors of Berlin in 1948, the US supplied the city though an airlift. **NATO** was created and the **Korean War** began against this background.

underclass

The underclass refers to those – generally living in the most disadvantaged inner-city neighbourhoods – who are in long-term, entrenched poverty. The term is also associated with particular cultural images that many liberal critics see as unwarranted. These include welfare dependency, drug abuse, criminality and teenage pregnancies.

Vietnam

In 1954, following a war of independence against French colonial rule, Vietnam was divided between the north, under communist rule, and a western-oriented south. However, the government of South Vietnam faced increasing opposition from the National Liberation Front (NLF or 'Vietcong'), guerilla forces backed by North Vietnam. US policymakers feared that if the south fell to the NLF, and Vietnam was reunited under a communist government, other countries in south-east Asia would fall – like a row of dominoes – to the communists. President **Kennedy** sent military advisers to aid the South Vietnamese forces. However, in 1964, following an alleged attack on US vessels in the Gulf of Tonkin, Congress responded to a request by President **Lyndon Johnson** and passed resolutions authorising measures to prevent further attacks. Although later criticised as a 'blank cheque' allowing almost any form of military action in south-east Asia, the resolutions were passed in the Senate by 8 votes to 2 and in the House by 416 to 0. In these circumstances, US ground troops were committed to Vietnam. The war led to the loss of 58,000 American lives. Faced by increasing domestic opposition to the war effort and repeated military setbacks, American forces were eventually withdrawn. In April 1975, the South Vietnamese government collapsed. The NLF and North Vietnamese forces captured Saigon and Vietnam was, as the US had originally feared, reunited under communist rule.

Wall Street Crash

During the 1920s, stock prices rose dramatically. Increasingly, their value bore no relationship to the profits that the company might yield. However, the continuous price rises encouraged the purchasing of shares. In many cases, people borrowed so as to buy them. However, from September 1929 onwards, prices began to fall and selling began. In October 1929, as prices tumbled, panic selling set in. In just twenty-six days, the market lost 47 per cent of its value. Banks were driven to closure. Both companies and consumers cut their spending thereby initiating a sustained economic depression.

war of independence
The war of independence – or the American revolution – led to the overthrow of British rule following their defeat at Yorktown in 1781.

Washington, George (1732–99)
George Washington led the American armies from 1775 onwards. He was later a signatory to the US Constitution and served as the first US president (1789–97). His presidency established foreign policy as primarily a responsibility for the executive branch.

WASP
WASP is an acronym for 'white Anglo-Saxon Protestant'. Although sometimes applied more broadly, the term is used to describe the earliest English settlers and their descendants.

Watergate
Following a break-in at the offices of the Democratic National Committee at the Watergate building in Washington DC during the 1972 election campaign, it became evident that there were links between the burglary and administration officials in the White House. Over the months that followed the election, there were efforts to conceal these ties and hinder investigations. A number of President Richard Nixon's most senior aides were compelled to resign. Against this background, the Supreme Court ruled in *US* v. *Richard M. Nixon* (1974) that the president must hand over tape recordings of his conversations that had been routinely made in the Oval Office. Shortly after this, the House of Representatives' Judiciary Committee voted to recommend three articles of impeachment to the House as a whole. In the face of this, the president resigned on 9 August 1974.

Wilson, Woodrow (1856–1924)
Woodrow Wilson was US president between 1913 and 1921. Although critics have pointed to his role in extending **segregation** in Washington DC and have suggested that many of his

deeds failed to match his words, he is particularly remembered for his commitment to the building of an international order structured around principles of democracy and the self-determination of nations.

In 1917, he described the US's entry into the First World War as a crusade to make the world 'safe for democracy'. In January 1918, he spelt out US war aims in terms of Fourteen Points. It promised 'mutual guarantees of political independence and territorial integrity to great and small states alike'. However, despite his crusade to ensure that the Senate ratified the Versailles Treaty that created the League of Nations, it failed to gain the two-thirds majority required under the US Constitution.

Wobblies
The 'Wobblies' were members of the Industrial Workers of the World (IWW) a radical trade union committed to the overthrow of capitalism. At its peak – in 1915 – it claimed 100,000 members. However, like other leftist groups and organisations in the US, the IWW proved to be short-lived.

Woodstock
The Woodstock festival was held in August 1969 in upstate New York. It reputedly attracted half a million young people and the event came to symbolise the social and political changes of the 1960s. It drew together new forms of music, the emerging hippie generation, the notions of freedom associated with the **sexual revolution** and the sense of radicalisation engendered by the protests against the **Vietnam** War.

5 AMERICA IN NUMBERS

POPULATION

Table 5.1 US resident population, 1980–2000

Year	Population
1980	226,545,805
1990	248,709,873
2000	281,421,906

Source: adapted from J. W. Wright (1999), *The New York Times Almanac 2000*, New York: Penguin, p. 276, and US Census Bureau, *US Census 2000*, www.census.gov/main/www/cen2000.html

Table 5.2 US population projections by race and Hispanic origin (percentages of the total US population), 2000–60

Projections suggest that the US will have a non-white majority population by 2060. They are based upon immigration patterns and differential fertility rates. However, many Hispanics (or 'Latinos') are also white. Furthermore, there are significant demographic differences between the metropolitan regions and the 'heartland' regions. The latter are likely to remain overwhelmingly white.

Year	White	Black	Hispanic	Asian	American Indian
2000	69.1	12.1	12.5	3.6	0.7
2025	62	12.9	18.2	6.2	0.8
2050	52.8	13.2	24.3	8.9	0.8
2060	49.6	13.3	26.6	9.8	0.8

Source: adapted from US Census Bureau (2003), *Projections of the Resident Population by Race, Hispanic Origin, and Nativity*, www.census.gov/population/projections/nation/summary/pp-t5-f.txt.
Note: 'Hispanic' is an ethnic description and can be applied to those of any race. The figures for whites, blacks, Asians and American Indians exclude those who are also Hispanic.

ECONOMY

Table 5.3 Economic growth, 1990–2002 (%)

Growth refers to the rate of change of output, or Gross Domestic Product (GDP). It is the principal measure of a country's economic well-being. If growth is negative, the country is producing less than a year earlier and is heading towards or is in recession.

Year	% change in GDP (1996 chained dollars)
1990	1.8
1991	−0.5
1992	3.0
1993	2.7
1994	4.0
1995	2.7
1996	3.6
1997	4.4
1998	4.3
1999	4.1
2000	3.8
2001	0.3
2002	2.4

Source: adapted from Bureau of Economic Analysis (2003), *Gross Domestic Product – Percent Change from Preceding Period*, www.bea.doc.gov/bea/dn/gdpchg.xls

Table 5.4 Unemployment, 1990–2002 (%)

Unemployment rose sharply during the recession at the beginning of the 1990s. It then dropped until the economy slowed up a decade later. Although it fell below the level that some economists felt would inevitably trigger inflation, (the non-accelerating inflation rate of unemployment, or NAIRU), the price level remained stable and low.

Year	Unemployment
1990	5.6
1991	6.8
1992	7.5
1993	6.9
1994	6.1
1995	5.6
1996	5.4

1997	4.9
1998	4.5
1999	4.2
2000	4
2001	4.7
2002	5.8

Source: adapted from Bureau of Labor Statistics (2003), *Employment Status of the Civilian Noninstitutional Population, 1940 to Date*, ftp.bls.gov/pub/special.requests/lf/aat1.txt

Table 5.5 Inflation, 1990–2002 (%)

Inflation refers to increases in the price level. High levels of inflation can destabilise an economy and undermine growth. Rising inflation may indicate that a boom has become unsustainable. Despite the sustained growth of the mid and late 1990s, inflation levels remained low and stable.

Year	Change in consumer prices
1990	5.39
1991	4.22
1992	3.01
1993	2.98
1994	2.6
1995	2.76
1996	2.96
1997	2.35
1998	1.51
1999	2.21
2000	3.38
2001	2.86
2002	1.58

Source: adapted from Economic History Services (2003), *What was the Inflation Rate then?*, www.eh.net/hmit/inflation/inflationr.php

Table 5.6 Per capita GDP, 1990–2002

Per capita GDP figures are often used as a shorthand measurement of average living standards. They are calculated by dividing the value of a country's output by its total population. However, used in this way, per capita GDP statistics can be misleading. As an average, they obscure the extent to which income is concentrated in the hands of relatively small numbers and in particular regions of the country. Quality-of-life considerations – such as educational and health provision – which may reveal rather more about living standards, are also neglected. Nonetheless, the statistics do offer a 'snapshot' of relative prosperity. After falling in the recession at the beginning of the 1990s, per capita GDP rose steadily until the economy faltered in 2000–1.

Year	GDP per capita
1990	$26,891
1991	$26,480
1992	$26,980
1993	$27,401
1994	$28,229
1995	$28,709
1996	$29,462
1997	$30,475
1998	$31,479
1999	$32,471
2000	$33,386
2001	$33,169
2002	$33,678

Source: adapted from Economic History Services (2003), *What was the GDP then?*, www.eh.net/hmit/gdp/gdp_answer.php

SOCIETY

Table 5.7 Life expectancy (at birth), 1930–2000

There has been a steady rise in life expectancy. This owes much to a decline in infant mortality. There are still, however, significant racial differences.

Year	All races	White	Black
1930	59.7	61.4	48.1
1940	62.9	64.2	53.1
1950	68.2	69.1	60.8
1960	69.7	70.6	63.6
1970	70.8	71.7	64.1
1980	73.7	74.4	68.1
1990	75.4	76.1	69.1
2000	76.9	77.4	71.7

Source: adapted from National Center for Health Statistics (2003), *Life Expectancy*, www.cdc.gov/nchs/fastats/pdf/nvsr51_03tb12.pdf

Table 5.8 Percentage of persons without health insurance coverage, 2001

Health provision has long been a significant political issue. Those who lack insurance – who are disproportionately drawn from the minorities – are dependent upon a uncertain patchwork of provision by Medicaid, states and charities. For their part, liberals want to see an extension of government-directed coverage. Conservatives stress the importance of the private sector.

Under 18s	% without insurance
Total	10.8
White	7.2
Black	10.5
Hispanic	24.1
18–64-year-olds	
Total	18.1
White	13.5
Black	22.8
Hispanic	40.1

Source: adapted from National Center for Health Statistics (2003),*Trends in Health Insurance Coverage by Race/Ethnicity among Persons under 65 Years of Age: United States, 1997–2001,* www.cdc.gov/nchs/products/pubs/pubd/hestats/healthinsur.htm

Table 5.9 Sedentary individuals (who never engage in physical activity for at least 20 minutes) as a proportion of the adult population (%), 1997

There are growing concerns about the health of the US population. Only a minority engage in the forms of regular activity recommended by the health profession.

	No leisure physical activity
All	40.1
Men	36.5
Women	43.2
White	36.3
Hispanic	53.5
Black	52.2

Source: adapted from National Center for Health Statistics (2002), *Prevalence of Sedentary Leisure-time Behavior among Adults in the United States,* www.cdc.gov/nchs/products/pubs/pubd/hestats/3and4/sedentary.PDF

Table 5.10 Overweight and obese people as a proportion of the population (%), 1999–2000

Lack of exercise and the hegemony of 'junk food' have led to weight problems among a significant proportion of the population.

	Overweight	Obese
20 years and over	64.5	30.5
Male	67	27.7
Female	62	34

Note: the definitions of 'overweight' and 'obese' are based upon body mass index (BMI) figures of 25 and 30 respectively.

Source: adapted from National Center for Health Statistics (2002), *Healthy Weight, Overweight, and Obesity among Persons 20 years of Age and over*, www.cdc.gov/nchs/data/hus/tables/2002/02hus070.pdf

Table 5.11 Legal abortions

Abortion – which was established as a constitutional right by the US Supreme Court's *Roe* ruling in 1973 – is a deeply divisive and controversial issue. It repeatedly appears on the political agenda. Although there are some methodological difficulties in collecting the figures, there was undoubtedly a significant fall in the number of abortions during the 1990s.

Year	Number of legal abortions
1973	744,600
1980	1,553,900
1990	1,608,600
1991	1,556,510
1992	1,528,930
1993	1,495,000
1994	1,423,000
1995	1,359,400
1996	1,360,200
1997	1,335,000
1998	1,319,000
1999	1,314,800
2000	1,313,000

Source: adapted from Robert Johnston (2003), *Historical Abortion Statistics, United States*, www.johnstonsarchive.net/policy/abortion/ab-unitedstates.html

Table 5.12 Percentage of households with internet access by income, 2001

Income	Percentage of households with internet access
Under $5,000	20.5
$5,000–9,999	14.4
$10,000–14,999	19.4
$15,000–19,999	23.6
$20,000–24,999	31.8
$25,000–34,999	42.2
$35,000–49,999	56.4
$50,000–74,999	71.4
Over $75,000	85.4

Source: adapted from Economics and Statistics Administration (2002), *A Nation Online*, www.esa.doc.gov/images/ANationCharts/ Charts_21589_image001.gif

LAW AND ORDER

Table 5.13 Crime rates (number of victimisations per 1,000 population age 12 and over)

Crime levels have been falling from the early 1990s onwards. This has been attributed to a range of variables including tougher policing, the large numbers who are imprisoned, growing economic prosperity, changes in urban planning and demographic shifts.

Year	Numbers reporting violent crime (per 1,000)
1980	49.4
1990	44.1
1991	48.8
1992	47.9
1993	49.1
1994	51.2
1995	46.1
1996	41.6
1997	38.8
1998	36
1999	32.1
2000	27.4
2001	24.7

Note: the National Crime Victimization Survey figures are based upon surveys of the population and are widely seen as more accurate than the statistics that are constructed from crime reports.

Source: Bureau of Justice Statistics (2003), *National Crime Victimization Survey Violent Crime Trends, 1973–2001,* www.ojp.usdoj.gov/bjs/glance/tables/viortrdtab.htm.

Table 5.14 Numbers of persons executed, 1960–2002

Almost all executions are carried out under state law, although a handful of recent executions – most notably that of Timothy McVeigh who was convicted for the Oklahoma City bombing – have been for federal offences. It seemed, for a period, that capital punishment had been brought to an end. There were no executions while the US Supreme Court considered claims brought by defendants and then ruled in *Furman* v. *Georgia* (1972) that the imposition and implementation of death sentences was a form of 'lottery' depending upon the quality of a defendant's lawyer, the nature of the court, and the widely used system of 'plea-bargains'.

Year	Number executed
1960	56
1961	42
1962	47
1963	21
1964	15
1965	7
1966	1
1967	2
1968	0
1969	0
1970	0
1971	0
1972	0
1973	0
1974	0
1975	0
1976	0
1977	1
1978	0
1979	2
1980	0
1981	1
1982	2

1983	5
1984	21
1985	18
1986	18
1987	25
1988	11
1989	16
1990	23
1991	14
1992	31
1993	38
1994	31
1995	56
1996	45
1997	74
1998	68
1999	98
2000	85
2001	66
2002	71

Source: adapted from Bureau of Justice Statistics (2003), *Key Facts at a Glance – Executions*, www.ojp.usdoj.gov/bjs/glance/tables/exetab.htm

Table 5.15 Lifetime chances of imprisonment, 1991

There are high rates of imprisonment in the US. One person in twenty will go to prison at some point in his or her life. As individuals get older and – if they have not served a prison sentence prior to that time – the chances of imprisonment fall. For black men, however, the figures are dramatically different.

Not yet incarcerated by age	Percentage chance of going to prison during rest of life		
	All persons	White men	Black men
Birth	5.1%	4.4%	28.5%
20	4.5	4.1	25.3
25	3.1	3.0	17.3
30	2.1	2.1	10.8
35	1.4	1.5	6.5
40	0.9	1.1	3.6

Source: adapted from Bureau of Justice Statistics (1997), *Lifetime Likelihood of Going to State or Federal Prison,* www.ojp.usdoj.gov/bjs/pub/pdf/llgsfp.pdf

PART II
Study Skills

6 SKILLS FOR STUDYING AMERICAN STUDIES

This section of the book outlines some of the study skills that are required at university. It includes advice on settling in, reading books and articles, and the development of writing skills. It also surveys the role of seminars and lectures and considers ways of approaching examinations at the end of a course

STARTING OUT AT UNIVERSITY

'Make sure you read any information that you get sent by your department. If some books need to be purchased, get them in advance. Online sellers usually provide a fairly quick service. If information is not provided then phone the department and ask for a list of set books. If there are no set books then try to read around the area you will be expected to study. This will be useful because it gives you a head start.

'It is vital that you get to know your way around the department. You need to find out if there is a departmental library and where it is. Look and see where the departmental office is and when it's open. You should also find out who will be lecturing you, as well as who the year tutors are and where they're based. If, then, you find yourself in difficulty you know where to go for help.

'The amount of work that you do is up to you. Unlike school there aren't people to make sure you get your work in on time. You have to motivate yourself into working. The amount of work that has to be handed in is also a lot less. Most people have just one or two essays per semester. However, you should try and think ahead and start early. If you leave it to the last minute then you make more problems for yourself. The main problem is that there is a limit on the amount of resources at the university. If you leave things until a late stage then by the time you get to the library most of the better texts have gone and you will be left with the materials that no one else wanted. The other thing that happens is that you sit down to start your essay and you realise that you don't really know what you are supposed to be writing about. If you have started early then you can go and discuss this with the relevant people but if you've left it until the night before then you're stuck on your own and you have to do the best that you can.

'It's important to find out the way in which the course is assessed. Some don't have exams. Some are assessed at various intervals throughout the semester. If you do have exams then it is important to prepare well in advance. If you have done the reading as it has been set then this pays off. Instead of having to start from scratch you are able just to review the material.'

Amy Voyle-Morgan, American Studies
student at the University of Keele, 2002

Starting out at university can be a difficult and challenging process. You cannot settle down to study effectively unless you are familiar with all the practical details and procedures.

The class booklet

Most courses have a course booklet with essential information such as course content, reading lists and a timetable. It will also explain the assessment and examination registration procedures. It may also tell you how essays and other written work should be presented.

The noticeboard

Any changes to class times and locations will be posted on the class/course noticeboard, sometimes at short notice. It is the place to look for tutorial lists, exam details and so on.

The departmental secretary

The departmental office may not be open to student enquiries all day. Find out when the secretary is available. This is where to go if you miss a lecture and need the handout, if you want to double-check dates and places for exams, if you can't get hold of a particular lecturer or if you change your address.

IT support

You will need to make use of computing facilities. A growing number of university departments insist that written work is typed and not handwritten. This is useful. Word-processing packages such as Microsoft Word allow you to change, edit and revise your work. They also incorporate spell and grammar checkers. For longer pieces of work, such as dissertations and theses, word processing and desktop publishing packages will allow you to choose from a range of layouts and presentational forms.

There will almost certainly be introductory courses on computing for new students. These are essential both for those who are computer literate and the complete beginner.

University computing networks offer other advantages:

- There will be online access to the library catalogue, enabling you to check the availability of books and periodicals as well as your own borrowing record.

- They provide an internet connection. Although it is easy to be overwhelmed by the number of websites that are available – and sometimes difficult to assess their credibility and reliability as sources – search engines such as Google (google.co.uk) offer an essential means of locating material on core topics. The university will also have online subscriptions to a range of journals and databases.

You will almost certainly be given an e-mail address during your first week. Check your inbox frequently. Tutors, lecturers or the departmental secretary may need to get in touch. Staff would also appreciate an e-mail if circumstances compel you to miss a class.

MATURE STUDENTS

Some mature students face particular difficulties. They may have family commitments or young children. The prospect of returning to education can – after a break – seem daunting.

However, despite these anxieties, mature students have significant advantages and strengths that often prove to be of considerable value. They are often more effective in organising themselves and their time than younger students. They have a range of experience – and knowledge of world affairs – that can be of direct or indirect relevance to the course. They are usually more effective in communicating ideas and arguments.

READING

Reading and study outside of classes will prove crucial. Essays and assignments require a range of reading that must go beyond the standard textbooks. In some cases, there may also be preparatory work for a class. At other times, there could be a follow-up activity. Students inevitably gain a much fuller and more developed understanding of the course if they undertake this work. In particular, it ensures that the material covered in lectures, seminars and tutorials can be understood and assessed in a critical and contextualised way. This is the way to gain higher grades.

Some texts are essential reading and will be recommended for purchase. It may be possible to buy second-hand copies, although older editions of a book can have drawbacks. Many of the examples may be outdated. Other books – and journals – will be found in the library. Introductory sessions for new users are always held within the first week or so of the university year. These outline and explain the cataloguing system that enables users to either find a particular book or a number of books that cover a broadly similar theme.

Alongside the different rooms, sections and shelves, nearly all university libraries will have a dedicated section that includes books that are – because they are crucial for a particular course – only available on a restricted basis. They might, for example, only be available for loan for a few hours. Alternatively, they might only be for use in the library itself.

Many books and articles can be challenging. They are rarely written with a first-year undergraduate audience in mind. It is, however, important to persist. You will eventually become familiar with the concepts, theories and terminology that initially seemed difficult.

- Do not feel that a book or article should be read from beginning to end. Instead, get used to 'dipping' in and out of a text.

- Build up an overview of the arguments used in a book before looking at the individual chapters or sections. The back of the book or the introduction may offer a summary. Many articles begin with an abstract that presents the core arguments in a much shortened form. A number of websites – including online booksellers such as Amazon (Amazon. co.uk) – provide summaries and reviews of books that will offer insights into their principal themes.

- At the same time, try and find out if the author is associated with a particular viewpoint. For example, many of the studies of the US economy published during the late 1970s and 1980s were written by conservatives. A number described themselves as 'supply-side' economists. Their analyses of the American economy were premised upon the assertion that economic growth requires a free market, deregulation and the dismantling of government regulatory mechanisms. It is much easier to understand a particular text or argument if you are familiar with the author's background

- It is a mistake simply to read without a purpose. Approached in this way, the level of concentration that is required cannot generally be sustained. Instead, adopt a pro-active approach. Note down the principal themes. The details are secondary. Try to rephrase the text in your own words. However, include page numbers so that you can come back to the text at a later point and find out more about it. If you use a direct quotation, ensure that it is placed in inverted commas or perhaps written using a different colour of pen. This is important because you may otherwise use a phrase or sentence and claim it as your own when it is – in reality – derived from a book or article.

- Start your work on a topic by using the broad introductory texts. Once you have built up a solid knowledge of the topic you are in a position to move on and consider specialist books, articles and websites. It is a mistake to begin with very advanced or highly detailed texts. Those who do this tend to become lost in the topic and lose sight of the principal themes or core ideas.

- Be ready to use reference works such as the *Oxford English Dictionary*. There are also some important resources that are of particular value for those pursuing American Studies courses, particularly during the second and third years. They can be found in most university libraries and include:
    Matterson, Stephen (2003) *American Literature: The Essential Glossary*, London: Arnold.

Stanley, Harold W. and Richard G. Niemi (2003), *Vital Statistics on American Politics: A Comprehensive Reference of Over 200 Tables and Figures: 2003–2004*, Washington DC: CQ Press.

Stein, Hebert and Murray Foss (1999), *The Illustrated Guide to the American Economy*, Washington DC: The AEI Press.

Thompson, Peter (2000), *Cassell's Dictionary of Modern American History*, London: Cassell and Co.

US Census Bureau, *Statistical Abstract of the United States*. Published annually (an online edition is available – www.census.gov/statab/www/).

SELF-DIRECTED LEARNING

Many students who arrive at university directly from a school or college find the process of adjustment challenging. Although Sixth-Form life is generally more relaxed than in classes for younger pupils, there is still a degree of discipline. While each teacher or lecturer will have had his or her own approach, the regulations will almost certainly have required regular attendance at classes and insisted upon the proper completion of homework assignments. The school or college may also have had rules about behaviour and activities out of class. There may, for example, have been a code of conduct governing the use of free periods by students.

There will still be deadlines at university – and marks may well be deducted if work is submitted late – but students will often be given far longer to complete each assignment. Instead of relatively short pieces or work, set on a relatively frequent basis, the assignments will be longer. Students will be given a number of weeks – perhaps longer – before they are due to be submitted. Sometimes – perhaps inevitably – assignment deadlines will be at around the same time in a number of subjects.

It can sometimes be difficult for students to become self-motivated, particularly if they had to be 'pushed' through their A-levels. However, unless they can make the shift to these new ways of working, there is a danger of missing deadlines, losing marks, building up a backlog of work, and joining the ranks of those who are compelled to drop out of a university course. It is, therefore, important to think about ways of organising your days so that you can work in an effective and purposeful way.

- Libraries often provide useful places to study. Although there are sometimes instances of poor behaviour in libraries, there are usually fewer distractions than in a hall of residence or flat.

- If you do work at home with other students, try to make sure that there are clear and understood guidelines about not interrupting each other's study time.

- Structure your study time. It is difficult to work effectively if you go for much more than an hour without a break. Make sure that you vary the form of activity that you are undertaking. Read and make notes for a while. Then look at the questions and exercises that may be included in the textbook or have been set by the lecturer taking the course. Some people also find it useful to reward themselves – with, for example, a rest – when a particular goal has been achieved.

ESSAYS, ASSIGNMENTS AND DISSERTATIONS

Essays form a crucial part of the learning and assessment process at university. Essay writing assists in building up a solid knowledge of a subject but – even more importantly – helps in understanding a particular argument or theory. It is only when we have to explain an idea, event or process in a clear and unambiguous way that we come to appreciate the gaps in our own knowledge and understanding. Connections that had not previously been evident become more readily apparent.

University-level essay writing requires a particular ap-

proach, although there will, of course, be differences between
the different institutions and courses. It is important to adopt a
degree of formality and an impersonal style so that the writer
does not get in the way of the subject. Vocabulary and
grammar have to be carefully checked to make sure there is
no possibility of misunderstandings. Sources should always be
cited.

Planning

It is easy to become impatient. Many students simply begin
writing with no clear sense of direction. This simply will not
work. Approached in this way, the essay may include substantial description and detail, but it will lack structure and
coherence. Even more importantly, there will be little effective
analysis or evaluation.

How, then, should American Studies essays be planned,
structured and organised? There is, of course, no rigidly fixed
or prescribed format. Lecturers and tutors will suggest different approaches and designs. However, course programmes
will usually spell out the basic requirements that should be met
if a particular grade is to be awarded.

The award of a high grade is likely to depend upon factors
such as:

- a comprehensive knowledge of the topic

- accurate evidence and an impressive range of examples

- a wide range of well-developed concepts and theories

- an awareness and understanding of differing and competing
  viewpoints

- a clear sense of direction culminating in a conclusion which
  flows from the discussion.

This is a formidable list and it can be difficult to think of ways in which all these criteria can be incorporated. Experience suggests, however, that the need to consider differing or contrasting viewpoints offers the most useful starting point. Many of the issues raised in examination questions are the subject of controversy among commentators and essay answers need to reflect the character of those debates.

A plan can therefore often begin with a simple line down the middle of the page. You can then jot down points that 'fit' on either side of the argument. At both the planning and the writing stage, it is best to keep the lines of argument entirely separate. There is, otherwise, a danger that the essay will 'zigzag' between arguments in a way that will prevent the reader from following its overall flow and structure.

On US government and politics courses, students are sometimes asked to write essays about the overall character of the principal American parties. A representative question might be:

Are the American parties locked into long-term decline?

An essay seeking to answer this would initially survey the arguments raised by those who suggest that the Republicans and Democrats have indeed lost much of their former strength and influence as organisations. It would outline and explain the arguments associated with writers such as David Broder in his book, *The Party's Over*. It would need to consider:

- the loss of the parties' nomination function through the growth of primaries and caucuses which have enabled the voting public to select candidates;

- the emergence of candidate-centred forms of organisation;

- the rise of thinktanks and their role in displacing parties as a source of new ideas and policy-development;

- the relatively low levels of party unity in Congress and the state legislatures;

- the dependence of candidates on sources of finance other than the parties.

The other side of the argument – which points instead to party revival – requires rather different points. A full and comprehensive answer would cite observers who have made the claim. It would then cite appropriate forms of evidence by pointing to:

- the role of the party apparatus in winning back the nomination function by backing particular candidates during the primary season;

- the growing role of leadership organisations – such as the national committees – within the parties;

- the sense of party discipline in Congress during the 1990s as partisan disputes became increasingly embittered;

- the failure of most independents and minor parties to make significant electoral inroads.

Examples

Many essays make a reasonable range of points, but do so in a way that lacks depth and substance. The second stage in the planning process is to ensure that each point is supported through the use of relevant examples. The rise of thinktanks could, for example, be illustrated by pointing to the work of bodies such as the Heritage Foundation, the Cato Institute and the Progressive Policy Institute. A well-developed answer would record their political character. They are mainstream conservative, right-wing libertarian and 'New Democrat' respectively. All of these points will require illustration.

Although you will need to draw upon illustrative material from a range of sources, *Politics Review* (published by Philip Allan Updates, *www.philipallan.co.uk*) frequently includes articles on topics such as the American parties. These articles are aimed at an A-level and undergraduate readership and are therefore very accessible. You should also be able to find examples of party activity from the Republicans' and Democrats' national committee websites, although it is important to approach the information that they offer in a cautious and critical way. It is, after all, designed to 'sell' the party. See:

www.democrats.org
www.rnc.org

Structure, order and theory

It is important to think about the order in which the points and examples are placed. Often, it may be sensible to begin with the most significant of the points and work through to those that are of lesser relevance or value. However, this is not always a straightforward process. Points are commonly associated with each other. Where there are ties and interconnections, it may be most appropriate if one point follows on from the next so as to ensure a sense of structure, order and continuity.

Wherever possible, the points should draw on – and incorporate – appropriate concepts, models and theories. In a discussion of parties and their relationship with the electorate, it would, for example, be useful to discuss the concept of 'partisan dealignment'. This is a concept suggesting that there has been a process of detachment between the parties and the electorate. As the parties have lost some of their former hold, the electorate has become more volatile and may well switch between parties. Formerly ingrained loyalties have been lost. At this point, it is particularly useful to cite the names of relevant theorists and commentators. For example:

Martin P. Wattenberg has stressed the extent to which there has been a process of partisan dealignment. This means that there has been a decline in the proportion of strong party identifiers. Wattenberg emphasises, in particular, the growing number of voters who are 'ticket-splitters'. They vote – in elections that are held at the same time – for candidates from different parties. The percentage of voters splitting their ticket between candidates for the Senate and the House of Representatives rose from 9 per cent in 1952 to 27 per cent in 1988.

Introductions and signposts

The introduction has not, so far, been discussed. This is because – in planning terms – it needs to be considered once the essay has been organised rather than at the beginning of the process. There are different opinions about its role.

- Some suggest that the introduction plays an important role in outlining the structure that the essay will follow and the arguments that will be employed.

- Others argue that it should attract the reader's attention, set the scene and establish the context for the essay. They believe, however, that the structure of the essay should emerge as it proceeds. From this point of view, the plan does not need to be outlined or explained.

Whatever approach is adopted, the introduction should be fairly brief and concise. Although some lecturers and tutors will ask for introductions that outline the principal themes that will be surveyed, introductions usually attract relatively few marks when compared with the more substantial sections of the essay.

'Signposts' are, however, worth thought and attention. It is important to remind the reader – and perhaps yourself – that you are answering the exact question that has been posed.

Without repeating the question verbatim, some links should be included on a periodic basis. It is, in particular, important to refer back to the themes raised in the question at the 'changeover' point between the two sides of the argument and at the beginning of the conclusion.

Types of questions

Most of the essay questions that you are set will probably adopt a 'discuss', 'assess' or 'evaluate' format that lends itself to this approach, even if these particular words are not used. It is simply assumed that you will do this. There are, however, a number of exceptions. Some questions are divided into separate and distinct parts. Others specify a structure. In these cases, you should follow the order and flow of the question, but look for opportunities to discuss and evaluate the issues that have arisen.

Most questions, however, lend themselves to the construction of distinct lines of argument. This includes those that begin with the word 'why'. A question could, for example, ask:

Why are racism and civil rights still important issues in US politics?

When addressing a question such as this, it is tempting to discard the rules for essay writing and present a fairly random list of points. However, this would be a mistake. It is always important to evaluate issues and weigh arguments even when the question does not include a direct invitation to do so. There are always different and contrasting arguments and the relative weighting of these needs to be considered and assessed.

You would be well advised to begin the essay with the most widely accepted explanation. In this case, many commentaries suggest that civil rights continue to cause controversy because African-Americans and other minorities are still economically, socially and politically disadvantaged. You could – at this point – outline and explain the scale of the differences between whites and blacks in terms of income levels, educational achievemen, and occupational status. The second half of the essay could consider the *other* reasons why civil rights are still high on the political agenda. A number of observers, for example, point to the campaigns organised by African-American interest groups such as the National Association of Colored People. Others stress the closeness of the relationship between these organisations and the Democrats. The role played by the Congressional Black Caucus is also a factor. Some conservatives go so far as to talk of a 'civil rights industry', claiming that these organisations foment hostility and antagonism. It might also be worth examining the historical legacy of segregation and institutionalised racial discrimination. Although the 'Jim Crow' laws – which confined blacks in the southern states to a separate and unequal status – were abolished in the 1960s, they left a sense of bitterness and resentment that has lasted to this day.

Not a science

There may, of course, be different ways of achieving the same purpose. In general terms, those responsible for assessment will reward all attempts to discuss relevant issues and arguments. They will be less generous to those who simply list points, particularly those who do so in a way that lacks depth or an intelligible structure.

All of this may seem highly prescriptive. There is, however, scope – within the approach that has been suggested – for the development of an individual style, particularly in the conclusion. It is easy to forget that although essays can be strong or weak in character, the writing of them is an art and not a science.

There are some other guidelines that should be borne in mind in all forms of writing.

- When you use a pronoun, can you identify the exact word or phrase it replaces? *This*, *these*, *that* and *those* are danger words. At the end of a long passage, essays often include the words, 'This means . . .' when it is not at all clear what 'this' was.

- Be careful when starting a sentence with an *-ing* word or an *-ed* word. Make sure that the *-ing* or *-ed* word really does relate to the subject of the sentence or you could end up with a point that cannot be understood.

When you are writing essays, it is very easy to fall into the trap of thinking that this is between you and the page and you forget that a real person will be reading it. Your reader will take you and your essay seriously. She or he will also expect a professional approach. A fairly formal style is therefore required. This does not mean that it has to be long-winded. It is very often the people who understand their subject best who can explain it most simply and directly. Those who have only half a grasp of what they are talking about are the ones who are most likely to dress up relatively shallow knowledge in dense language. They think they know what they want to say, but when it comes to putting it down on paper, the words won't come because they have not thought everything through. If you can say what you mean with absolute clarity, you will demonstrate your knowledge effectively. Look at every single sentence you write and ask yourself whether it is crystal clear. The process will often expose gaps in your understanding. This makes essay writing a valuable learning opportunity.

Preparing for submission

Course booklets will often include a departmental stylesheet telling you how to set your work out. If not, here are a few suggestions:

1 Make sure that the typeface you use is sufficient in terms of size; 12 pt is preferable.
2 A page with plenty of white space is more attractive than a black, solid block of text. Make sure you use big margins so that the marker can write helpful comments. Separate your paragraphs with a blank line instead of indenting.
3 Use a conventional font such as Arial, Arial Narrow or Times New Roman.

Footnotes and endnotes

Footnotes or endnotes matter and should not be regarded as a mere afterthought. They allow the reader to ascertain from where a quotation, statistic, or argument has been taken. They also enable you to follow up and develop your work on the topic at a later stage. It is therefore important that the footnotes or endnotes include the name of the author, the title of the book or article, the date of publication, the publisher, and the page number:

Author, A. N. (1995) *Book Title in Italics*, Place of publication: Publisher.
Author, A. N. (1996a) 'Article title without capitals', *Italicised Journal Name*, 10 (3): 1–55.
Author, A. N. (1996b) 'An essay in a book', in S. Cribble (ed.) *Book Title*, Place: Publisher.

Should you use footnotes or endnotes? Universities and departments may have their own policies. However, if you are in doubt, adopt an approach that will be of most help to the reader. For a few short notes that are important to an understanding of the text, the foot of the page is probably best. If there are many notes and references, they should be placed at the end.

Bibliographies

The bibliography brings together all the sources that have been used so that the reader can see the processes that have been followed in constructing and writing the essay. It should incorporate the sources that have been cited in the references and other materials that may not have been cited but have been consulted. Again make sure that you include essential information: the author, the title of the book, the date of publication, and the publisher or, in the case of an article, the author, the title of the article, the name of the journal, the date of publication and the page numbers.

Plagiarism

Plagiarism or the copying of work – whether intentional or unintentional – is a form of cheating. In recent years, universities have come to see it as a major problem and they are increasingly vigilant to ensure that students do not reproduce material from other students, from published sources, or from websites. Some institutions use computer programs so as to detect plagiarism.

Of course you will present and discuss other people's ideas, opinions and theories in your essay, but you must state where you found them and be very careful not to claim them as your own original thoughts. All direct quotations must be acknowledged as such through the use of inverted commas and proper references. Close paraphrasing should be avoided as this reproduces someone else's work much too directly.

Some universities will ask you to submit a plagiarism declaration form when you hand in an assignment. This affirms that an assignment is a student's own work.

Proof-reading

Always check your work. There will inevitably be some errors and problems. The proof-reading process involves a number of stages.

Stage one
Take a break between writing the essay and re-reading it. It is very difficult to check your own work because you are over-familiar with it. Put some distance between writing and re-reading.

Stage two
Read the essay so as to ensure that it makes sense and is effective in terms of communication. It may feel odd, but it can be useful to read it out aloud. Are there any words, sentences or sections that are unclear or simply sound wrong? At this stage, do not stop to correct things or you will lose the big picture. Just make a mark in the margin. At the same time, you also need to ask yourself other questions. Is the balance right? Have you devoted the most time to the important points?

Once you have read right through the essay, wrestle with the awkward sentences. Be careful to ensure that any improvements do not introduce new errors. When you are sure that that essay or assignment flows and is as you would wish it to be, you can move on to the next stage.

Stage three
There are some mechanical tasks that are required. Use the spellchecker but do your own check for things that it will miss. Ensure that you have correctly used *it's* or *its*. Sometimes *where* and *were* are confused. A very common kind of mistake is to mistype the little words, *on* instead of *of* for example. Is your punctuation helpful? Work out all the sums. Double-check names and dates. When checking your grammar, common errors to look out for include verbs changing tense and pronouns. It is easy to drift between *one* and *you* or construct sentences without main verbs.

Stage four

Give the essay to someone else to read. It is perhaps better if it is a person who is not a specialist in American Studies. Ask them to make sure they can completely understand every sentence. (Offer to do the same for them. You can learn a lot about your own writing from helping to make other people's writing clearer.)

Problems

What should you do if you have failed to hand your essay in on time? You may have a good reason, such as illness. If so, you should provide a medical certificate. Your director of studies or personal tutor should be notified of serious personal problems that may interfere with your work and they might be taken into account if you find you need an extension. As soon as you feel you are behind schedule, have a word with your tutor.

Further reading

Creme, P. and M. Lea (1997) *Writing at University: A Guide for Students*, Buckingham: Open University Press. This is a very approachable general introduction to university writing.

IMPROVING WRITTEN COMMUNICATION

As you progress through university, you will have to deal with more and more complex concepts and those who teach you will ask for more demanding standards of precision and accuracy. This will require changes in your writing style.

Paragraphs

Topic sentences

You should have one topic or core idea per paragraph. It is a good idea to summarise it in a topic sentence. The best place for the topic sentence is at the beginning of the paragraph because it makes for easy reading if your reader knows what you are writing about. If your reader is scanning through your work, the first sentence of each paragraph will catch the eye. You can put it at the end, which is also a position which gives emphasis, but that makes it harder work for the reader. Of course, if you really want to drive a point home, you can put it at both beginning and end, although excessive repetition serves little purpose and is often wasteful. As you write, keep your topic sentence in mind. When you find yourself straying from it, it suggests that you should have begun a further paragraph.

Conversation

Your reader must be able to follow the direction and flow of the essay. It is worth keeping the reader in mind as you write. Will he or she be able to follow what is being said? If your paragraphs are well planned, your reader should be coming to the same conclusion as you, just before you state what has just become obvious. Or, at least, he or she will be formulating the question that your next paragraph is just about to answer.

Linking

The process of helping the reader is of particular importance when moving from one paragraph to the next. In the best forms of writing, one paragraph naturally and necessarily flows onto the following paragraph. Take time to reflect:

• What did I establish in the last paragraph?

• How does my next paragraph relate to it?

In case the relationship is not immediately clear, it might be helpful to have some words ready to use as signals. Paragraphs could begin:

However . . .

First . . . Second . . . Finally . . .

Another example . . . Furthermore . . . Moreover . . .

By contrast . . . On the one hand . . . On the other hand . . . Alternatively . . .

There is a danger, however, that if these links are overused, they may become intrusive and irritating.

The length of paragraphs should be varied. A long paragraph is hard reading and it is good to put in short, signpost ones, just to say where you have got to or where you are going, if you think you might be overloading your reader. The more important the point, the longer the paragraph, but an occasional, very short, punchy paragraph can be used very effectively to hammer home a vital point.

Sentences

The important thing about sentences is to keep the words in the right order. Do not alter the natural word order for rhetorical effect unless you really know what you are doing and you are really sure that your meaning will be made more rather than less clear.

The subject of the sentence goes at the beginning. It is no accident that the grammatical 'subject', the one that 'does' the verb, goes before the verb. The subject is what the sentence is about and the rest of the sentence is saying something about the subject. The second most conspicuous position in a sentence is at the end. Occasionally, it can be effective to build up to a climax at the end of a sentence.

A sentence is as long as it needs to be. If you are building complex relationships, your sentence might have to be very long but, if you keep the structure simple, a long sentence does not have to be difficult. Do not try to include too many additional bits of information into a sentence or your reader will loose the main thread. Too many short sentences sound rather ugly and fail to develop links and relationships but the very occasional short, sharp sentence can give a dramatic emphasis. Try to give the reader some variety in terms of sentence length.

Be positive
Negatives can overstretch your reader's logical abilities:

   There are no conditions under which the president will not be re-elected.

Be concise
Word limits take into account the number of words necessary to deal with the set topic. Using unnecessary words so as to provide padding out or to reach a word limit does not help the process of essay writing.

Vocabulary

Jargon
One person's technical term is another's jargon. In choosing your words, keep your target reader constantly in mind. When you are writing for your tutors and lecturers, you should be able to show that you have understood the technical terms and can use them correctly and appropriately.

Big words
Do not use big words where a little one will do the same job. If by *termination* you mean *end*, then use *end*. There is nothing to be gained by substituting *utilise* for *use*. There is a place for big words where they are the best ones to convey an accurate

meaning, but they are not to be used unnecessarily for the sole purpose of sounding authoritative. You will just end up not knowing what you are talking about. Be especially self-disciplined about avoiding words whose meaning you are not completely sure about. Either consult a dictionary or use a word you know.

Formality
You need to maintain a certain level of formality. In selecting short, commonly used words, you should avoid any slang terms and colloquialisms.

Premodifiers
Consider the following sentence:

> *The build-up of long, heavily premodified, fluency-impairing noun phrases is a common failing in academic writing.*

This could be rephrased:

> *Too many adjectives before a noun often impair the fluency of academic writing.*

More verbs
Verbs make your text bounce along. Nouns and adjectives and prepositional phrases describing nouns are solid and slow your reader down. If you can use more verbs and fewer adjectives and nouns, you will sound much less boring:

> *After expulsion of the breath by the lungs . . .*
> *After the lungs expel the breath . . .*

You can increase the proportion of verbs to knows by rewriting phrases like:

> *make an adjustment to > adjust*
> *come to the conclusion > conclude*

Other examples which can be shortened to a single verb are:

arrive at a decision
make an examination of
conduct an investigation into

Inference

In a real conversation, there is a lot of creativity coming from both sides. How many interpretations can you put on the following?

Where was I?
Are you on the phone?

These sentences work in conversation because you can rely on inference. You can give signals with your own facial expressions and other gestures. You alter your tone of voice. If an appropriate, unambiguous inference cannot be made, your hearer will ask what you mean. You can see if there is a blank or bewildered or angry or approving expression on a hearer's face. You can ask little 'tag' questions just to make sure the conversation is going as you intend. Right? When you write, you are deprived of all these safety checks. You cannot assume that just because your reader is an expert in the subject, he or she will know what you mean anyway.

Rhetoric

Figures of speech are more likely to be found in writing where the purpose is to persuade or entertain than in the dispassionate prose of academic discourse. They should be used sparingly. However, some can help in getting a point across.

1. Simile
A simile suggests that something is 'like' something else. If you

are going to use similes, make sure that you do not choose one that is overused. Some are mere clichés.

2. Repetition
Usually, you go to quite a lot of effort to vary your sentence structure. If used very sparingly, a deliberate repetition of a pattern can therefore attract and hold the reader's attention.

> *I came. I saw. I conquered.*

Here, the third time comes with a little extra. This is repetition and variation. Effective writers have always exploited this device. Think of repetition with variation as the delivery of some weakening punches followed by a decisive blow.

3. Questions
It can sometimes be useful to employ questions during the course of a discussion. For example, 'What have been the consequences of the Iraq war for the role of the presidency?' Again, this device should not be overused.

Professional spelling

Spelling mistakes create a poor impression especially when you make mistakes with technical terms specific to your subject; you undermine your reader's faith in your professional ability. Use your spell checker or dictionary to ensure correct spelling. If a word keeps coming up, take a moment to learn it.

Punctuation

Punctuation is there to help the reader. Too much can get in the way of fluent reading. Too little can lead to misunderstandings and prevent the reader following the structure of a sentence, particularly if it is fairly long.

Full stops
Between the capital letter and the full stop there should be one, and only one, complete statement.

Commas
Commas separate out the sections of a sentence or the component parts of lists. Note that there is no comma before the *and* in British English.

> *The president's constitutional powers include his position as commander-in-chief, his right of veto, his ability to appoint senior officials and his power to conclude treaties with other nations.*

If a section in commas is in the middle of the sentence, make sure that the commas come in pairs.

Dashes
Dashes can be used in much the same way as commas and brackets, for sectioning off an optional extra but they should not be used to hang afterthoughts onto the end of sentences.

Brackets and dashes can be useful if commas start nesting. Compare

> *Poor writers, who frequently compose long-winded sentences, rendered, as this example shows, incomprehensible, more or less, to the average or even skilled reader, by the interpolation of little, badly positioned, extra bits, should be ostracised by the academic community.*

with

> *Poor writers (who frequently compose long-winded sentences, rendered – as this example shows – incomprehensible to the average, or even skilled reader, by the interpolation of little, badly positioned, extra bits) should be ostracised by the academic community.*

The second version is still dreadful, but not quite so nightmarish as the first.

Semicolons

If you feel that two sentences are so closely linked that you want to draw attention to the fact, you can use a semicolon instead of a full stop:

> *The students gained very high marks; nothing in their answers was irrelevant to the question.*

Semicolons are also useful for lists where the items consist of more than one word, especially if the individual items contain commas.

Colons

You will notice how colons are used to introduce lists and examples in this book. They are also used to introduce quotations when no verb of saying is present.

Exclamation marks

Although often used in personal correspondence, they have very little place in academic discourse.

Hyphens

These can be useful for resolving ambiguities. Hyphens should also be used to avoid weird spellings: *de-ice* rather than *deice* and *go-between* rather than *gobetween*. If you are not sure whether a compound word is hyphenated or not, and you cannot find it in your dictionary, make a decision and stick to it.

Apostrophes

Apostrophes are the punctuation marks that people seem to find hardest. In fact, they are really easy. In very formal writing, you will not use apostrophes for shortened words. *Do not write don't. It's it is, isn't it*?

Apostrophes are used to show possession:

If the possessor is singular, use 's (*The president's powers*)

If the possessor is plural and ends in -s, use ' (*citizens' rights*)

If the possessor is plural and does not end in -s, use 's (*women's rights*)

In other words, make the plural first and the possessive second.

This is not all that there is to say about punctuation, but it might be enough to prevent the most common errors. When checking your punctuation, the question to ask yourself is always, 'Does it help the reader?'

Recommended reading

In addition to a dictionary and thesaurus, you might invest in one or two of the following, or find them in the library:

G. J. Fairburn and C. Winch get down to detail in *Reading, Writing and Reasoning* (1996) Buckingham: Open University Press. This is an excellent book.

J. Peck and M. Coyle provide help with the mechanics of writing in *The Student's Guide to Writing: Spelling, Punctuation and Grammar* (1999) Basingstoke: Macmillan.

Philip Gaskell combines a useful summary of the basics of good writing with some well-chosen examples of different styles in *Standard Written English* (1998) Edinburgh: Edinburgh University Press.

R. Quirk and S. Greenbaum's *A University Grammar of English* (1973) Harlow: Longman, is a useful book to refer to on occasion.

The Chicago Manual of Style (1993) Chicago: University of Chicago Press, is widely used as a standard reference book. It covers bookmaking and all you are ever likely to need on production and printing as well as giving a comprehensive and authoritative ruling on all matters of style.

WRITING SKILLS SELF-ASSESSMENT

When you have completed a piece of work, measure it up on the table below. Note down your strengths and weaknesses. Now and again when you write, look back on your comments on earlier work. Have you taken your own criticisms on board?

First impression:
    Layout
    Word processing
    Attention to detail

Content:
    Definitions
    Adequate research
    Argumentation
    Evaluation
    Balance of argument
    Fairness of presentation
    Answering the question
    Overall integrity of structure

Paragraphs:
    Length
    Signposting
    Conversation
    Linking

Sentences:
    Length
    Clarity
    Grammar:

Vocabulary:
    Consistent formality
    Accuracy
    Clarity

Spelling:

Punctuation:
    Accuracy
    Helpfulness

Other comments:

SAMPLE ESSAY QUESTIONS

Although most courses rest upon a combination of term-time essays and an examination paper, some assess students on the basis of essays alone. The University of Hull's Topics In American Culture And History course requires the writing and submission of two essays during the first semester. Each has to be approximately 1,500–2,000 words in length.

Students may – if they wish and after consultation with the relevant tutor – decide upon their own essay titles although they must be related to a lecture that has been given as part of the course. The essays have to include notes/footnotes and a bibliography.

Alternatively, they can draw on the list of sample questions offered by the University.

- 'The disciplines of American Studies and Cultural Studies are so compatible as to be at times synonymous.' Discuss.

- 'American culture is characterized by a schizophrenic split between rapacious materialism and the most exalted forms of idealism.' Discuss.

- Consider the cultural implications of America's shift, during the course of this century, from industrial capitalism to consumer capitalism.

- Discuss an example of American culture that exposes the country as being in a state of crisis. (Avoid examples discussed at length in the lecture.)

- Apply a Cultural Studies approach to an example of ONE of the following: Jazz, Cinema, Pop Music, Soap Opera, Sport, Fast Food, Advertising, Fashion, Sci-Fi.

- How should historians come to terms with the problem of subjectivity/objectivity?

- To what extent is history objective?

- In what ways do historians' political sympathies colour their work?

- Compare and contrast oral histories and memoirs as sources.

- Evaluate the difficulties of the work of the Federal Writers' Project and Freedmen's Bureau interviews as source material for understanding slavery.

- Account for and illustrate the shift in American historical writing in the wake of the Second World War.

- Account for and illustrate the shift in American historical writing in the 1960s and 1970s.

- To what extent do the arguments of postmodernists represent a fundamental challenge to the American historical profession?

- Women in jazz.

- Jazz and Discrimination.

- Jazz autobiographies

- Jazz and the historian

- Consider the influence of John Coltrane on Pharoah Sanders.

- By what means does West Coast jazz popularise be-bop?

- Write a book review of *The Swing Era* by Gunther Schuller.

- Assess the contribution of Johnny Hodges to the music of Duke Ellington.

- After reading Leroy Ostransky's *Understanding Jazz* do you feel you understand jazz?

- Discuss Philip Larkin's objections to Charlie Parker and the be-bop movement.

- Select no more than ten tracks to provide a musical illustration of Whitney Bolliett's chapter on Bob Wilber in *Improvising*.

- 'No matter what their race or religion, the new immigrant groups entering the USA in the late nineteenth century were the targets of regular stereotyping in newspaper cartoons and illustrations.' Discuss.

- Analyse the stereotype of ONE of the following groups as promulgated by the American popular press: Jews, the Irish, African-American, Chinese immigrants.

- What were the origins of the 'Sambo' stereotype?

- Explore the minstrel tradition.

- What was the place of African-Americans in Hollywood?

- Racism and historians.

- Would it be true to say that by putting the 'noble savage' on a pedestal, Americans were admitting to an inability to accommodate the native American in mainstream society?

- What effects have native Americans had on the culture of the United States?

- Discuss the issue of reliability in native American historical sources.

- 'For writers working in Hollywood, the Hollywood Novel was the perfect vehicle for revenge.' Discuss.

- Compare the depiction of Hollywood by an American writer with that by a British writer.

- 'Writers who complained about their lot at the Hollywood studios often overlooked one important fact: they simply could not do the job for which they were paid.' Discuss.

- 'Ironically, although many writers hated working in Hollywood, it was in Hollywood that a number of them produced the finest fiction of their careers.' Discuss.

- Compare a portrait of an artist figure in one novel with that in any film.

- Assess the career of any writer working in Hollywood during the 1930s and/or 1940s.

TUTORIALS

Tutorials are probably the most efficient and engaging way of learning. Indeed, they are the principal basis for teaching at the universities of Oxford and Cambridge. They usually consist of a small group of students and a tutor. It gives you the opportunity to get to know at least some people. Apart from anything else, there will be people you know to sit next to in the first few lectures. It also means that, if for any reason you have to miss a lecture, you can borrow the notes.

The official aims of a tutorial are to reinforce lectures, to clarify any points in the lectures that you did not understand and to explore topics in more depth than can be attempted in lectures, perhaps moving on to related topics that were not covered in the lecture but which are still relevant to the course. To get the most out of a tutorial, you need to tell your tutor where your difficulties and interests lie.

Do not be afraid of asking something silly or giving a wrong answer. In tutorials, you are very unlikely be assessed on what you know (although you should clarify any criteria for assessment with your tutor). If tutors award a mark for tutorial performance at all (and not all courses have tutorial assessment) it will be based on attendance and participation. If you make a mistake in a tutorial, you and your tutor can get to the bottom of it and clear up any misunderstandings. Better to make a mistake there than in the exams or essays.

Attendance at tutorials is usually compulsory and if your attendance is poor, the tutor will be obliged to inform the course organiser and your director of studies or personal tutor. This is partly for academic reasons, to make sure you are not falling behind with your work. It is also for pastoral reasons, to make sure you are not ill or in some kind of difficulty. Please try to let your tutor know if you are going to be absent. Because tutors are the members of university staff that students come into contact with most frequently, they are often the first person that a student will consult about a non-academic problem.

In the last tutorial before the exams, look for clues. Your tutor will probably tell you about the exam layout. You may go over past examination papers and be given hints on question spotting or on the structuring of answers. If the course has changed recently, past papers can cause confusion and concern because they will include questions about topics with which you are not familiar, and your tutor will be able to reassure you. If the tutor does some exam revision work with you, which topics are the focus of attention? After the exam, ask your tutor about any mistakes you have made if you cannot see for yourself how to put them right.

The better prepared you are for a tutorial, the more you will get out of it. Obviously, you will do any reading that the tutor has asked you to do and you should attempt the exercises that you might have been assigned as out-of-class work. Often, some of these exercises will prove very difficult at first. If that happens, do as much as you can and try to work out exactly where you are getting stuck. Do, however, let your tutor see your work, however much concern it causes you. You are not going to be the only one in the group who faces problems. The tutor needs to know what areas of the course need extra consolidation and which sections are straightforward enough for you to revise on your own. If there is no set homework, make sure that you have understood the lectures and the recommended reading that goes with them. Tell the tutor about the topics and themes that are not clear.

If you have special needs, tell your tutors if there is anything they can do to assist. For example, if you are partially deaf and need to lip read, suggest to the tutor that you sit where you can see the tutor's face clearly and in good lighting. Ask the tutor to help by speaking clearly. If the tutor lapses and starts talking to the blackboard, a quick reminder will not cause any offence and would be appreciated.

SEMINARS

The structure and purpose of seminar classes varies, as do their length, which is either one or two hours. For some modules, you must make individual presentations or work in small groups. Whatever their structure, seminars (and workshops if appropriate) are essential to each module. They aim to provide a supportive environment for debate and discussion and provide an important opportunity for the expression of your own ideas and interaction with those of others. In general, the tutor's role is to guide discussion, and you will be encouraged to risk expressing your arguments in order to develop your ability and confidence. You should find positive contributions well rewarded by the rest of the group, as well as by the tutor.

University of Keele

Seminars lie between the full-scale large lecture and the small, relatively intimate tutorial. However, different members of staff will approach seminars in different ways. Some regard them as large tutorials and others see them as small lectures. Nonetheless, there should be opportunity for questions and comments in a seminar. You should, therefore, come well prepared so that you can contribute but, because it is a larger gathering, you must also let other people speak and take care not to monopolise the lecturer's time. You cannot expect the same level of individual attention that you may be given in tutorials.

ORAL PRESENTATIONS

Some tutors ask students to give oral presentations in tutorials. It is not very likely that this will happen at the start of the first year. By the time you have to give a talk, you will be familiar with your subject and on fairly friendly and relaxed terms with the other members of the tutorial group.

Your oral presentation will be based on a written paper, produced with all the skills you would use for writing an essay. Some tutors will be quite content if you simply read from your written paper. Other members of the tutorial group will, however, be bored. Therefore:

- Try to keep your voice interested and interesting.

- Be sufficiently well prepared so that your nose is not always buried in your paper.

- Mark the important points in your paper (probably topic sentences) with a highlighter pen, so that you can find your way at a glance.

- As you speak, watch your fellow students and make eye contact with them and the tutor.

- Smile from time to time.

- Invite questions and comments and be prepared to deal with them

- Admit that you do not have all the answers.

- Make use of any appropriate audio-visual aids (whiteboard, overhead projector, computer screen, recordings).

- Provide a handout if you think it would be useful.

LECTURES

Lectures can be quite large. It is a good idea to arrive in good time and get a seat quite near the front, where there is less chance of being distracted and you will be able to hear. If the lecturer is inaudible or if the visual aids are not visible, let the lecturer know at once. If you have a hearing problem consult the university's special needs adviser. If you have a motor or visual problem and cannot take notes, ask the lecturer if you can use a tape-recorder. Recording devices should not, however, be used without specific permission.

Lecturing styles vary quite considerably and so you must be able to adapt your note-taking and listening. Many lecturers provide a course outline in the class booklet and it is a good idea to take a look at this and get a general picture of where the lecturers are heading. A number of lecturers follow a published book (sometimes their own). If there is not a suitable book to refer to, you may well get a handout at the lecture or handouts may be collected together in a class booklet. If there is such a booklet make sure you take it with you. If the lecturer sticks closely to the handout, it might be enough just to make marginal notes on it. If there is no handout, or if the handout goes beyond the content of the lecture, be sure to take notes. You may think you will remember it all but this simply will not work. A good lecturer will have planned the lecture and it will have a structure. In fact, even although the lecturer may sound quite spontaneous, the lecture should have been constructed in sections and paragraphs like a well-thought-out essay. The lecturer may tell your the gameplan at the start of the lecture. Try to structure you notes accordingly. Use bullet points and numbers where possible. Use a different coloured pen to highlight key terms and VIPs (Very Important Points). This will help with exam revision. You would be very exceptional if your concentration did not lapse occasionally in lectures but train yourself to waken up rapidly if the lecturer gives any VIP signals.

Not all lecturers are charismatic and riveting. You may have to make a big effort to stop your attention from wandering. On these occasions, you could try active rather than passive listening. Imagine you are in a radio discussion programme and you are going to have to respond to what the lecturer is saying. What can you agree with? What would you question? What stimulates you to think in fresh directions? This approach can help prevent lapses of concentration and also assist in the taking of notes.

At the end of a lecture, there will probably be a short time for questions. It can be daunting, but do not hold back. If, however, you cannot bring yourself to speak in front of a large audience, have a word with the lecturer afterwards. Questions are useful feedback for lecturers, who need to know whether their lectures have been pitched at an appropriate level.

Always take a look over, and make sense of, your lecture notes the same night, while the lecture is still fresh in your mind and, if there is recommended reading to do, do it as soon as possible after the lecture. You might like to revise your lecture notes with a friend, in the hope that your absent moments do not coincide and that if one of you has a gap in your notes, the other can supply the deficiency. By the same token, if you miss a lecture, borrow notes for the same lecture from at least two people.

Make a particular effort to attend the last lecture of every lecture block or module. This may well be directed towards the end-of-course examination paper.

EXAMINATIONS

The assessment process is usually based upon both the assignments that have been set during the semester and an examination at the end of the course. You can improve your exam technique greatly by planning how much time you are going to spend on each question and sticking to it. You know the duration of the exam and you know the number of questions. Assuming that each question is worth the same number of marks, you simply divide the time equally among the questions. This may sound self-evident, but significant numbers of students sacrifice examination marks and grades by devoting disproportionate amounts of time to a limited number of questions. It is relatively easy to gain the first few marks when answering a question. After that, the rate at which you collect marks slows down and eventually you reach a plateau. It is therefore important to spend time writing a full answer even if you feel that it is less than adequate. By the same token, avoid spending additional time on a question even if you feel that your answer is of a very high quality. In short, it is better to begin three questions than to finish two and neglect one altogether.

Examination practice should, therefore, begin with a calculation. Work out how much time you can have for each question. Remember to allow for the time it takes to complete the administrative details, question-reading time, thinking time and essay-planning time. For essay-type answers, note the time at which you must start to draw each question to a close. Even if you have not completely finished when your time is up, move ruthlessly on to the next question. Usually, each answer should be written in a separate book, but, if this is not required, leave a significant gap between the answers.

Getting ready for exams

Look at past papers. Read the instructions. How many questions are you going to be asked? How many topics have you covered? How many topics do you need to revise? There may well be some bits of the course that you find easier or more absorbing than others. These are the ones to concentrate on. Just make sure that, if you are question spotting, you cover a safe amount of material. It is a good idea to have at least two 'spare' topics in case one of your chosen subjects does not appear on the paper or if the question on it is asked in an unexpected way.

Pick your questions carefully. If you lack confidence, there are some questions types that can help you. It is possible to do really badly in an exam essay if you misread the question or wander off the point. Structured questions requiring short answers may, therefore, be a better bet. With questions like these, you can see exactly where the marks are coming from. The same applies to sectioned, short-answer-type questions. You might be asked for a definition of something you are not sure about, but you might manage to find something sensible to say about it and even if you do not, you can still get 80 per cent for getting all the rest right. You cannot get less than zero, so it is always worth making an attempt at an answer.

Plan your revision. You should be able to go over all your selected topics several times. Instead of planning to do one topic to death before going on to the next, aim to revise all your exam question topics once and then revise them all again, and again. That way, everything gets a fair turn and nothing gets skimped.

Active revision. Instead of just reading over your notes, which can put you to sleep or make you think you're learning when you're not, try making notes of your notes and notes of the notes of your notes until you have reduced the material down to a very small size for each question. Then, check that you can expand it all again to exam-answer size. A glance at these notes before you go into the exam will give you all the confidence you need.

Become familiar with past papers. You might like to brainstorm a few past papers with friends to get ideas on how to structure answers, and at some point, when you are far enough on with your revision, but well before the examination date, set yourself a paper under exam conditions. The most frequently asked question is 'How much should I write?' and this is the best way to find out. How well can you fit your answers to the time allowed for each question? You may be able to do exercise-type questions in less than the allotted time. Essay-type questions and definition-type questions, however, should take up all the time allowed. If you run out of things to say, you will have to go back to the books. Always learn more than you need, to allow for all the things that go straight out of your mind under the stress of the exam.

Look at more past papers. Now that you have the information needed to answer the questions, think how you would manipulate what you know to fit the different ways the questions are worded.

Make sure you know where and when the exam is. If necessary, get an alarm call or ask someone to see that you are up in time.

On the day

(If you are unable to attend an exam, you must give your reason to the course organiser as soon as possible. If the reason is illness, you will have to produce a medical certificate.)

Get to the examination room in plenty of time so that you arrive feeling calm and confident. However, do not get there too early. If others are nervous, it can prove infectious. Be sure you have everything you need: identification if required, watch, spare pens, handkerchief. If you want to, take a last look at your postcard-sized notes just to remind yourself that you really do know a lot. When you go into the examination hall, you will be asked to leave your notes, your coat and your bags at the back of the hall.

The best response to exam nerves is the knowledge that you have studied to the best of your ability. Remind yourself that you are as well prepared as you will ever be and look forward to displaying your knowledge. The examiners want you to pass and they are actively looking to reward you for displaying relevant knowledge. They are not going to try to catch you out. If nerves do begin to get the better of you, before or during the exam, breathe. Breathe very slowly and deeply, counting to seven as you breathe in. Then see how slowly you can breathe out. Three breaths like this can prove very helpful.

Now read the instructions carefully. You will probably be asked to use a fresh examination book for each answer. Remember to put your name on each book, and your tutor's name if it is asked for.

If there is anything you need to ask the invigilator, just put your hand up. It does occasionally happen that misprints occur on exam papers, in spite of careful proof-reading. If something is missed out from the instructions, or they are not clear, the invigilator will be glad to hear about it and will inform the rest of the class. If you run out of paper, feel unwell, need to go to the toilet, or need to borrow a pen, put your hand up and the invigilator will come to you.

Read through the questions and choose the ones you are going to do. Decide on the order in which you are going to do them. Make a note of the time at which you will need to start drawing each question to a conclusion. Make a note of the time at which you stop doing the each question, finished or not. Do not be tempted to overrun. Use any time left over to check through your answers, but do not start dithering and changing things that were right in the first place. If in doubt, go with your first instincts.

After the exam

When the exam is over, avoid people who ask, 'What did you write for question two?' It is over, finished, and there is nothing you can do to change it. Try not to think about it again until you get the results. When you get your exam paper back, look at the examiner's comments, even if you have gained a very high grade.

Marks are most commonly lost because of:

- Not reading the instructions and doing one question too few or one too many.

- Not reading the question.

- Poor time management.

- Irrelevance.

- Not providing enough examples.

SAMPLE EXAMINATION PAPERS

American history

This University of Keele paper was set at the end of an introductory American history course. It asks about events and developments between the revolutionary war in the late eighteenth century and the Reconstruction era that followed the Civil War (1861–5).

1. What prompted the majority of American colonists to reject British imperial rule after 1763?
2. What were the main conflicts or tensions in debates to establish a new Federal Constitution in 1787?
3. What sort of republic did Thomas Jefferson envision at the beginning of the nineteenth century?
4. What were the principal political themes of 'Jacksonian Democracy'?

5. How did the antislavery movement change after 1831?
6. Account for the expansion of black slavery in the southern states during the first half of the nineteenth century.
7. Examine the role of the West in the coming of the Civil War.
8. Why did Union war aims in fighting the Confederate States change after 1861?
9. Evaluate the North's motivation in its attempts to 'reconstruct' the South after 1865.

This is another University of Keele history paper. It asks about the period between the late nineteenth century and the end of the twentieth century.

---

1. Why, towards the end of the nineteenth century, were cities increasingly seen as threatening by rural and small-town America?
2. Why did mass immigration between the Civil War and the First World War focus ever more upon the growing cities of the Northeast and the Midwest?
3. How 'progressive' was the Progressive Era?
4. Some historians have argued that in the First World War, the US won the war, but lost the peace. Explain.
5. In what ways can the period of the 1920s be considered the beginning of modernity in American society?
6. What were the causes of the Great Depression? In your answer discuss both domestic and foreign factors.
7. Why did the US–Soviet wartime alliance so quickly fall apart after 1945?
8. In what ways did the Second World War and the Cold War both promote and hamper the cause of Civil Rights in the US?
9. What is it that makes the Vietnam War, according to George Kennan, 'the most disastrous of all America's undertakings in the two hundred years of its history'?
10. How do you explain the conservative resurgence in the US since the late 1970s?

American literature

This is a University of Hull American literature paper. Students were asked to answer three questions.

1. Compare Anne Bradstreet and Edward Taylor as 'reluctant poets in a society unsympathetic to poetry'.
2. Does Benjamin Franklin's *Autobiography* depict an eighteenth-century Puritan?
3. EITHER – (a)
   'Thoreau's experiment in simplicity and isolation has, as its natural conclusion, the fate of Melville's Bartleby.' Discuss.

   OR – (b)
   Define Transcendentalism through a discussion of EITHER at least TWO of Ralph Waldo Emerson's essays OR Henry David Thoreau's *Walden, or Life in the Woods*.
4. EITHER – (a)
   Compare the depiction of evil in TWO of the following authors: Edgar Allan Poe, Nathaniel Hawthorne, Herman Melville.

   OR – (b)
   >Use 'The Philosophy of Composition' as the basis for the analysis of at least TWO works by Edgar Allan Poe.
5. Discuss the view that, in the poetry of Walt Whitman and Emily Dickinson, form reflects content.
6. Is *Adventures of Huckleberry Finn* a realist text written by a romantic or *vice versa*?
7. Compare the ways in which *Daisy Miller* and *The Awakening* dissect courtship rituals and the bourgeois marriage code.

American government and politics

> This is a University of Keele paper. It asks students
> about the defining features of the US political system.

1. Does the separation of powers work?
2. How has the balance of power between national and state governments changed in the last forty years?
3. Can the president lead the US political system?
4. Are the Congress and its procedures too complex to function effectively?
5. Does the Supreme Court have unlimited power?
6. Do US political parties have a role beyond getting people elected to government office?
7. Why do so few Americans vote?
8. How do interest groups try to influence the US political process?

WEBSITES

American and British History Resources

This site (Rutgers University) offers access to many different resources including those covering the Civil War (1861–5) and African-American history.
    www.libraries.rutgers.edu/rul/rr_gateway/research_guides/history/history.shtml

American Memory Project (Library of Congress)

This site is aimed at both students and teachers who are interested in US history and culture. It provides access to over 100 collections and more than 7 million primary-source documents, photographs, films, and recordings.
    memory.loc.gov/ammem/ndlpedu/index.html

American Studies Resources Centre

The website hosted by the American Studies Resources Centre offers an excellent starting point for those studying US politics and government. Based at John Moores University in Liverpool, the site provides information about learning resources, student conferences, study days and degree courses in the UK. It incorporates *American Studies Today*, an online journal with a wide range of articles, news and book reviews.

www.americansc.org.uk

InfoUSA

This site offers information on a broad range of topics and themes. It is hosted by the Department of State.

usinfo.state.gov/usa/infousa/homepage.htm

Internet Movie Database (MDb)

This is one of a number of sites that provide detailed and comprehensive coverage of both past and recent American films.

www.imdb.com/

The New American Studies Web

This site – hosted by Georgetown University – offers links to a broad range of texts and other resources. These are organised under headings that include the economy, gender and sexuality, literature, music and performance, media cultures, war, science and religion.

cfdev.georgetown.edu/cndls/asw/

US Embassy (London)

The US Embassy website provides information for travellers to the US and American citizens living in Britain. It also offers information about events from an American perspective.
www.usembassy.org.uk/

US House of Representatives

The House of Representatives is one of the two chambers of Congress. It consists of 435 members, each of whom represents a district.
www.house.gov

US Senate

The Senate is the other chamber of Congress. Each state is represented by two senators, regardless of its population.
www.senate .gov

Voice of the Shuttle

This site – hosted by the University of California, Santa Barbara – offers links to a broad and eclectic range of sites. Its coverage includes less conventional themes such as anthropology, archaeology, architecture, cyberculture and gender studies.
vos.ucsb.edu/

ORGANISATIONS

These websites are directed towards researchers and lecturers, but they do, nonetheless, incorporate features that may be of value to students.

American Politics Group (Political Studies Association)

www.psa.ac.uk/spgrp/apg

American Studies Association

www.georgetown.edu/crossroads/asainfo.html

British Association for American Studies

www.baas.ac.uk/default.asp

European Association for American Studies

www.eaas.info

LTSN Subject Centre for Languages, Linguistics and Area Studies – American Studies (Niall Palmer, Brunel University)

www.lang.ltsn.ac.uk/index.aspx

REFERENCES

Bailey, C. (1990) 'Political parties', *Contemporary Record*, February: 12–15.

Baritiz, L. (1985) *Backfire: A History of How American Culture Led Us into Vietnam and Made Us Fight the Way We Did*, New York: Ballantine Books.

Bennis, P. (2003) *Before and After: US Foreign Policy and the September 11th Crisis*, New York: Olive Branch Press.

Bradbury, M. and D. Corker (1975) 'The American Risorgimento: the coming of the New Arts', in M. Cunliffe (ed), *American Literature since 1900*, London: Sphere.

Campbell, N. and A. Kean (1997) *American Cultural Studies: An Introduction to American Culture*, London: Routledge.

Davidson, R. and W. Oleszek (1998) *Congress and its Members*, Washington, DC: Congressional Quarterly.

Dumbrell, J. (2000) 'Foreign policy and foreign policy making', in A. Grant, *American Politics: 2000 and Beyond*, Aldershot: Ashgate, pp. 85–101.

Etulain, R. W. (ed) (1999) *Does the Frontier Experience Make America Exceptional?* (Historians at Work), New York: Bedford Books/St Martin's Press.

Fernandez-Armesto, F. (2003) *The Americas: A History of Two Continents*, London: Weidenfeld and Nicholson.

Fox-Genovese, E. and E. D. Genovese (2001) 'Surveying the south', *Southern Cultures*, 7:2, Spring, 76.

Glazer, N. and D. P. Moynihan (1967) *Beyond the Melting Pot: The Negroes, Puerto Ricans, Jews, Italians and Irish of New York City*, Cambridge, MA: The MIT Press.

Gleason, P. (1980) 'American identity and Americanization', in S. Thernstrom (ed), *Harvard Encyclopedia of American Ethnic Groups*, Cambridge, MA: Harvard University Press, 31–58.

Gone with the Wind, www.filmsite.org/gone.html

Hall, S., D. Held and T. McGrew (1999) *Modernity and its Futures*, Cambridge: Polity Press.

Johns, J. (1996) *A Brief History of Nature and the American Consciousness*, xroads.virginia.edu/~cap/nature/cap2.html

Kennedy, P. (1989) *The Rise and Fall of the Great Powers: Economic Change and Military Conflict from 1500–2000*, London: Fontana Press.

Kennedy P. (2003) 'The perils of empire', *The Washington Post*, 20 April, MGG Pillai: Journalism and Commentaries, www.mggpillai.com/sections.php3?op=viewarticle&artid=2459

Kristol, I. (1996) *A Post-Wilsonian Foreign Policy*, American Enterprise Institute, 2 August, www.aei.org/publications/pubID.17311/pub_detail.asp

Matterson, S. (2003) *American Literature: The Essential Glossary*, London: Arnold.

Pells, R. (1997) *Not Like Us: How Europeans Have Loved, Hated and Transformed American Culture since World War II*, New York: Basic Books.

Prestowitz, C. (2003) 'Imperial America: time to scale back', *The Times*, 1 July.

Rossiter, C. (1963) *The American Presidency*, London: Harvest.

Roth, J. K. (ed) (1995) *American Diversity, American Identity: The Lives and Works of 145 Writers Who Define the American Experience*, New York: Henry Holt and Company.

Rubin, L. D. Jr (1991) *The American South: Portrait of a Culture*, Washington, DC: United States Information Agency.

Snyder, J. (2003) 'Imperial temptations', *The National Interest*, 71, Spring.

US Census Bureau (2001) *Historical Income Tables – Households*, www.census.gov/hhes/income/histinc/h06.html

INDEX

A
SPELLBOOK
for the
SEASONS

Distributed in North America by Red Wheel Books
An imprint of Red Wheel/Weiser, LLC
with offices at:
65 Parker Street, Suite 7
Newburyport, MA 01950
www.redwheelweiser.com

British Library Cataloguing-in-Publication data available on request.

ISBN 978-1-59003-537-5

10 9 8 7 6 5 4 3 2 1

Printed in China

A
SPELLBOOK
for the
SEASONS

Welcome natural change with magical blessings

TUDORBETH

Red
Wheel

CONTENTS

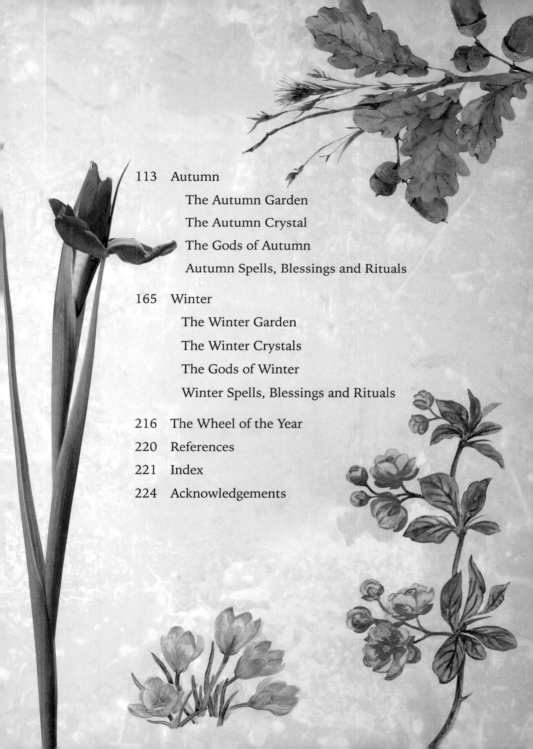

INTRODUCTION

We are governed by the seasons whether we live in the northern or southern hemisphere of this magnificent world. It has been that way since the beginning of creation and for as long as humans have walked this earth. Over the centuries, seasons and magic have journeyed together. We have watched nature unfold before our eyes and related our needs and desires to this earthly dance. Plants, flowers, even the seasons themselves, became allied to magic and we harnessed it to our soul's memory.

The wonder of magic and witchcraft is that it changes with each generation. We base spells and potions on the original associations with nature and add something new each time. Our magic and witchcraft are the product of our time and all the trials and tribulations we face today are mirrored in the magic we create. We may no longer use cauldrons to cook or broomsticks to sweep the house clean but we still use the spells.

The Wheel of the Year – the term pagans use to describe the year of festivals and celebrations – is part of our belief system's central core and much has been written of this Turning of the Wheel and the festivals that are celebrated. In this book we shall investigate these festivals, the practical magic that flows through our seasons and the gods that rule over the different times of the year. Each season is presided over by a set of deities. The Norse gods and goddesses have authority over the winter months, while spring is presided over by Celtic deities, summer belongs to Ancient Greek gods and goddesses and autumn comes under the watchful gaze of the Ancient Roman deities.

Never before has the world and nature needed magic so much. The oceans are filling with micro plastics, and the world's largest single organism, the Trembling Giant, an aspen forest in Utah, is dying. Fires and droughts are spreading throughout the globe and yet nature still leaves us gifts – the seasons.

Use the gift that nature brings with these spells, but in return give something back; plant trees and flowers, sow seeds, pick up litter, recycle whenever and wherever you can. We are all connected to one another and everything around us. We are nature.

BLESSING FOR SISTERS AND BROTHERS AROUND THE WORLD

Sisters and brothers, world's apart,
Embrace the magic in our hearts.
Upside down, turn around,
Connected are we for power abound.
Spring, summer, winter and fall,
Children of nature, blessed be to all.

Season's Blessings

Summer, autumn, winter and spring,
Blessed be to the Turning of the Wheel.
Let me embrace all the good you bring,
All the season's changes I will feel.
Peace and love in every month in every day,
In every rain drop, in every snowflake that comes my way.
Glory to the scorching sun, glory to the breeze,
I am grateful to the cool summer seas.
To rainbows and storms blessed be,
To the Turning of the Wheel.
Summer, autumn, winter and spring,
So mote it be.

Spring

SPRING

'No matter how long the winter,
spring is sure to follow.'

Traditional proverb

Spring is a season of such wonder that we can feel the magic in everything from the daffodils and tulips to the baby birds demanding food. There is so much life to spring and everywhere is bursting with change. The dark days of winter are over as the nights shorten and the days grow longer. The changes in weather can bring with them snow, rain, gales and thunderstorms. Yet, there may be beautiful rainbows and the warm spring sun is kind to both humans and animals. The butterflies come out of hibernation as caterpillars now change with the growing heat of the sun. Bees also begin to appear as flowers start to blossom.

There are many changes and extremes of weather in the spring months. Warm, wet, mild weather can be a breeding ground for life-threatening illness, such as influenza. However, spring is also a time for beauty.

Gardens begin to burst with colour during this season and over the following pages the magic spring flowers hold will be revealed. Harness the power of the season through spells, blessings and rituals and learn about the pentagram of spring crystals and the Celtic deities that rule these bountiful months of the year.

THE SPRING GARDEN

The spring garden is full of such wonder and magic. In the Celtic world the enchanted inhabitants are very much welcome, as the plants and flowers of the spring garden are the nectar to all manner of fairy folk. Some of the most well-known spring flowers are daffodils, tulips and crocus. Other spring flowers that are perfect for enticing the fae into your garden are given here.

WINTER ACONITE

The winter aconite (*Eranthis*) is the witch's friend. Despite its name, it flowers in the spring months. This plant is a member of the buttercup family and can be used for many magical purposes and in many spells. *Eranthis* has many names, but some people may know it as monkshood or wolf's bane. Remember that it is highly toxic and if any part of this plant is ingested then it can kill, so when handling it always wear gloves, as even touching the plant can cause an allergic reaction.

BLUEBELL

The wild bluebell, or wild hyacinth, is native to the British Isles and some parts of Europe, although cultivated versions are available around the world. It is well known how the fairies and other beings of nature love the sound of bluebells (*Hyacinthoides*), that only they can hear. The wild bluebells are usually a beautiful violet blue colour, although they can also be white. The best time to see them is in the spring, when they carpet the floor of ancient woodlands. These beautiful flowers are also known as wood bells and fairy flowers. The Spanish bluebell, that you can grow in your garden, is either pink or blue, and it flowers at the same time as other spring flowers such as tulips, narcissus and hyacinths.

BABY'S BREATH

Gypsophila or baby's breath is a beautiful spring plant that can be both an annual and a perennial. The flowers are either white or pink and they make the perfect table decoration for an Ostara Wiccaning (*see page 35*). The plant usually flowers from late spring through summer, although you can get early flowering species. It is often also called Bristol fairy.

HYACINTH

The highly scented *Hyacinthus* is a favourite with fairy folk and mortals alike. The flower, a native of eastern Europe, is used to symbolize the spring equinox in eastern new year celebrations. Its flowers can bloom in a range of colours including blue, pink, white, red, orange, pink and yellow, and appear throughout the season.

LILY OF THE VALLEY

The lily of the valley (*Convallaria majalis*) blooms from mid-to-late spring. It is associated with the goddess of spring, Ostara (or Eostre), and is often used in wedding bouquets. This lovely little plant was known to our ancestors for its medicinal properties as it has a similar effect on the heart as *Digitalis* or foxglove. However, this plant is toxic and no part of it should be eaten. Only qualified practitioners should use this plant in a medicinal way.

When planted, these five wonderful and magical plants will entice the inhabitants of the enchanted world into ours. If you can, make room in your garden for the fairies of spring and then watch the mushrooms and toadstools pop up in autumn. Plant these flowers in a wild but orderly fashion. Despite their love of nature and wild gardens, the fae actually like gardens that have order to them.

By also planting herbs you can create a sensory garden full of sight, smell, touch, taste and sound. Try growing some of the more unusual ones, such as bronze fennel, or tricolour sage. You may also want to add a water feature as the trickling sound is not only a calming addition to any garden, but wildlife such as birds and squirrels may welcome it in the height of summer. Finally, fairies love bells so, if you can, dangle some little bells around your garden and trees.

Pixie Garden Blessing

Say this pixie garden blessing in your garden while planting your spring plants. You could also write this on a sign in the shape of a little door so the fairies know it is for them.

Welcome pixies, welcome fae,
Enter my garden both night and day.
Please feel free to skip and play,
But leave some magic on your way.
Blessed be and so mote it be.

THE SPRING CRYSTALS

There are many symbols of spring and one of the most powerful is the rainbow. Fortunately, the earth has given us five crystals that yield the power of spring and they form the pentagram of rainbows (*see page 20*). If you are able to invest in a crystal, choose one of these rainbow crystals as your spring crystal. Then, during the spring have that crystal on your altar so it can remind you of the power of nature that always surrounds us.

RAINBOW PYRITE

Rainbow pyrite or Russian rainbow pyrite, as it is sometimes known, is a perfect crystal for working with all earth and water elements. You could keep a piece of it in your garden, especially if entertaining outdoors, as this stone is excellent at imparting people with confidence. It may be beneficial to guests who do not know everyone at your gatherings. Rainbow pyrite is also a good ghost hunter's stone as it keeps negative forces at bay. It shimmers with all the colours of the rainbow, including yellows, greens, pinks and blues.

This crystal is found in the bottom, left of the spring crystal pentagram and governs security, values and material possessions.

RAINBOW OPAL

The rainbow opal crystal is truly beautiful. The rainbow effect occurs in both black and white opals but it is worth finding the rainbow version, for it is a stone of wishes. It is also a wonderful stone for connection with the spirit, as it is an uplifting, healing stone. The rainbow opal sits at the top of the pentagram in the place of the spirit.

Rainbow Quartz

The rainbow quartz is a double gem for it has the combined benefits of clear quartz plus the enchanting properties of the rainbow. As a result, this amplifies the known qualities enhancing confidence and courage.

It lies in the bottom, right of the rainbow crystal pentagram. This is where passion, creativity, enterprise and faith lie. The dual action of the rainbow quartz amplifies all of these characteristics.

Rainbow Moonstone

Rainbow moonstone is often regarded as the original moodstone as it changes in tone, either becoming brighter or duller in certain conditions and with different people. It is a perfect stone to entice the fae, so keep a piece in the spring garden. The rainbow flashes of this stone catch the eye and enhance wonder and magic. Place it around your spring herbs to increase their healing energies.

As a moonstone, its powers are charged best in full-moon light. In the pentagram, the rainbow moonstone sits to the left and governs emotions, moods, dreams and romance, which are all expressed by this amazing stone.

Rainbow Obsidian

Rainbow obsidian is an incredibly powerful stone. Its energy can be too intense, and for this reason it is best kept from view when not in use. It is a deep black, but when held against the light a striking iridescent rainbow is revealed. Like all obsidians, it makes the perfect divinatory tool. Indeed, our first mirrors were made of obsidian.

In the pentagram, the rainbow obsidian sits to the right and governs ideas, communication, truth and justice – the very core characteristics of being human.

The Pentagram of Rainbows

Rainbow Opal

Rainbow Moonstone

Rainbow Obsidian

Rainbow Pyrite

Rainbow Quartz

Obsidian Scrying Spell

With a highly polished rainbow obsidian, use this spell to ask what the coming months may bring. Light a white candle and holding up your rainbow obsidian say:

Stone of wonder, stone of spring,
Show me what the summer will bring.

Let the flickering candlelight shine through the rainbow inside the obsidian and watch the images of the coming months.

THE GODS OF SPRING

The months of spring are traditionally associated with the Celtic deities. Indeed, the main festivals of spring are named for two of them. Through centuries and millennia all the Christian and Norse influences could not silence the voices of our Celtic ancestors. The festival of Ostara is named for the goddess Ostara (or Eostre) and Beltane was named for the god Belenus.

In the Celtic myths and legends of the British Isles we find Arthur and Avalon, Finn MacCoul, Brigit and Cernunnos, among many others. In the British Isles every spring, every waterfall, every cave, hill and mountain has a deity and legend associated with it.

Day	Colour	Deity	Stone
Sunday	Red	Lugh	Garnet
Monday	White	Ana	Diamond
Tuesday	Green	Cernunnos	Tree Agate
Wednesday	Blue	Manannan	Turquoise
Thursday	Yellow	Taranis	Fulgurite
Friday	Orange	Branwen	Carnelian
Saturday	Silver	Cerridwen	Quartz Crystal

Other Celtic deities include Lir, the sea god, and Gwynn, king of the faeries. Branwen, the white blossom daughter of Lir, is often compared to Venus and Aphrodite of Roman mythology. Brigit is the poetess goddess and the goddess Ana is the queen of healing, while Manannan is the wind god. Cerridwen rules over nature and is viewed as the Celtic goddess of witchcraft. Gods and goddess of air, fire, sea, earth, trees and wind – the Celtic world had them all.

Some of the Celtic deities and their correspondences are shown below. These can be used throughout the spring or throughout the rest of the year if you have a particularly strong connection to the Celts.

Oil	Tree	Herb
Cedar	Ash	Basil
Juniper	Beech	Myrrh
Patchouli	Hawthorn	Vervain
Lotus	Apple	Lavender
Fennel	Oak	Sage
Honeysuckle	Hazel	Valerian
Jasmine	Willow	Mugwort

SPRING SPELLS, BLESSINGS AND RITUALS

FLOWER SEASON SPELL

The work of the busy gardener is never-ending, yet the delight and visual show the garden gives us is phenomenal. To encourage your spring flowers to bloom, step into your garden on a bright, sunny spring morning and say this spell:

From gentle flowers meek and mild,
To tame roses and the wild.
Show your splendour this spring,
In summer your beauty bring.
In autumn bloom forever bright,
In winter sleep beneath the snows.
Dearest garden you are a colourful show,
You are a seasonal magical sight.
All year round and blessed be,
An' it harm none so mote it be.

PELARGONIUM LUCK SPELL

When planting a pelargonium in your spring garden,
say this little spell over the plant to encourage good luck:

Mighty plant with horseshoe leaf,
To this garden bring good luck.
Let all who pass this garden,
Enjoy and give you a second look.

Daisy Love Answer Ritual

Daisies are a beautiful little flower and when we see three of them growing on the lawn, it is a gift from the goddess. The three daisies not only signify that spring has sprung, they also signify Maiden, Mother and Elder, or Maiden, Mother and Matriarch, the leader of the family and wise spiritual counsel.

Daisies are also the plant that young lovers use, with the wise spirit of the Matriarch watching over, to find out if their chosen one loves them in return. To discover if your true love returns your feelings, try this ritual.

Fill a small bowl of with water and light three matches. As you light each match say these words:

They love me,
They love me not.

Drop the lighted match into the water. If they all sink to the bottom then they do not love you. If they all float, then they do love you. If some sink and some float, there is potential but it will be hard work to keep the relationship alive.

CHERRY PASSION OIL SPELL

To find passion in the spring time, try this spell. You will need:

3 drops cherry blossom essential oil
15 ml (½ fl oz) sweet almond essential oil

Mix the oils together in a dark bottle while saying these words:

Cherry sweet, cherry divine,
Let my lover be mine.

Then, dab the oil on your wrists and neck. Label and date the cherry blossom oil. If it is kept in a dark place, such as a drawer, it can last up to a year, depending how frequently it is used.

SPRING ILLS SPELL

The damp weather of spring brings with it colds and the dreaded flu. Along with a boost of vitamin C, use this spell to keep sickness at bay. Light an orange candle and say:

Weather chills and spring ills,
Stay away do not come this way.

OSTARA RITUAL

Ostara, or Eostre as she is more commonly referred to, is a spring goddess. She is often depicted as the maiden goddess with flowers in her hair. She is dressed in robes of white, a sign of purity and spirituality.

Many of the traditions of the Christian celebration of Easter were part of the pagan Eostre festival. Ostara (Eostre) is celebrated on the spring equinox, which falls between 20–23 March in the northern parts of the world and between 22–23 September in the southern hemisphere. It is a physical changing of time and seasons when the days get longer as the sun's strength returns to life and we feel energized with its heat and begin to look forward to the summer.

Perform this ritual on Ostara Eve. It is the beginning of new life and new hope. The Ostara ritual embodies that hope. On your altar, place a yellow candle, a bowl of salt, a selection of spring flowers still growing in their pots and a cup of wine or water.

Take the bowl of salt and walk deosil (clockwise), gently throwing a couple of pinches of salt as you make a circle. Say these words as you go around:

> This circle I summon
> Circle of life summon I,
> Only energies of love and light
> To welcome spring this night.

After you have cast your circle you can begin your Ostara ritual, which can involve spell casting; write out something that you want for the coming season on a piece of paper, then put the paper in a plant pot and cover with soil. Then plant seeds in the soil – herbs such as basil if it is a money spell. Water the seeds and as you do say:

> With this intent,
> May my dream grow as these flowers.
> An' it harm none so mote it be.

Then imagine the flowers growing and as they bloom your dream coming to fruition.

OSTARA BLESSING

An Ostara blessing can take different forms, and can be done in gratitude
or for healing purposes or pure spell casting. However, the blessing is
always rooted in the natural world, and often involves the sowing of
seeds, but it could involve taking care of plants, looking after animals
through a healing prayer or even planting trees. The blessing can be
made to suit the individual. Say these words over seedlings about to be
planted, an animal in need of healing or as is required.

Blessed be Ostara,
Blessed be season of spring.
Let this season,
Be full of new things.

Ostara Magic Salt

Make Ostara magic salt on the night of the full moon in March in the northern hemisphere and September in the southern hemisphere. Take a bowl of salt and say:

Goddess Ostara blessed be
Make this salt, magic for me.

Leave the salt in view of the full moon overnight. Then place in a glass jar and tie a yellow ribbon round it so you know it as Ostara salt. This salt can be given as a gift at an Ostara Wiccaning (*see page 35*) and when sprinkled around your home or office, will ensure bright ideas and business success.

OSTARA DECLUTTER

Early spring is a time of changing seasons when we clear away the clutter and dirt from the winter. Keep the spirit of Ostara going by spring cleaning and decluttering. Undertake a deep clean of the house, starting with the smallest room and see what can be thrown away. Deep clean the oven or wash down walls ready to be painted for the coming summer. Have a spring clean of your wardrobe and donate any clothes or shoes you have not worn for over a year. Those items you have not worn take to the charity shop or sell. Place a small Ostara charm (*see page 32*) for seven days in a place where you have cleared a space; it will help stop you re-cluttering!

CHARM OF OSTARA

Ostara represents the spring and flowers. Hers is the domain of fresh, new vitality. If you would like to make a charm of Ostara you will need some fresh sprigs of lavender or rosemary tied together with a piece of yellow ribbon. Attach a small key and the Ogham symbol of the pine or Alim, which is a 't' shape, if possible. It is Ostara's charm and can be hung anywhere in the house. An office would be ideal as Ostara instils vibrancy and new ideas and the Alim symbol will give your business enterprise a boost of fresh ideas. When hanging up your Ostara charm say these words:

Goddess Ostara blessed be,
Bring new ideas to me,
Let spring be full of wonder,
For those close to me.
An' it harm none so mote it be.

Ostara Fresh Air Spell

Spring is a time of deep cleaning, fresh flowers and rain, and has a fragrance all its own. Open all the windows and let the air flow through your home, taking with it the winter gloom. To create your own air freshener to enhance that spring feeling, you will need:

2 tablespoons Ostara salt (*see page 30*)
8 drops lilac essential oil
10 drops rosemary oil
20 drops cedar oil
Spray-top bottle

Mix ingredients together in the bottle and shake. Spray around your home while saying these words:

> Blessed Ostara hear this spell,
> Clear this house of all unwanted smells.
> Clean and fresh, pure and light,
> Put this house just right.
> So mote it be.

You can also dab some lilac or honeysuckle essential oil on furniture around the house for a fresh spring smell. Alternatively, fill a small ceramic water holder with the spray mixture and place it on a radiator. The water and essential oil will evaporate with the heat, leaving a fresh smell of Ostara around the house.

Ostara Fertility Spell

The goddess Ostara is a symbol of fertility and one of the old ways to increase fertility was to sprinkle periwinkle flowers under the bed. This small blue flower has five petals. Anything in nature that has five strands or five petals can be used for magical purposes. In the case of the little periwinkle, or lavender-blue, as it is sometimes called, its connections with love and fertility are often called upon.

For this spell, sprinkle five periwinkle flowers under your bed and say the following words:

Oh goddess from blessed lake,
This infertility from me take.
Help to fill this empty womb,
With a babe's laughter in every room.
Help to make parents of we,
An' it harm none so mote it be.

OSTARA WICCANING

A Wiccaning is the naming ceremony of a newborn child, similar to a baptism or christening, an example of which is offered on the following pages. The importance of the Wiccaning is to not only name the child with their earthly name but also to ask ancestors and the goddess to protect the child for now and evermore. The other purpose is to also give the child a magical name. This secret name is the binding defence against the negative forces who would do the child harm. Many choose magical names from nature such as Fox, Bear, Willow or Lily. Friends of the parents of the child will be chosen as guardians (or god/goddess parents) and will take part in the ceremony, during which the child is given the magical name that only the child and guardians know. The magical name is never uttered and never spoken of for fear the fairies may hear and take the babe to the enchanted land while leaving a child of the fae, a changeling, in its place.

The ceremony is usually performed in a protective circle with the congregation standing all around. It can be performed outdoors, but if the weather is wet and cold bring the outdoors inside by decorating the house with plants. Hang your Ostara charm (*see page 32*) up in plain sight of the ceremony.

The gifts a child can be given for their Wiccaning are traditionally silver. Silver is a metal that is highly revered as not only does it keep werewolves at bay, it also symbolizes wealth.

Traditionally, Ostara magic salt (*see page 30*) is also given, either blue moon salt (salt made on the night of a blue moon) for a boy or midsummer salt (*see page 82*) for a girl. Another symbolic gift can either be a book, as it represents knowledge, or an egg, as it represents fertility. Some god/goddess parents buy a crystal egg made from the child's birthstone. These are symbolic Wiccaning gifts that the child keeps and become family heirlooms, passed onto each generation.

OSTARA WICCANING/NAMING CEREMONY

HIGH PRIEST/PRIESTESS
Blessed be to one and all on this Ostara Day.

ALL
Blessed be.

HIGH PRIEST/PRIESTESS
We are here today to bless this child and to name them in our tradition. I ask the maiden goddess Ostara to bless this child with her presence today. I ask the guardian of this child to step forth and name them.

GOD/GODDESS PARENTS
(Child's name.)

HIGH PRIEST/PRIESTESS
Then in the name of the goddess I ask the ancestors of this child to bear witness to the name of (child's name). I ask all present in Spirit to protect this child of grace. So mote it be.

ALL
So mote it be.

HIGH PRIEST/PRIESTESS
And now god/goddess parents whisper into (child's name) ear so that they may recognize and know their name of magic.

(God/goddess parents step forth and whisper into child's ear.)

HIGH PRIEST/PRIESTESS

I ask the goddess and ancestors to protect this child for now and evermore, whose name in magic is known. Blessed be.

ALL

Blessed be.

HIGH PRIEST/PRIESTESS

I thank the goddess Ostara for her blessing and I thank the ancestors of this child for their never-ending protection of (child's name). May the goddess bless you all always, so mote it be.

ALL

So mote it be.

HIGH PRIEST/PRIESTESS

Blessed be to one and all.

ALL

Blessed be.

GOD OF WEATHER AND MISTS

Spring weather can be both beautiful and changeable. Cold and frosty mornings can turn into warm sunny spring evenings followed by nights of rain. You can experience great contrasts from hail, snow, sleet, rain and thunderstorms to rainbows. It is due to the highly changeable nature of this season that you may also see mists and fog as moisture from the earth meets the heat of days and nights.

Manannan is the god of weather. He is responsible for mists but also for that which clears mists and fog, for he is the Celtic god of wind. Often associated with the spirit realm and the mysteries we can find there, he is the god of the Isle of Man and to this day Manx people still honour him in a midsummer ceremony. Bundles of yellow flowers, meadow grasses and reeds are offered to him to ensure safety and protection throughout the year.

Manannan has many magical items, from the goblet of truth to a flaming helmet, and also a magical horse that could travel on both sea and land. Yet it is his magic cloak of colours that is the most memorable. The cloak, which can change from blue to green, silver to purple, brings mists and a change of weather with it.

Springtime can be grey, but it is also a time of rainbows with their seven-dimensional multi-colours pouring out or the golden rays of the sun peeking out from behind a grey cloud. Think of the rainbow as the magic cloak of Manannan and make a wish upon it or ask Manannan to help and protect you in all you do.

TRUTH SPELL

One of Manannan's key magical items is the goblet of truth. Create your own goblet of truth and use it when you feel someone is not being entirely honest with you. Have a cup or mug that appeals to you the most. Light a silver or grey candle. Hold the cup or mug in your hands and say:

> From this cup you shall drink,
> Let truth come from your lips.
> No more lies you shall think
> For now and evermore,
> The truth with each sip you will speak.

When the person, friend or lover you doubt comes for a drink, make sure they always use that same cup or mug to drink from and their truth shall be set free.

Charm of Manannan

In Celtic myth, the god Manannan is a foster father to the many children he takes under his care, and as a protector god he cares deeply for all his children. He gathers the mist around them to protect them from their enemies. He is a kindly god and in many ways one that prefers peace.

Harmony in the family and household is important, so create a charm of Manannan to bring about a loving and caring environment in the family home. Collect two or three twigs from an apple tree and tie them together with a turquoise ribbon. As Manannan is the son of the Irish sea god Lir, add two or three shells to your charm. If relevant, each shell could represent a child in your family.

Anoint your charm with a few drops of lotus essential oil and hang in the room you use most as a family. Say these words:

> Manannan blessed be,
> Bring love and respect to my family.
> Let all who dwell here live in harmony,
> An' it harm none so mote it be.

BLOSSOM LOVE SPELL

If you have a love that you desire to come to you, this is the spell to perform. Collect some fallen blossom that lies on the ground in late spring; a cupful will do. Place all the blossom on a flat surface like a table and light a pink candle. Then with your index finger write the initial of your intended in the blossom while saying this spell:

Blossom fair blossom breeze,
Grant my love come to me
Before the blossom fall from trees.
An' it harm none so mote it be.

HEATHER STRENGTH SPELL

Heather has a strong connection to the Celtic lands. There are many different types of heather – purple, white, pink – and the plant's honey is prized for its wonderful taste. Many myths surround this flower, such as if you find a wild white heather then give it as a gift for it will bring good fortune – good fortune because, as it is white, it belongs to the goddess. White heather is also often used in wedding bouquets. If you plant heather in your garden, say this spell to ask for its Celtic strength:

Little heather plant of mountain mist
Celtic wonder and preferred of bees,
Bring your strength and majesty
To all who live here so mote it be.

ACCIDENT-PRONE SPELL

At times, we can be clumsy – tripping over the pavement, spilling water or wine, walking into things. If clumsiness is a pattern for you, call on Manannan to help carry your accident-prone habits away on the wind. Say these words upon a gust from the heavens or light a turquoise candle.

> Father Manannan hear my plea,
> I am a total calamity.
> Help me to go through my day,
> Without fall or accident in my way.
> No more the clumsy fool for me,
> An' it harm none so mote it be.

Blow out the candle and watch the smoke rise through the air. The spell is carried upon the wind to Manannan himself.

Spring Showers Magic

Spring showers are magical. They can descend quickly, as if the goddess herself is stopping us in our tracks. When accompanied by a thunderstorm, the air fills with magic and electricity. Some of us can see sparks of light due to the built-up energy. Spring showers can awaken our spirits. If you have been suffering from sadness or lack of energy then go outside in a rainstorm and ask the goddess to refresh your soul. If you see a spark of blue light from the build-up of thundering energy, close your eyes and make a wish.

RAIN BLESSING

Droughts occur in all parts of the world. A blessing for rain – rain being welcomed as a gift from the gods – can help those in need. Summon your circle (*see page 28*), place a white candle (preferably protected in a hurricane lamp) on your altar.

A white candle is always appropriate when saying a blessing or prayer but first go out in a rain shower and get absolutely soaking wet. Hold out your hands as if you were drawing down the moon and with your hands raised upwards towards the skies say these words:

Gods above and gods below
I honour you with light and love,
Hear my prayers and grant my wish.
Blessed rain I embrace you,
Your wonder and your might,
Do not hide from needed sight.
Shower your graces upon those in need,
In countries starved of your deed.
Rain not so much where there is no need,
Balance the world by day and by night.

Afterwards, meditate for a while and imagine the rain coming down in those lands where it is needed, while also wishing for less rain in those parts of the world affected by floods. When you have finished, give thanks to the gods and let the candle burn down.

RAIN ENERGY SPELL

If you're feeling lacklustre and in need of energy you can harness the power of the spring rains using this spell. Go outside when it is raining, stretch your hands up to the sky and feel the raindrops upon your face as you say:

> Rain, rain come this way,
> Wash away my sadness today.
> Rain, rain give me energy,
> An' it harm none so mote it be.

SLOW THE PACE SPELL

Here is a spell to help slow the pace, when we need space to breathe. Light a blue candle as you watch the rain. Remember what the rain feels like when you have been caught in a shower; how it taps and touches the skin. When you're ready, say these words:

> Drip drop, drip drop
> Rain on my face,
> Help me to slow the pace.
> Smooth and soft, light and free,
> That's how I want my life to be.

Yellow Umbrella Creativity Spell

Yellow is the colour of the flowers that are offered to Manannan. Here is a
spell of enchantment to call upon him, and to call upon the colour yellow,
if you feel you need more creativity in your life. Yellow reminds us of the
sun, of the warmth and of happiness. Buy a yellow umbrella, as using one
on a grey, rainy spring day is very magical. Use this spell to charm your
umbrella so that every time you use it you feel empowered and inspired.
In the light of a yellow candle hold the yellow umbrella in your hands
and say:

> Yellow umbrella, yellow bright,
> Forever burn bright as can be.
> Grant my life full of creativity,
> Give me constant energy.

Every time you use your umbrella feel energy and creativity surging
through you.

Rainbow Rain

Rainbows are beautiful – their cascading colours pouring into one another are a magical sight. They are the bridge to the Otherworld, the bifrost of Norse mythology, connecting the gods with humanity; they are often thought to evoke forgiveness and bring peace and serenity – the hope that the sun will soon follow the storms. It is for these reasons that catching the rain from a rainbow is worthwhile, as it is an excellent magical resource.

It is said that, if there be a rainbow in the eve, it will rain and leave. When it does rain and there is a rainbow at the same time, take a glass jar and leave it in the rain outside. Collect as much of the rainbow rain as you can. Afterwards, take it inside and tie a rainbow-coloured ribbon round the jar. If you do not have one of those, then braid red, yellow and orange ribbons together and use that instead. This is your rainbow rain and can be used for all manner of magical work, including in the spell given opposite.

HELP YOUR GARDEN GROW SPELL

If you would like to add a magical boost to your garden and houseplants then put some rainbow rain (*see opposite page*) in a spray-top bottle. Spray around your houseplants and garden while saying:

> Rain from the rainbow,
> Help my garden grow.

BELTANE TRADITIONS

Late spring is a time of flowers, fun, fairies and love. There are so many Celtic customs associated with the month of May in the northern hemisphere, primarily because of Beltane, the festival of the god Beli, or Belenus, as some refer to him, which is celebrated on 1 May. In Ireland, 1 May is viewed as the first day of summer. A public holiday is held on the first Monday in May in the British Isles. In the southern hemisphere the same festival is celebrated at the end of October.

There are ancient places in the British Isles that were named in honour of Beli. Cornwall is one such place, as its ancient name was Belerion or 'the place of Bel'. Bel or Belenus was a sun god and is often referred to as the 'shining one'.

At Beltane the veil between our world and the enchanted world is lifted, allowing fairies, sprites, elves and goblins to run free. Traditionally, young women washed their faces in the morning dew believing it would keep them young and beautiful for ever. People would sing May carols and songs. To this day the choir at Oxford's Magdalene College rise early and climb to the top of the bell tower to welcome the sunrise with the May hymn. Children would make a flower garland of two hoops with a doll in the centre called 'the lady' which they carried round the village. They would call for treats for themselves, although usually the treat was money.

In the Beltane festivities there is also often a man covered by a cage of leaves. He has many names, including the Green Man, Jack in the Green, Leaf Man, Wild Man and George Green. He symbolizes the death of winter and the birth of spring.

The Morris men of Britain are another traditional part of the Beltane festivities. They wear hats with ribbons, have large handkerchiefs or sticks and also have bells on their legs. The idea of the stick and the bells was to stamp and drive out evil spirits. The stamping and the ringing of bells was said to waken the spirits of the earth after their long winter sleep. In other parts of the British Isles the ground was beaten with sticks to drive out the spirits of winter to ensure a good harvest in the coming months.

Beltane is held halfway between the spring equinox and the summer solstice, around 1 May in the northern hemisphere and end of October in the southern, and for some it is called Walpurgis Night. It is an important witch's festival, although some people believe 30 April is the unluckiest day of the year to be born on, because malevolent fairies abound at this time. Traditionally, people would protect their houses with crosses made from rowan wood with elder leaves, a combination of Christianity meeting the pagan traditions. Alternatively they would decorate houses with blue, yellow or pink flowers. The branches of the sycamore tree and the wonderful hawthorn would also decorate houses and important buildings and monuments, such as the goddess shrines, in villages.

The dressing of wells and homes with flowers and garlands was a beautiful custom. You can replicate this in your own home by decorating it with flowers. Many plants begin to flower in late spring, so there should be something in your garden or garden centre that you can use. Try making garlands or bouquets to put in vases around the house and enjoy the sensual nature of spring.

In different parts of the British Isles many customs and tradition were in force during Beltane. In the north of England villagers would go May Birching. It was actually rather a cruel tradition and a bit similar to the Trick or Treat of Halloween. People would creep round their neighbours' houses after dark and hang branches that signified the character of the owner or occupant. The language and meaning of the trees that were used was important and it was rather similar to Cockney rhyming slang in the way it rhymed. Thus, a thorn branch meant 'scorn', a holly branch 'folly', and a briar branch meant 'liar' and so on. Some of the most commonly used branches are listed here:

Lime = Prime	Thorn = Scorn	Pear = Fair
Holly = Folly	Briar = Liar	Plum = Glum

Another tradition in the British Isles during Beltane was 'Bless the Sea'. Being an island race, blessing the sea ceremonies were held around the coast from Whitby to Southampton. Many of the Beltane traditions had elements of fertility ritual plus tree and water worship as well as purification such as the cleansing of the body and soul.

Cleansing Detox Ritual

The god Belenus is the god of purification, healing and hot springs. Hot springs, such as those found throughout the world from Iceland to California, are all healing. The volcanic mud draws out toxins from our bodies through our sweat and skin. If you can't get to a natural hot spring or spa, then create a healing and purifying bath for yourself by creating a cleansing detox ritual.

This ritual requires dedication and takes at least 24 hours to be performed properly. It is not just a case of having a deep soak in the bath. It begins with you making the ritual cleansing salt (to be made the day before the ritual, *see below*). This is then followed by an opening ceremony (*see opposite*) to acknowledge Belenus and promise him your intent. The ritual ends with a day of fasting.

Cleansing Salts

225g (8oz) sea salt
225g (8oz) Epsom salt
1–2 drops chosen essential oil
Handful chosen herbs and flowers, ground or left intact

In a bowl mix together the salts. Slowly add the essential oil along with the herbs and flowers. Combine and then store in a sealed container. Sprinkle a few tablespoons into a warm bath and allow to dissolve before soaking and purifying yourself. Use for your ritual as described opposite.

OPENING CEREMONY

Decorate your altar with spring flowers that are in bloom and cast your circle (*see page 28*). Have red, orange and white candles to hand, along with the cleansing salts (*see opposite*) and bottled water. Say the following words:

> God Belenus, I call upon you,
> To grant me strength in all I do.
> These next 24 hours,
> Increase my cleansing powers.
> Winter has now gone,
> Help me to cleanse all spring long.
> Bless these salts and water too,
> I am dedicating this purification ritual to you.

Drink some of the water and bless the salts with your index finger. Fast throughout the rest of the day, drinking the blessed water. In the evening, and when you know you won't be disturbed, light red, orange and white candles and place them round the bath. Pour three scoops of the cleansing salts into the bath water and say these words:

> Cleansed and pure
> My body and soul will be,
> Belenus, so mote it be.

Bathe and meditate in the bath for at least 20 minutes and afterwards close the ceremony as you are drying off by repeating this spell three times:

> I am renewed and I am cleansed,
> May this purity never end.

After this, write down how you feel and how you want to continue with a monthly routine of cleansing and fasting for a day.

SPRING SAGE CLEARING RITUAL

Cleansing in the spring doesn't just mean detoxing your body but also your home, your sacred space. To do this, you can make your own smudge sticks. Traditionally, white sage alone was used, but it is lovely when combined with lavender. Lavender and sage are two of the most important magical herbs because their uses are endless. They can be used in spells for happiness, healing, health, lust, psychic awareness and money.

Cut the sage into 15–20cm (6–8in) lengths (you need quite a bundle). Bind together tightly with a few sprigs of lavender, using thread or black or white cotton. Leave for the sage to dry out.

When the smudge stick is completely dry, you can use it in your space-clearing rituals. Set light to the end of the sage then blow out the flame and waft the smoke through the air, cleansing the sacred space. There is really no 'right' or 'wrong' way to create sacred space; magic is within you, so do whatever feels right.

If you feel as though you are not alone at home, or there is something different about your living space, as if perhaps there are 'unwanted guests', then try to clear it. Take back your power and reclaim your home. You have all the energy and power you need within you to clear the space. Light your smudge stick, then blow out the flame to create smoke and keep blowing into the stick to keep the smoke coming. Go to every room in the house while saying:

You are not welcome here,
Power of sage, make all clear.
Unwanted visitors, disperse from this place,
I now reclaim my living space.
Go back from whence you came,
And never come back again.

CHARM OF BELENUS

During the wonderful time towards the end of spring, we can feel summer in the air and happiness all around. Capture this feeling and welcome it into your home with the charm of Belenus. This charm can have many different items included. The main element are twigs from the hawthorn tree. Look for two or three twigs about 15–20cm (6–8in) in length and tie them together with an orange or red ribbon. If you have a little bell, then attach that too. A bell is very significant, as it not only has the name of Belenus (Bel), but is also an instrument used to call to the fae.

Hang your charm of Belenus in your house. This charm creates a happy and fun environment. Belenus is also the god of prosperity, so hang up the charm in your office to bring about a positive energy.

Summer

SUMMER

'A life without love is like
a year without summer.'

Swedish proverb

S ummer is a season that can burst upon us like a lover. The skies twinkle with sunbeams as bees take to the garden and migrating birds fly overhead. A time for welcomed rest, the summer months are traditionally associated with the Ancient Greek gods and goddesses. With midsummer's day being the longest day of the year, the sun god Apollo guides the month of June in the northern hemisphere and the month of December in the southern hemisphere. Litha, as midsummer is also known, is a day of great rejoicing and fun, though there is a hint of sadness as the once long summer nights begin to draw in by a minute of daylight every day as the Wheel of the Year turns towards autumn.

Summer is full of life, a time to choose new paths. We make affirmations and lists of new experiences to fill the long, warm summer days, while basking in the company of friends and family.

The following pages look at the bounty of the summer garden, the power of the summer crystal, along with spells, blessings and rituals to make the most of this glorious time of year.

THE SUMMER GARDEN

By creating a summer garden, you embrace all that is magical in your past. The Ancient Greek myths and magical entities are welcomed in our summer garden. Here are the five summer flowers that can be used in your summertime spell-making.

DELPHINIUM

The delphinium, also known as larkspur, is a beautiful, tall flower that is available in several varieties. The name delphinium means dolphin, due to its shape. In early to mid summer this flower blooms in varying colours, from reds, purples and blues, to yellows and whites.

Although this plant is highly toxic and poisonous it can be used in herbalist medicine. In small amounts larkspur is used for digestive problems and insomnia. The plant can also be used for healing, especially eye diseases caused by diabetes. Only qualified practitioners should use this plant in an medicinal way.

DELPHINIUM EYE SPELL

If you or a friend are suffering from eye problems, then send some healing. Have a delphinium flower next to you, light a blue candle and say:

> Flower light, flower bright,
> Help my/(friend's name) sight.

Blow out the candle and watch the smoke rise towards the universe. Imagine a swirling blue light returning, healing your eyes or your friend's eyes.

DIANTHUS

A lovely summer flower with many different species in its family, dianthus is also known as carnation, pinks or sweet William. There are five petals on the dianthus and they are usually frilled in varying shades of pink. Some perennial pinks are noted for their spicy fragrance. Anything in nature with five petals or five stems can be used in magic. As the flower is predominantly pink it can be useful in love magic in particular. The name dianthus roughly translates as 'god flower' from the Greek, as *dios* means god and *anthos* means flower.

DIANTHUS AFFECTION SPELL

As dianthus can be used in love spells and also to show affection, send a bunch of flowers to your loved one, or the person you would wish to have a relationship with, saying these words before you do:

> Little flower, fallen have I in love
> Show them how much.
> With this gift Dianthus
> Let them return my love.

IRIS 'TITAN'S GLORY'

The iris is a splendid summer plant whose name in Greek means rainbow due to the many different colours it is available in. The iris also has numerous species and varieties but this particular variety is most appropriate for us.

'Titan's Glory' has strong sword-shaped leaves and a full head of deep purple flowers. If you plant many together, the effect is stunning. The Titans were the forefathers of the Olympian gods and we cannot underestimate their power and strength. They represent the old order, the establishment, as it were. Trying to fight the past can become very draining. At times we need to accept the present in order to create a different future. Our only hope is trust in fate and hope that justice will do her best.

If you are trapped or in a situation in which you are up against many, the 'old guard', or tradition, and you want to bring in new ideas, then 'Titan's Glory' can act as a mediator between you and justice.

JUSTICE SPELL

Take an iris and write your name and problem on a piece of paper. Say this spell:

> I am right but they can do no wrong,
> They are many but I am just one.
> Mighty Iris I call upon you,
> To ask justice to be swift and true.
> Help me take the right path to be free.

Put the flower in a vase and place the spell underneath it. Each week take out the spell and think about what has changed. Is your path a little clearer? Has something been discussed?

If nothing has changed in a month, then do the spell again, picking another iris. Bury the old one in the garden and give thanks.

SALVIA NEMOROSA 'AMETHYST'

Salvia nemorosa is also called woodland sage. It has spikes of lilac-purple flowers. These plants look fragile but are actually very hardy, and bees and butterflies adore them.

The salvia family is huge with over 900 species stemming from it. Both the herbs mint and sage are a part of this magnificent family of plants. There are many different varieties of sage, including *Salvia apiana*, or white sage, which is sacred to Native American tribes. Another useful variety, *Salvia divinorum*, is also called the diviner's sage, while *Salvia officinalis* is the common sage used in cookery. *Salvia sclarea*, or clary sage, is grown not only as an ornamental plant, but as a source of essential oil. In magic, it is associated with vision and clairvoyancy.

You can treat woodland sage the same way as white sage and create a sage stick from it to cleanse the air in your home (*see page 58*). This particular variety is also excellent for connecting with elemental beings of nature such as nymphs. The nymphs are divine spirits who are different from goddesses and muses. Just like the *salvia* there are different varieties of nymph. There are celestial nymphs, water nymphs and underworld nymphs. The ones we are most familiar with are the land nymphs, the nymphs of the woods and plants. They are regarded as florists and protectors of the forests and woods. They are often depicted as beautiful young women.

Nymphs' Garden Spell

If you would like to acknowledge and welcome the nymphs into your garden then cast this spell. Make a sage stick (*see page 58*). Light it and waft it through the air in the garden while saying:

Here and now I clear the space,
For nymphs to come through time and space.
Walk freely in my garden and play,
Care for my plants in your own way.
Lady nymphs blessed be.

SUNFLOWER

No flower truly says it is summer more than a sunflower. There are many wondrous uses to the sunflower from making breads to medical ointments to dyes and body paints. Sunflower oil can also be extracted from the seeds. The seeds themselves can be eaten raw and are very nutritious, containing several B vitamins, vitamin E and they are also an excellent source of dietary fibre. Further, the sunflower is used to remove toxic chemicals from the soil such as arsenic and lead.

Sunflowers, because they are reminiscent of the sun, are also good flowers to use if you have a noisy or disturbing spirit such as a poltergeist. Sunflowers counteract the negativity within a family or with spirits.

Just as sunflowers are good at getting rid of toxins from the earth and the spirit realm, they are equally good for the body. Their oil is used as a carrier or base oil in aromatherapy and massage potions as it can also rid the body of toxic buildup via stresses and strains.

SUNFLOWER SPELL

If you have disharmony in your home or you suspect a negative presence.
Then have several sunflowers placed around the house. As you place a
sunflower in every room cast this spell.

> Sunflower of warmth,
> Take away this cold.
> Sunflower of light,
> Take away this dark.
> Sunflower of Grace,
> Take away this presence.
> Fill my house with love, light and peace,
> An' it harms none so mote it be.

When the sunflower has completely dried away keep the seeds for future
spells. If you find your house becoming a bit 'crowded' spiritually, then
invest in spirit quartz, or fairy quartz, and place it in the room with the
most activity. Never be afraid of the spirit realm, the things that go bump
in the night. This is your world and they are guests within it. If you do not
wish to have contact with spirits then merely say so out loud.

THE SUMMER CRYSTAL

There are a number of crystals that could be attributed to the summer, yet the one that stands out the most is the sunstone or feldspar and, in particular, the Iceland spar or the medieval sunstone. This stone, clear in colour, was used historically by seafarers as a navigation instrument to locate the sun in an overcast sky. The other type of sunstone is one that comes in a variety of colours such as yellows, reds, blues, greens and copper. The sunstone is a positive stone that represents the sun. On your altar you could place both a moonstone and a sunstone, representing both the god and goddess, especially at midsummer when their combined energies are heightened.

As this is such a positive stone, the sunstone can bring good luck to you in all manner of things, such as competitions, job interviews and all new business enterprises and opportunities. Further, if you are a seeker of fame then this stone is for you.

LOST DESTINY SPELL

If you feel adrift, with little idea about where you are headed, then use the Iceland spar to find your destiny. Hold the crystal in your hand as you say:

> I am lost,
> I am nowhere bound.
> I drift along,
> In hope to be found.
> Show me the path I must take,
> Show me the journey I must make.

Hold your Iceland spar up to the horizon and through your mind's eye, remember the images you see. These are hints as to where your destiny lies.

POWER OF THE SUN SPELL

The sunstone can help us when we are lost, it can also help us outshine others on our path. It is a powerful stone that harnesses the positive energies of its namesake the sun, which waxes and wanes throughout the year. If you are going to a job interview or you are hoping to set up a new business or enterprise, carry a piece of sunstone in your pocket or purse. Holding it in your hand say:

> Come to me power of the sun,
> Help me to be number one.
> I am the best,
> I will pass the test,
> I will beat the rest.
> Come to me power of the sun,
> I am number one.

The sun that brings positive benefits including life and nutrition can also burn too bright for those who prefer the dark. At times, the heat from our sun can create fires and cause destruction. Yet the sun is also the sign of nobility and strength. It is traditionally perceived as a powerful male force and is related to the god of the sun, Apollo. The sun's strength is no more felt than at midsummer.

THE GODS OF SUMMER

There were many tiers of gods in the Ancient Greek world. In the beginning there was Gaia, who was followed by the Titans, led by Kronos. His children became the Olympian gods we know today, who are known as the Dodekatheon, or the twelve gods.

In magic, numbers are highly significant and hold all manner of meanings. In this case, the number twelve can be used to relate to the twelve months of the year but it is also the symbolic number of the divine. It is the number of completion – a full circle. In Ancient Greek mythology, the twelve Olympians are the major deities of the Greek pantheon who resided on Mount Olympus. There is some debate about which gods are included. Hades (the god of the dead and the underworld) is commonly believed not to be one of the twelve, but some scholars believe that Hestia (goddess of hearth and home) gave up her Olympian seat to Dionysus, so she has some claim.

Aphrodite – goddess of love and beauty
Apollo – god of light and sun
Ares – god of war
Artemis – goddess of the moon and the hunt
Athena – goddess of the heroic endeavour
Demeter – goddess of the earth and fertility
Dionysus – god of wine and merriment
Hephaestus – god of fire, blacksmith to the gods
Hera – goddess of women and marriage, the mother of gods
Hermes – god of flight
Poseidon – god of the sea
Zeus – king of the gods

Zeus, Hades and Poseidon can be viewed as the triple gods of creation. They split the world between the three of them and Poseidon became god of the sea, Hades god of the underworld and Zeus the heavens, thereby making him supreme ruler. Zeus is the King of the gods and like Thor in winter, Zeus wields the power of lightning.

In the wider pantheon of Greek gods are the children of these gods. A further layer of the divine includes the demi gods, such as Perseus and Herakles, who are the result of divine unions between mortals and gods.

The chart below shows the correspondences of just a few of the gods and goddesses of Ancient Greece.

Day	Colour	Deity	Stone
Sunday	Orange/Gold	Apollo	Goldstone
Monday	Yellow	Hestia	Jade
Tuesday	Red	Hera	Ruby
Wednesday	Blue	Poseidon	Aquamarine
Thursday	Silver	Zeus	Diamond
Friday	Green	Aphrodite	Rose Quartz
Saturday	Black	Hades	Jet/Obsidian

Each god and goddess has their own symbol and correspondences. Athena, warrior and protector of her namesake, Athens, is the goddess of heroes and warriors. Her symbol is the owl.

The middle of summer is governed by Aphrodite, the daughter of Uranus, who was born from the sea off the Greek island of Cyprus. The wife of Hephaestus and lover of Ares among many others, she is associated with the sea and has many related symbols including shells, pearls, dolphins, doves, swans, apples, pomegranates, rose and lime trees. She is the understated goddess of love who holds sway over our hearts. Her son, Eros, is the god of desire and attraction.

Oil	Tree	Herb
Frankincense	Elder	Vanilla
Rosewood	Bay	Sage
Cinnamon	Apple	Basil
Thyme	Willow	Vervain
Lotus	Oak	Myrrh
Rose	Peach	Valerian
Sandalwood	Pine	Mint

SUMMER SPELLS, BLESSINGS AND RITUALS

CHARM OF APHRODITE

To make the charm of Aphrodite, take three sea shells with a hole through and thread a pink ribbon to join them. Rose quartz, the stone of Aphrodite, helps build strong and loving relationships so tie a piece to your charm. Add a rose, preferably red or pink, then hang up your charm anywhere in your house, as you want the love to flow through. As you put up your charm say these words:

Mighty Aphrodite hear my plea,
Let love flow here in my home.
Here in my family,
An' it harm none so mote it be.

LEFT: Aphrodite, goddess
of love and beauty

Sun Day Love Spell

The hot sunny days of summer can inflame the heat of love. Passion and love go together in the summer sun, the sun can penetrate even the coldest of hearts with warmth. Here is a spell to say when thinking of your love and when you want them to feel what you are feeling. Say this spell as you stand in the sun's rays. Imagine the same ray beaming on your intended, infusing them with your thoughts and feelings for them.

> Drifting by on summer sun,
> Let me love the one.
> Let them feel what I feel,
> Let us be together in summer sun.

CHARM OF APOLLO

To call on the powers of Apollo, the god of knowledge and healing, make a charm by taking three twigs of the elder tree, a yellow flower, and wrap them with an orange ribbon. A buttercup is a perfect addition to this dainty little charm of such power. When hanging your charm of Apollo, charge it with the following spell:

Blessed Apollo,
Grace this house.
Protection and healing abound,
Blessed Apollo thank you.

CHARM OF EROS

Eros is the son of Aphrodite and the god of desire and affection. If you feel your love life diminishing, then invite desire and passion into your house by creating an Eros charm.

Eros is associated with a number of symbols, many of which come via his mother, but particularly with hearts, wings, kisses, bows and arrows. Create a specific charm of Eros using any of these symbols. A heart shape is the most popular.

Write Eros in his Greek form Ἔρως directly onto a heart-shaped item – magnet, greeting card, brooch – and place in clear view, such as on your bedside table. If you do not have anything that is heart-shaped, write Ἔρως on a post-it note and stick it on your fridge door in the kitchen. Every morning and evening when you look at your bedside table, or go to the fridge, think of the love you want. Actively bring it into your life by visualizing it and saying these words:

Eros god of desire,
Ignite the passion and fire.
Affection and love be mine,
Give me a love so fine.

APHRODITE'S TRUTH SPELL

Aphrodite's power is not confined to love. She is also associated with the sea and everything in it, including the sea shells, have been graced by her. Bring the power of this Greek goddess into your home to help show you the truths you seek.

Create a frame for your bathroom mirror with gifts from the sea. Collect sea shells, pebbles and sea glass, enough to decorate a mirror's frame. As you decorate, say these words:

> Sea shell, sea find,
> Aphrodite blessed be.
> Let this mirror show truths for me.

GLIMPSING THE FUTURE SPELL

There are many magic mirror spells in witchcraft, just like the one used by Snow White's evil stepmother in the fairy tale. A mirror that tells us the truth is very useful. A divining mirror is another way in which we can see the power of the sea. If you would like to create your very own magic seeing mirror then attach your objects of the sea round your mirror. As you do, say these words:

Gifts of the sea
Hear me Aphrodite,
Show me only what I can see.

By candlelight look into your mirror and think of the future. What images do you see forming? Always keep a pen and notebook close by when you are scrying as you want to record every detail that you see in order to make sense of it later on. It could just be random images, but remember and record everything you witness while staring into your mirror. After you have finished with your mirror, keep it somewhere safe and secure. Cover it with a piece of black velvet or with a scarf you may have. This mirror is for your eyes only.

THE UNKNOWN GOD RITUAL

If you would like to work with a particular deity but are unsure which one
to choose, then you can perform an unknown god ritual. On the night of
the full moon perform this ritual before you go to bed. Scatter salt around
your bed to summon a protective shield around you while you sleep. Place a
purple candle by your bed and stare into the flame as you say:

> Gentle gods I call upon you all,
> To bear witness to my request.
> I wish to know the name of the Lord,
> Or to serve a goddess?
> Help me please through this night,
> That I may know the deity right.

Then blow out the candle and watch the smoke rise upwards, carrying
your thoughts and wishes to the gods.

Go to bed and sleep; telling your mind to remember what you dream.
The gods act in different ways to us, and working with them takes serious
effort. Always be respectful when communicating with any deity.

In the morning when you wake, write down what you remember. You
may know immediately which god you should work with, while others are
a bit more elusive. Some may take a while to come through but leave clues,
such as images of flowers, animals, colours or even days of the week.

Check the charts of the gods (*see pages 76–7*) and see if you can find the
deity who wishes to work with you. Remember, we are connected and
there are symbols and correspondences for everything in this world and
the next.

Midsummer's Eve Ritual

The hedgewitch is traditionally a solitary practitioner whose magic comes from her garden and plants. The term hedgewitch most likely comes from the Saxon word *haegtessa*, which translates to hedge-rider. A hedge-rider refers to one who journeys to the other side and has the gift of second sight. She is the mediator between the elemental beings and humans, living in both the human and elemental worlds. She is the guardian of the forests and cares for all fauna and especially flora. The Midsummer's Eve ritual for many hedgewitches is by far their favourite – full of magic, anticipation, creativity and imagination. Midsummer, it could be said, is the hedgewitches' Christmas!

For midsummer, the altar is decorated with flowers of the summer, cakes, sweets, mead or wine or fruit juice and honey. Also placed on the altar is a symbol or statue of the gods you adhere to. The colours of the candles used are yellow, black, red and orange. The reason for this is yellow represents the sun and black represents the dark, which is now beginning to creep back into our world, as this is the strongest and longest the sun will shine during the day. We are acknowledging the Turning of the Wheel and know that time is changing once more.

There is music playing, dancing and lots of merriment all within the protection circle to begin with and then it expands and grows to the whole garden or wherever you are performing this ritual. Ideally, though, a Midsummer's Eve ritual should be performed outdoors. One last thing on your altar is a bell, as it is used to ring for the fae and elemental beings to join in the celebration.

To begin your ritual, summon your circle with salt (*see page 28*), casting away negative energies and embracing the positive ones that come with love. Then raise your hands to the moon saying the words:

> Gods above, hear me now,
> Happy am I to embrace all at this midsummer.
> Allow the healing energy of sun and moon,
> Bring prosperity and love to all this June.
> Long may the sun shine to grow the crops,
> May the sun shine all summer long.
> Blessed are the gifts this midsummer bell rings,
> Let all be merry and free to sing.
> Rejoice and enjoy the magic this night brings.

Ring the bell and notice your surroundings, be aware of nature around you. Do the trees rustle? Does a gentle wind begin? Do you hear strange music, not in the distance but carried on the breeze? Do the candle flames flicker or blow out? The gods have heard and embrace all that follows. Afterwards, bow your head to the gods, then drink the mead and eat the cake and sweets.

MIDSUMMER SALT

The summer solstice or midsummer can fall anywhere between 20 June and 22 June in the northern hemisphere. In the southern hemisphere, midsummer falls on 22 December. For many though, midsummer celebrations take place not on one day but often over a very long weekend spanning three to four days.

This is a turning point in our calendar and every opportunity should be taken to enjoy the day and draw down the benefits of this yearly spectacle. Midsummer is the perfect opportunity to capture the energy in salt. Simply fill a bowl with sea salt on midsummer's eve and leave it from dawn to dusk on the longest day.

Cast this spell over the salt:

> God of healing
> God of knowledge,
> Mighty Apollo hear my plea.
> Bless this salt with your gifts
> An' it harms none so mote it be.

This salt draws down the energies of the day and is superb to use in any future spells in which you require the positive energy of the sun. Keep it in an airtight jar and tie a yellow ribbon round it so that you know it is midsummer salt.

Nectar of the Gods Spell

Bees and their honey have been revered since the beginning of time. The Ancients knew the importance of honey, calling it the 'nectar of the gods'. An amazing product that can be used for healing and cleansing, it can be made into lotions and bath potions for the ultimate relaxation. With its antiseptic qualities, honey can also help us to heal. Today, we can buy propolis, a hive product, in health food shops, which can be used to ease sore throats.

To encourage bees into your garden, plant a bee-friendly plant, such as lavender or buddleia, and as you plant say these words over it:

> Welcome to this garden bees,
> Feel free to do as you please.

POWER OF THE SUN CHARM

Use golden topaz to capture the power of the sun and enhance your business and financial success. Hold a piece of golden topaz in your hands and enchant it with this mantra:

Summer sun,
Help me be number one.

Say it over and over again with the stone firmly clasped in your hands. When you feel it charged with your energy, the stone will feel hot and your fingers may be tingling. Keep the stone in your pocket or wallet and take it with you when you go to work or embark upon a business venture.

Demeter's Labyrinth Spell

The time towards the end of summer is governed by the goddess Demeter and brings with it the harvest celebration know as Lammas. Demeter is the goddess of the harvest and is associated with wheat, oats and barley. During Lammas, give your thanks to Demeter by offering her the first fruits of the harvest.

Demeter is also a guiding light during times of uncertainty. If you are feeling lost and troubled on your present life journey, do this spell before bed.

> I am a seeker of the labyrinth,
> I know my journey will be long.
> But help me in all my endeavours,
> Goddess Demeter, blessed be.

That night, or subsequent nights, you will dream the path you should be on. You may dream of fields, trees or plants; all images of Demeter telling you she has heard your plea. Stay with the dream and ask your questions: What should I be doing?, Where should I be going?, and any other questions that will help you feel less adrift. Keep a notebook by your bed and write down everything you remember from your dream when you wake.

LAMMAS

A powerful day for both the natural and supernatural worlds, Lammas is the first harvest festival of the year, falling at the start of August in the northern hemisphere and the start of February in the southern hemisphere. It was also often called 'rent day' as traditionally land tenure and rights of pasture were settled on this day.

On Lammas, it was not only custom to offer the first fruits to the goddess Demeter to give thanks, but also to give her a baked product, such as bread or biscuits. In many parts of the world, it was also customary to make gingerbread on Lammas.

At Lammas fairs, which were essentially agriculture shows, a couple could have a trial marriage that lasted the duration of the fair – roughly eleven days. If, after that time, they found themselves incompatible, they would 'divorce' and go their separate ways. Today we live together to find out whether a relationship will work, but in times of deep religious belief and spiritual law this was not possible. The Lammas fair ritual at least gave couples a chance to see what marriage would be like.

Another belief attached to Lammas is that if couples suspected their child had been swapped by the fairies (*see page 35*), then this is the day when the reverse could happen and the changeling child would be replaced.

Lammas Gratitude Ritual

Make sure to have a loaf of bread, some barley and lentils on your altar. One of the symbols of the goddess Demeter is wheat, so try to represent this, perhaps in the shape of St Brigid's cross, or a corn doll. Also place beer and gingerbread on the altar. The candle colours for this ritual are brown, orange, yellow and red. This is to symbolize that the sun is still strong but the Turning of the Wheel is now changing to the harvest.

Summon the circle as before (*see page 28*) with salt and good intentions.

> Goddess Demeter I call to thee,
> Thank you for these gracious gifts.
> Grant us a bountiful harvest,
> May our oats be plenty and our wheat free of tares*.

Then share the gingerbread and beer, giving thanks to the goddess by raising your glass to her. During this gratitude ritual, you can also perform healing spells for the earth, including for both flora and fauna.

* Tares is an old term for 'weeds'.

CLOUD CLEAR SPELL

There is nothing worse than a grey, cloudy day on your summer holiday, so try this quick spell of cloud clearance to bring back a blue sky. Fill a bowl of water and start to gently stir it with your index finger. Pour three teaspoons of salt in and continue to stir. Then say:

> Move the clouds, skies clear all day,
> Mighty Apollo send your sun's rays.

Watch the water moving gently round the bowl and imagine the clouds being moved along by an unknown force. The clouds will disintegrate as the salt will.

ECLIPSE SUMMER'S MAGIC

Though they are quite common in the summer months, eclipses can occur throughout the year, and can bring so much mayhem, upheaval and general malaise that in ancient times people feared them. This spell honours eclipses but also asks the father of the gods, Zeus, to send positivity.

At the time of an eclipse, light one black and one white candle. Say these words while watching the light and flame of the candles:

> Power to the eclipse be,
> May negative become positivity.
> And dark becomes the light,
> Mighty Zeus make it right.

Imagine all your negative encounters being transformed by the light and becoming positive.

Summer Money Spell

If you don't know what to do regarding money, then ask the gods for help and guidance in trying to figure out your finances. Try to perform this spell on a Wednesday, as this is the day governed by the god Hermes, who was also the god of trade. Light a silver candle and recite these words:

> Mighty Hermes, your guidance I need,
> My money and finances are a mess.
> The best course of action I know not,
> Please Hermes, show me the way,
> The best paths to take for my pay.
> Thank you, Hermes, and blessed be.

When you go to sleep at night, have a pen and paper handy as the answer may come to you in a dream. But it could be at any time, so carry a pen and paper with you always. Repeat the spell for seven nights until you have an answer. When you do, remember to give thanks to Hermes.

SUMMER REST SPELL

The freedom one feels when the sun is shining is nature's blessing.
Give yourself permission to be at peace during this time. Find a restful
place in your favourite garden and say these words:

Sunny days of freedom,
Give me peace of plenty.
Relax and rest,
So mote it be.

Midsummer Enchantment

This is an enchantment for midsummer night using a favourite piece of jewellery. Enchanted jewellery can be used for many things, from gaining the attention of a new lover, to being a lucky talisman in business and financial affairs. Lighting one red and one yellow candle, place your piece of jewellery between the two candles and say these words:

Midsummer magic, midsummer madness
Grant me a wish this night,
Make my jewellery twinkle with fairy might.
He who looks upon this jewellery,
Will fall in love with me.
Fairy magic, come to me,
Grant this wish for me.
Blessed be to all fairie,
An' it harm none so mote it be.

SUNSHINE MINE SPELL

If there is something you have been wanting for a long time,
but it's just out of reach, then call upon the god Apollo to
help you achieve it. Write down what you want on a piece of
paper, sprinkle cinnamon over it and say these words:

> Summer sunlight, summer sunshine,
> Mighty Apollo, make it mine.

Afterwards, fold the paper carefully with the cinnamon inside
it and bury in the garden.

MAGICAL SQUARE OF THE SUN SPELL

It is thought that the earliest magical squares appeared in China over 3,000 years ago and were also found in Mesopotamia, India and Europe – including Ancient Greece. The magical square of the sun is one of the most famous, and powerful, squares. Adding the numbers in all six rows equals the number 666 – the symbol for the sun since Babylonian times.

When in need of extra energy concerning a spell or something that you are after, draw down this power.

Start by writing the square, opposite, out on yellow card. Write what it is you desire most of all for the summer on a piece of paper and then place it on top of the square. Keep the square in direct sunlight all day and in less than seven days the thing that you desire should be yours or making its way to you. If that does not happen, repeat the spell again.

6	32	3	34	35	1
7	11	27	28	8	30
24	14	16	15	23	19
13	20	22	21	17	18
25	29	10	9	26	12
36	5	33	4	2	31

The Muses Spell

In Ancient Greek mythology the Muse can be called upon for all manner of requests and blessings from the divine, but most of all they give us inspiration. Below is a chart of their correspondences.

Use the spell opposite to harness the power of a particular Muse in your life, adapting the wording to fit your intention. For example, you may choose to make this a money spell (green candle), a healing spell (blue candle), a career spell (yellow candle) or a love spell (red candle), or anything else that is important to you. Light a candle of the colour corresponding to the intention of the spell and say the following words:

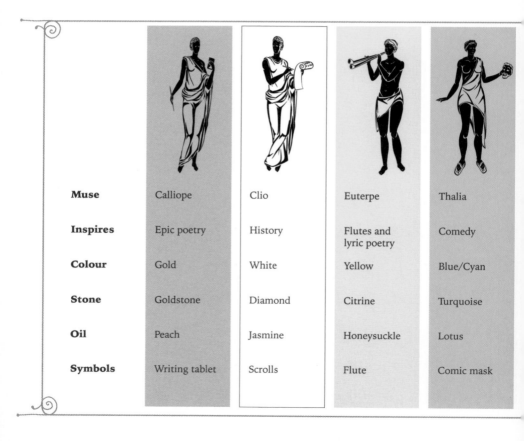

Muse	Calliope	Clio	Euterpe	Thalia
Inspires	Epic poetry	History	Flutes and lyric poetry	Comedy
Colour	Gold	White	Yellow	Blue/Cyan
Stone	Goldstone	Diamond	Citrine	Turquoise
Oil	Peach	Jasmine	Honeysuckle	Lotus
Symbols	Writing tablet	Scrolls	Flute	Comic mask

Oh sacred muse,
Daughter of Zeus,
Your music divine.
Grant this love/money/healing spell of mine.

As a general rule, whenever you are spell casting, think of your favourite piece of music, something that makes you feel happy. Put it on and dance to it, lift your spirits and allow it to raise your energy.

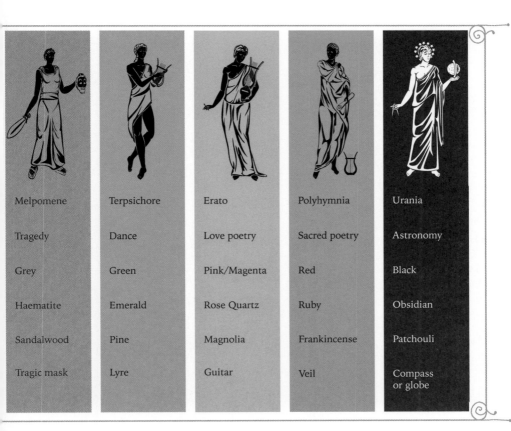

Melpomene	Terpsichore	Erato	Polyhymnia	Urania
Tragedy	Dance	Love poetry	Sacred poetry	Astronomy
Grey	Green	Pink/Magenta	Red	Black
Haematite	Emerald	Rose Quartz	Ruby	Obsidian
Sandalwood	Pine	Magnolia	Frankincense	Patchouli
Tragic mask	Lyre	Guitar	Veil	Compass or globe

Summertime Sleep Spell

In the summer, it can be difficult to sleep, with the heat, with
light nights and early mornings. Our sleeping patterns may
be adversely affected in the summer, but we need to sleep,
we need our energy to carry on with our daily lives. Use the
Ancient Greek god Hypnos to help you sleep using the spell
given here.

Hypnos, the Greek god of sleep, put people to sleep with
a touch of his wand or by fanning them with his wings. The
mask of Hypnos is quite a beauty to behold. If you can, place
an image or replica of the mask in your bedroom and focus
on that while you train yourself to astral project – when the
spirit/soul leaves the body and travels through the realms.
You could also ask Hypnos to grant you safe passage in your
dreams, by saying this spell before you go to sleep:

> Dear god of sleep,
> I ask my soul to keep.
> Grant me safe passage in my dreams,
> Let me wake without screams.
> Dear Hypnos, blessed be.

WISHFUL HEARTS SPELL

If you take a holiday to the beach, collect as many seashells as you can.
When you come home, cut some stiff cardboard into a heart shape and
write the word 'WISH' in the centre, glue the seashells on both front and
back, around the word. Make a little hole at the top for a piece of ribbon
to go through, as you are going to hang up your heart so you can see it all
year round. Hang the heart up and as you do, say these words:

> I wish I may, I wish I might,
> Let my family have their wish this night.
> Blessed be to one and all.

Throughout the year, when the family needs a little boost, touch the hearts
and remember your holiday and how happy you all were.

Summer Blessing Spell

As summer draws to its inevitable close, take a moment to offer a blessing to all the season has bestowed upon you. Perform this spell by lighting an orange candle, and as you look into the glow of the soothing flame, say these words:

> Bringer of happiness and sun,
> All that was is now done.
> You have given much to me,
> An' it harm none so mote it be.

Autumn

AUTUMN

*'Autumn is the hush
before winter.'*

French proverb

Autumn for many, is the most magical of seasons – it's full of wonder and mystery, yet tinged with shadows and darkness. This changeable season brings the festival of Mabon (the autumn equinox), which is typically celebrated, depending on the year, on a day between 21 to 24 September in the northern hemisphere and 20 to 21 March in the southern hemisphere.

The months of autumn provide such contrast. In the early part of the season, we feel the last of the sun's warmth and the days are still quite long. Trees can appear green and flowers are still in bloom. Soon the leaves on the trees turn many colours including reds, browns, golds and orange and the warmth is replaced with colder days. In some parts of the world this is a time of gales and storms. Autumn also sees the turning of the clocks.

There are so many customs and sayings for autumn; a whole book could be written on them alone. Yet it is the magic that concerns us here. If a falling leaf literally lands in your hand, then accept it and make a wish upon it; this is a gift from the season to you. Keep the leaf in a safe place for the duration of autumn and see if your wish comes true. Continue reading to learn more about the autumn garden and crystal, the deities that preside over this mystical time of year and the spells, rituals and blessings that enhance the season.

THE AUTUMN GARDEN

Autumn in the garden is a very busy time. There is plenty to do, from planting bulbs that give life and colour to the garden in spring, to creating a safe haven for wildlife to hibernate. This could be done by turning a plant pot on its side and placing dry leaves inside for hedgehogs and other hibernating creatures to burrow down into during the long winter. There are five herbs which dominate the season: fennel, rosemary, mint and oregano. Plant them along with the following flowers to bring your autumn garden alive with colour and magic.

FALL DAFFODIL

The *Sternbergia lutea*, sometimes called the fall daffodil or yellow autumn crocus due to its bright yellow petals, flowers throughout the autumn months into winter. The beautiful flowers bloom soon after the leaves appear. When the sun may not be shining quite so brightly, these flowers give off a shine like a miniature sun in the garden.

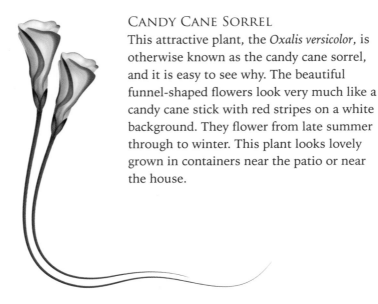

CANDY CANE SORREL

This attractive plant, the *Oxalis versicolor*, is otherwise known as the candy cane sorrel, and it is easy to see why. The beautiful funnel-shaped flowers look very much like a candy cane stick with red stripes on a white background. They flower from late summer through to winter. This plant looks lovely grown in containers near the patio or near the house.

SAFFRON CROCUS

The *Crocus sativus* is more commonly known as the saffron crocus. A prized flower throughout the ancient world, the spice saffron comes from the red stigma inside the lilac flowers, and has been used for flavouring dishes and making dyes since Roman times.

MONARDA 'SQUAW'

The *Monarda* plant is a member of the bergamot family. Its scarlet flowers have wonderful colour in early autumn and the subsequent black pepperpot seed heads last through the winter too. The crushed leaves of the *Monarda* plant exude a fragrant essential oil that has been used for centuries by the indigenous peoples of America. The *Monarda* is of the mint family and so has a bitter spearmint or peppermint taste. Its other names are bee balm, horsemint and bergamot, due to the fragrance of the leaves. However, it should not be confused with the actual *Citrus bergamia* from which we get the tea.

BARBERRY

Berberis is an amazing shrub with colours that encompass the colours of all seasons. The leaves change from green into red, orange and yellow. It also has flowers and some varieties have black fruits. Historically, the barberry has been used for everything from yellow dyes to cooking and herbal remedies. Scientists are now discovering that its effects are better than conventional drugs in treating certain ailments such as polycystic ovarian syndrome.

The autumn garden with its colours of wonder is enhanced by the magical beings that can be welcomed inside. In folklore, the Will-o'-the-Wisp is a delightful little fire sprite who carries a fleeting 'wisp' of light, which sometimes leads foolish travellers astray and into the marsh. Often called 'corpse candles', some say Will-o'-the-Wisps are omens of death, though nowadays, the term has come to mean any impossible or unattainable goal.

To encourage your dreams or impossible goals to become more than just fleeting wisps of light, allow Mr Wisp to help you manifest your potential.

As you tidy your autumn garden, or plant your spring bulbs, speak the following words:

MR WILL-O'-THE-WISP GARDEN INVITATION SPELL
Mr Will-o'-the-Wisp blessed be,
Welcome to my garden.
Bring your power of possibility,
Help me to turn my dreams into reality.
Will-o'-the-Wisp you are most welcome,
Show me the wonders yet to come.
Mr Will-o'-the-Wisp blessed be.

THE AUTUMN CRYSTAL

There are many stones that could be chosen for the autumn crystal, yet one outshines them all. Alabaster is a magnificent stone of transition, healing and spiritual connection to the divine. The stone was a favourite in Ancient Rome, where it was widely used for carvings. Alabaster is also an ecclesiastical stone as historically many Christian carvings were made from it.

Alabaster is found in a range of shades that are reminiscent of autumn, including red, brown, yellow, orange and white. Black alabaster is extremely rare but can still be found in Italy. It is the stone of transition and autumn is most certainly the season of change. If you have a piece of alabaster in your home, as an ornament during autumn it can help in the shift from one season to another.

As it is a stabilizing stone, alabaster is believed to help bring feelings of calm, which is of direct benefit for those overcoming grief. If there has been a passing in the family, then place a fragment of alabaster in the family home to help heal the wounds of this painful and final voyage. Any piece of alabaster would be good for this purpose, but a piece of black alabaster is especially powerful at such a time. You could also dab some anise or clove oil on the alabaster to help healing and ease the spiritual upheaval.

ALABASTER ENERGY SPELL

Alabaster is also known as the 'drawing' stone, not just because of the carvings and drawings one can make from it, but because it can draw things to you or away from you, depending on the energy and intent you wish to work with in magic. It is also used as a meditation vehicle. Further, alabaster can help 'charge' other stones by placing a stone on top of the alabaster and leaving it overnight.

Alabaster has a deep connection to the moon and sun due to its translucent appearance. When held against either one, the light will shine through. Thus, alabaster can also act as a conduit, allowing energies to flow through it and into other stones. To draw these energies to you, hold your piece of alabaster or alabaster ornament in your hand and light an orange candle as you say:

> In this season of change,
> Bring me the courage,
> To face that which I cannot see.
> Help me to have flexibility,
> An' it harms none so mote it be.

THE GODS OF AUTUMN

The deities that dominate autumn are the Ancient Roman gods and goddesses, who have an unspoken sense of strength and power that still echoes in our modern world. Indeed, the names of the week in many modern European languages are still based on the names of the Roman gods. For example, Thursday, or *Jeudi* in French, is named after Jupiter in Latin – *Dies Jovis*. Some of the months are also named after Roman gods,

Day	Colour	Deity	Stone
Sunday	Gold	Jupiter/Sol	Goldstone
Monday	Silver	Diana	Moonstone
Tuesday	Red	Mars	Ruby
Wednesday	Yellow	Mercury	Opal
Thursday	Blue	Juno/Jupiter	Amethyst
Friday	Green	Venus	Emerald
Saturday	Black	Saturn	Onyx/Jet

such as January for the god Janus. The faces of the gods still peer out at us from monuments, buildings and statues in many major cities. The physical influence of Roman civilization on the West is still evident in some part of the world in the roads we walk and drive down.

This chart shows some of the most important Roman deities and their correspondences.

Oil	Tree	Herb
Almond	Oak	Basil
Magnolia	Willow	Valerian
Juniper	Ash	Sage
Honeysuckle	Pine	Tarragon
Jasmine	Hazel	Myrrh
Vanilla	Apple Tree	Fennel
Patchouli	Hawthorn	Vervain

ROMAN PENTACLE OF THE DIVINE

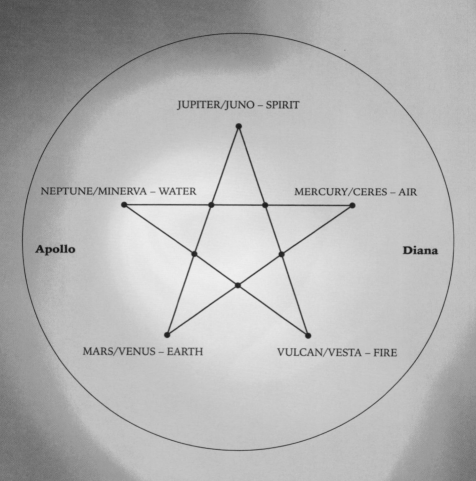

JUPITER/JUNO – SPIRIT

NEPTUNE/MINERVA – WATER

MERCURY/CERES – AIR

Apollo

Diana

MARS/VENUS – EARTH

VULCAN/VESTA – FIRE

The Roman Pentacle of the Divine (*see opposite*), is an encircled five-pointed star representing the five elements from which man is made – fire, air, water, earth, spirit – by way of the twelve most prominent gods and goddesses in Roman mythology. Placed in gender-balanced pairs, the pentacle is represented by Jupiter and June who crown the star as the Spirit, while Minerva and Neptune – god and goddess of water – sit to the left and govern emotions, dreams and fantasy. Mars and Venus represent the earth and are located bottom, left of the pentacle and govern love, war, money, work and security.

Vulcan and Vesta – god and goddess of fire – can be found bottom, right, and are associated with faith, action, passion, creativity and enterprise, while Mercury and Ceres represent air and can be found to the right, representing ideas, communication, truth and justice.

Apollo and Diana feature on either side of the pentacle and represent the sun and moon respectively, ruling over all. The pentacle, thusly completed, is a powerful symbol of life, love, unity and the quest for divine knowledge.

Invoke the power and protection of these elemental forces and Roman deities by drawing a pentacle on your altar, using it along with the magic in this book by placing objects and casting spells in the specific areas.

AUTUMN SPELLS, BLESSINGS AND RITUALS

FENNEL CLARI-TEA

Like the autumn weather with its mist and fog, we may feel lost in a fog of unknowing at this time of year. One of the most important herbs that helps with clarity and learning is fennel. A key herb during Roman times, it was used in both medicinal and culinary practices. Indeed, it has so many wonderful uses that the Roman writer Pliny listed over twenty-two remedies that use fennel.

Fennel is used in a number of spells regarding education and learning as fennel promotes mental clarity. If you need a clear mind, make yourself some fennel tea. However, if you are pregnant, fennel is best avoided as in large doses it is a uterine stimulant. To make fennel tea you will need:

1 teaspoon fennel seeds, crushed
Orange slice, cut thin
Honey, if desired

Place fennel in a teapot and pour over boiling water. Leave to infuse for 5 minutes. Strain and serve with the orange slice. Add honey to sweeten if desired. Slowly sip the tea and allow the mental blocks to be shifted, while breathing in the clarity of the fennel.

CLARITY SPELL

If you are starting a new course or educational training and you need to be clear about why you are doing so, then try this spell. On a piece of paper write down a simple list of things that will change if you complete the course. For example, 'It will boost my earnings', 'It will enhance my standing in the office', or 'I have always been interested in the subject'. Write down four or five reasons why you are doing the course and what you hope will come out of it. Then sprinkle some fennel seeds on the list and say:

Fennel seeds, bring me clarity,
In all my learning so mote it be.

Then fold the paper up and keep it somewhere safe. After you have completed the course, look at the list and see if your answers have become clear. Repeat the spell if necessary.

WEATHER SPELLS

By the middle of autumn many parts of the world experience stormy weather. In folklore, storms were often viewed as being witches' work, and perhaps there is some truth in this. Many witches throughout the world often prayed for rain. For example, rain sticks and similar instruments have been found in South America, Africa and Australia. The shamans and witch doctors would use these to draw down the rain.

If you are facing a water shortage then channel the energy of the ancients and summon the rain using your own rain stick, but be careful as weather spells have a way of manifesting their own energy and once let out, you can't reverse the spell or the weather!

NINE KNOTS RAIN ENERGY SPELL

Instead of rain sticks to cast rain, you can use string or ribbon. You will need a grey ribbon and some neroli essential oil. Dab some of the essential oil on your fingers and work along the ribbon, tying nine knots as you move along its length. Focus your mind on infusing the ribbon with rain energy. Then begin the spell:

> By the knot of one, this spell is now begun;
> This knot one weave is drizzle
> This knot of two is light rain
> This knot of three is rain
> This knot of four is heavy rain
> This knot of five is torrential downpour
> This knot of six, the storm spell is fixed
> This knot of seven is a deluge by earth and heaven
> This knot of eight is monsoon
> This knot of nine, is cloudburst.

When you have woven your spell upon the rain ribbon, undo the first knot, then wait three hours and see what happens. Work your way up the knots, undoing the first then the second, and so on. Always wait three hours in between each knot to give the heavens a chance to work their magic.

SAGE WATER HOUSE CLEANSE

Sage is a very effective herb, often used for healing. Indeed, its Latin name, *Salvia*, is related to the word 'salveo', which means, 'I am well'.

With heating, closed windows and reduced ventilation, a home in autumn can be a breeding ground for germs and bacteria. To counteract this, make some sage water and spray it round your house every so often. You will need:

3 sage leaves
3 drops eucalyptus or tea tree essential oil
Spray-top bottle

Place the sage leaves in the bottle and add the essential oil. Fill with water and spray around your home as needed. The sage liquid will keep for up to seven days.

Autumn Equinox Healing Ritual

The autumnal equinox is celebrated when the length of the day is equal to the length of the night, after which the longer, darker nights of winter truly take hold. Depending on the year, the equinox falls on a day between 21 to 24 September in the northern hemisphere and 20 to 21 March in the southern hemisphere. In magic, we call this day 'Mabon' – a sacred and magical day to cast many a spell and healing ritual.

Take advantage of this powerfully magical day by performing this healing ritual for someone in particular, or the world in general. On Mabon, light one black and one white candle. Place fruits and vegetables from the earth on your altar, especially an apple, it being a symbol of healing. You could also add cider or apple juice and a piece of apple cake.

Summon your circle (*see page 28*) then hold up your arms in a Y shape so your whole body becomes a Y. We call this 'drawing down the moon', but tonight we are drawing down the power of the equinox. Say these words:

Where I am here and now, I am Gaia,
The earth of gentle beauty,
Of violent temper hold fast my power.
I wax and wane,
As my children feel my pain.
I send healing carried on light,
To every corner of my world this night.
Fill their hunger from my harvest fruits,
Ease their suffering on lonely nights.
Calm my oceans and my seas,
I am Gaia and hear my plea.
Heal my earth so mote it be.

Imagine the light from the candles beaming throughout the world with healing energy. Pass round the cake and cider, or enjoy by yourself, then close the ritual by brushing the salt circle away.

CHARM OF MINERVA

Minerva, goddess of wisdom, is one of three Roman deities that rule over the months of autumn. Trivia, the goddess of crossroads and magic, is the second and Libitina, the goddess of funerals and death, is the third.

Influenced by the Greek goddess Athena, Minerva's domains include trade, the arts, strategy in war, medicine, poetry and handicrafts, and is, therefore, a deity worth welcoming into your home.

Harness the wisdom and power of Minerva by using a collection of her symbols to make a charm. Take an image of a wise owl, punctured with a small hole, and, using a green ribbon, tie it to a small branch from an olive or mulberry tree and three flowering geraniums. Hang the charm in a study, office or hall of your house. As you hang your charm say these words:

> Minerva goddess of wisdom, arts and trade,
> Grant your gifts to me.
> Bless all in this house,
> With enterprise and creativity.

If you do not wish to make a charm of Minerva you could simply place a vase or pot of geraniums in your house throughout the early part of autumn to honour this wonderful goddess.

MABON SUCCESS SPELL

Harnessing the power of the autumnal equinox and capitalizing on the energy of the goddess Minerva can make this time of year a success. To bring even greater success into your life, perform this spell. Begin by making a lemon and ginger tea. There are two ways to do this: either make ginger tea and add a slice of lemon, or pick a handful of lemon balm leaves, wash them, then pour over boiling water and add some freshly grated ginger. Leave for 5 minutes, then strain and pour into a cup and gently sip. As you drink, write a list of the areas of your life in which you would like success. These could be career, love, money or health. As you drink the tea and write your list, say these words:

> Mabon magic blessed be,
> Bring your power and energy to me.
> All my endeavours shall be a success,
> Mabon magic let me be the best.

As you say the words imagine what the outcome would be. Imagine what success looks like to you. Imagine how you would live, how you would love and how you would spend your time.

Minerva Success Water

Commemorate Minerva and welcome her energy into your life by making geranium water. You will need:

8 drops geranium essential oil
5 drops olive oil
Spray-top bottle

Place the oils in the bottle and fill with water. Shake well and spray while saying these words:

Minerva goddess divine
Success be mine.

Spray the water in your office, or dab a small amount onto your wrists, before you are going for an important interview or business meeting.

Equinox Salt Ritual Bath

If you have a special event coming up around the time of the autumn equinox, or you would like to prepare for this special day, then use this Minerva-inspired salt bath and scrub. You will need:

5 drops geranium essential oil
1 teaspoon olive oil
Juice of 1 lemon
1 tablespoon bicarbonate of soda
100g (3oz) sea salt

Mix together the oils and lemon juice. Blend in the bicarbonate of soda and salt. Stir and dissolve in a bath. Or, if you prefer, use this as a body scrub in the shower. Do not be tempted to use this scrub all the time as it can upset the gentle balance of the skin.

Autumn Wisdom Spell

At certain times of our lives, we deepen our understanding of the world. Here is a spell asking for wisdom to help guide our education. Light a yellow candle and say:

> Yellow candle light,
> Make this learning right.
> I am not too old to learn,
> It is for the benefit of what I earn.

CHARM OF PROTECTION

If you feel in need of extra protection, call upon the ancient energy of the
Roman gods by invoking the god Mars. You may also like to create a charm
of protection for a child. You will need three pieces of very thin ribbon,
one red, one fern green and one white. Weave the ribbons over each other
in a braid or plait and create a loop at the end so they can be easily tied to
something. As you weave them say these words:

> Hear me Mars,
> Protect my little one from harm.
> Place your power of protection,
> Upon these ribbons three.
> Thank you, Mars, and blessed be.

You are drawing down the energy and protection of Mars into this charm.
When the spell is completed, give the braided ribbons to the child or tie it
around their wrist or on to their school bag or pencil case. In this way it
will always be near to give protection.

Samhain

Samhain marks the start of the darker days of the year, when one harvest draws to a close and the next begins. Samhain usually occurs on 31 October – 1 November in the northern hemisphere and on 30 April – 1 May in the southern hemisphere – the beginning of a new year for many. Lanterns and bonfires were traditionally lit as this day was also the Day of the Dead, the day that preceded All Souls' Day. The festival of Samhain historically lasted over three days in many places, with bonfires, feasting, divination and much merriment.

A time for facing darkness and death, it is no surprise, then, that this time of year is ruled by the Roman goddess, Trivia. Trivia has dominion over magic and the underworld. Her delightful other name is 'Queen of Ghosts'. She governs sorcery and magic and is therefore the goddess of witches, wizards, sorcerers and the supernatural realm in general. Trivia is also the goddess of the crossroads and there is no greater crossroads than that of time. The crossroads of summer and winter is positioned when clocks fall back one hour as the dark nights now begin to take over daylight hours.

The Romans observed the 29th of every month as Trivia's sacred day. Traditionally there were three parts to the meal. The first part consisted of setting out the meal at a crossroads in Trivia's honour. The second was a sacrifice and the third was a ritual purification of the household. Today, you can mark Trivia's day with a special meal at home with friends on the 29th of any of the autumnal months.

SAMHAIN REMEMBRANCE POTION

Rosemary, one of the most essential Roman herbs for any magic kitchen, is about remembrance of those who have passed. Here is a simple method for making a remembrance potion for Samhain. (It is best to use fresh herbs, but dried herbs can be substituted if necessary.)

50g (2oz) fresh rosemary or 25g (1oz) dried rosemary
1 pint boiling water

Using a pestle and mortar, crush and bruise the rosemary and then place in a bowl. Pour over the boiling water and leave to stand overnight. The next morning, pour the contents of the bowl into a saucepan and add enough water to make up a pint of liquid. Bring to the boil then gently simmer for 20 minutes with the lid on. Remove from the heat and strain the water and herbs. Squeeze all the liquid out and then discard the herbs by sprinkling them on the garden giving thanks to the goddess for the nutritious potion.

Pour the potion into a glass bottle, label and date it. This standard potion will last for two to three days and can be taken neat. Use 2 tablespoons of it with boiling water to make rosemary tea, which is good for clearing the head.

Remembrance Day

Samhain is regarded as the time of year when the veils between worlds are at their thinnest and all manner of spirits can walk among the living once more. For those in the northern hemisphere, this is the time for Halloween. Yet Halloween is not just a fun party for scaring one another. There is also a serious side too: it is Remembrance Day.

There is a piece of art in the Brooklyn Museum in New York, which is a triangular table measuring about 15m (48ft) on each side. It is called *The Dinner Party*. The table has thirty-nine place settings for the most magical and brave women in myth and reality. In among these honourable women is one woman in particular that captures the eye. Her name is Petronilla de Meath. Petronilla is place setting number twenty-one and she sits in between Hildegard of Bingen and Christine De Pizan.

Petronilla was not a well-versed lady nor was she brought up in a convent. She was a servant of a fourteenth-century Irish noblewoman and the first person in British history to be burned at the stake for witchcraft heresy. The trial predated any formal witchcraft statutes but all subsequent witchcraft laws can be traced back to this trial. Petronilla was tortured, flogged and forced to declare herself a witch. She was burnt at the stake on 3 November 1324.

Petronilla de Meath is the starting point of the witch trials that continue even today in some form, in some parts of the world. The most recent case in Britain was in 1944. A medium named Helen Duncan told a worried mother that her son had been killed in a naval battle that had not been officially declared. The authorities became enraged and she was convicted under the Witchcraft Act of 1735 and subsequently spent nine months in Holloway Prison.

The exact number tried under the Witchcraft Acts are unknown. Yet throughout the world and centuries the figure runs to hundreds of thousands, possibly more. However, they did not die in vain and many people acknowledge the fallen by remembering them on this day.

A BLESSING FOR THE FALLEN

Whether you are in the northern hemisphere or southern hemisphere, mark a day of remembrance by setting a place for Petronilla de Meath and the fallen while lighting a blue candle and saying this blessing:

Brothers and sisters past,
Find peace at last.
Your lives were not in vain,
In your passing was great pain.
We send you love and eternal rest,
We bow our heads in your respect.
Go with love and be free,
Thank you to all and blessed be.

SAMHAIN RESOLUTIONS

Samhain is a time to plan and make magical resolutions for the forthcoming year. The plans of one year can now be let go while we look to the future with new ambition.

Light one black candle and one orange candle and place two pieces of paper and a pen nearby. Think of all you have done over the past year, including things you wish you hadn't done, and write them down. Then list your future goals and plans on the other piece of paper. Look at them side by side. Then roll up the past paper and burn it in the black candle's flame while saying these words:

> You are past I let you go,
> What cannot be,
> Is now history.

Then meditate for some time on your future plans while watching the flickering flame of the orange candle.

Samhain Ceremony

Give thanks to the passing year by performing this ceremony. It can be performed outdoors either with a coven or without.

High Priestess
Blessed be to one and all.

All
Blessed be.

High Priest/Priestess
We are here today to celebrate the passing of the year and all that has been accomplished. We are also gathered to give thanks to the goddess and the god. So mote it be.

All
So mote it be.

High Priest/Priestess
Mother goddess and Father god we welcome you into our circle this Esbat. We welcome you into our hearts this day of days. We are true to you and ask you grant these favours and blessings upon those that are gathered here this evening. So mote it be.

All
So mote it be.

High Priest/Priestess
Mother goddess and Father god, we give thanks and many blessings for your protection and care this past year. We are grateful that we have never gone hungry or have been cold. We give thanks that our loved ones are well also. We are truly grateful. Thank you, Mother goddess and Father god. Blessed be.

ALL

Blessed be.

HIGH PRIEST/PRIESTESS

Great Mother goddess and Father god we ask you to send healing this night of nights to the different lands of your world. To the people of (say name) who are suffering. We who stand here this night send healing and love to our brothers and sisters in other lands. Help us to increase our love by sending yours also. Blessed be.

ALL

Blessed be.

HIGH PRIEST/PRIESTESS

Mother goddess and Father god we ask also for your protection and blessing in all our magical work this coming year. So mote it be.

ALL

So mote it be.

HIGH PRIEST/PRIESTESS

Mother goddess and Father god on this night of nights we also ask for those that are now with you in the worlds beyond this one who join us here and walk freely with you on this night and when the dawn comes they return home with you. Our loved ones in the light world can hear how much we love them still and think of them often. To those that passed with pain their suffering is now ended. Those that passed with old age their youth has now returned, and those that passed with fear are now comforted. So mote it be.

ALL

So mote it be.

HIGH PRIEST/PRIESTESS

Mother goddess and Father god in the coming year grant us in
equal measure health, happiness and love. Let those we care
for always be in good health. Let us be prosperous in all our
endeavours this year. So mote it be.

ALL

So mote it be.

HIGH PRIEST/PRIESTESS

And now great Mother and Father we all give thanks for the
passing year and share our hopes for the coming year with you
as we all bow our heads in silence for a few moments.
(Everyone bows their heads in silence to give thanks and share
their hopes for the coming year in silent prayer.)

HIGH PRIEST/PRIESTESS

Blessed be.

ALL

Blessed be.

HIGH PRIEST/PRIESTESS

Thank you, Mother goddess and Father god, for joining as this
night. We ask you always walk beside us and guide us always
with your love and grace. We now close our circle as we enjoy
our Samhain feast. So mote it be.

ALL

So mote it be.

HIGH PRIEST/ PRIESTESS

Blessed be to one and all.

ALL

Blessed be.

THE MOURNING MOON

The weather at the end of autumn is heavy with fog. Mists prevail that echo late into the day as the strength of the sun can no longer burn them away. The end of autumn is known as the funeral of the year and the full moon is called the Mourning Moon. In every month of the year the full moon has a name, as shown below, with the northern hemisphere months listed to the left and southern hemisphere months listed to the right:

January – Cold Moon – July
February – Quickening Moon – August
March – Storm Moon – September
April – Wind Moon – October
May – Flower Moon – November
June – Strong Sun Moon – December
July – Blessing Moon – January
August – Corn Moon – February
September – Harvest Moon – March
October – Blood Moon – April
November – Mourning Moon – May
December – Long Nights Moon – June

Accept Change Spell

As the leaves turn from green to red and the wind blows from warm to cool, it's unsurprising that autumn is considered the season of change, and change is a part of life we must accept. It can be difficult to consider change as a learning experience, but everything that happens deepens our soul's knowledge and is carried with us throughout our life's journey.

Try this spell if you find it a challenge to accept change. On a Sunday, light a gold or orange candle. Place an oak leaf and acorn nearby. Hold the leaf in one hand and the acorn in the other as you say these words:

> Future, present and past,
> The world changes so fast.
> Like trees that grow,
> From seeds nature sow.
> Rising smoke upon the air,
> Help me accept the changes that come my way,
> Help me to adapt and bend both night and day.

Blow out the candle and watch the smoke rise with your spell in the air. Feel the leaf and acorn in your hands. See the changes of nature and begin to accept them.

LIBITINA GODDESS OF DEATH

As the end of autumn is known as the funeral of the year, it is apt that this season is governed by the Roman goddess Libitina, the goddess of death, funerals and a revered member of the underworld. Libitina's symbol is fire and during Feralia, a week-long Roman festival honouring those that had passed into the spirit world, written messages for the dead would be tossed into the fire for Libitina to answer.

This is very similar to what happens during a Wiccan funeral (*see pages 152–53*). Guests are asked to write something about the deceased. It could be anything from a goodbye note to asking for forgiveness. It is purely between the person writing the note and the deceased. During the ceremony the High Priest or Priestess will ask if anyone wishes to say or request anything. It is not read aloud and people walk up to the front and hold the paper over a candle flame then drop it into a heat-proof bowl. Normally the bowl contains water. This is all done very quietly and solemnly as each individual is letting go in their own way. There is something very therapeutic about writing a sentence about the deceased person, folding the paper then watching it burn away.

THE GIFT BLESSING

When we know a loved one is coming towards the end of their life, if often causes us to become introspective, to talk to friends and family about the past, or hopes for the future. We can sometimes take these conversations for granted, only giving them attention when prompted by the finality of death.

Our need to talk to friends or family during such a difficult time, is the soul's release, the soul knowing that the journey of someone we know and love, is nearing an end, though we are not always conscious of it.

Some refer to these conversations as the 'gift of knowledge' or simply, 'the gift'. It is a passing on of information that is important to the soul. When this has happened, light a white candle and say:

Thank you for the gift of knowledge (name)

Meditate quietly, staring at the flickering flame and thinking of the one who passed.

A Wiccan Funeral Ceremony

High Priestess/Priest

Welcome to one and all as we remember and say goodbye
to our sister/brother (name). We ask the goddess and god to
embrace (name) and welcome them home. For all is connected
and we return from whence we came. Like the cord that moves
into another vessel, we move through lives and touch those we
meet. (The High Priestess/Priest places a silver cord into a
chalice while saying this.) So mote it be.

All

So mote it be.

High Priestess/Priest

Let us at this moment think now of the laughter and memories.
For the love and the tears we remember our brother/sister and
all that they meant to us. If there are any of those who wish to
say any words now for our sister/brother, then come forward.

(Anyone wishing to say a few words about the deceased
now steps forward. Or they can silently read any words sacred
between themselves and the deceased. After, the paper can be
lit by a candle and burned in heat-proof dish.)

HIGH PRIESTESS/PRIEST

And now we say goodbye to our sister/brother. (If in a crematorium this is the time the curtains are closed and the coffin slips out of sight.)

HIGH PRIESTESS/PRIEST

Dear (name of deceased) beloved Spirit we bid you farewell for you await a new destiny. We shall see you again in the Summerland (the afterlife). Thank you for coming into our lives. Blessed be and go with love. So mote it be.

ALL

So mote it be.
(The High Priestess/Priest blows out the candle.)

REMEMBER THE DEAD

There is no charm of Libitina, as she is the goddess of death and we do not want to intentionally invoke her. Yet we can acknowledge those that have passed. Keep a shelf or an altar just for the pictures of family members that have departed. If you do not have photos of them, then place one of their belongings on the shelf or altar as a reminder. You may like to write out all the family members in a family tree. Roll it into a scroll and tie with a black ribbon. Keep the scroll on your remembrance shelf along with the photos and/or belongings of the departed.

THE THREE MATCHES CLARITY SPELL

Late autumn weather not only brings fog and mist to the sky, but to our lives. At home and work, we may feel that there is something unknown, the truth shielded from the light and we cannot see it. Clouded knowledge and falsehoods create negative energy, which should be dispelled. If you suspect you are not being told the truth on a matter, use this clarity spell.

Take a bowl of water and light three matches. As you light each one say these words and drop the lit match into the bowl:

> Scrying bowl let me see,
> Is the truth hiding from me?

If most of the matches sink to the bottom, the answer is 'yes', if most of them float, the answer is 'no'.

Smoke and Mirror Spell

If an answer to a question you seek is clouded with mystery, light a candle and look into the mirror. Clear your mind and say these words:

> Scrying mirror let me see,
> That which others hide from me.

Close your eyes and breathe in, hold your breath for a moment, then open your eyes as you exhale, looking into the mirror. What is the first thought that comes to mind, sound you hear, or even smell you notice? These will be a link or clue to your question. Keep performing the spell until you have your answer or more information presents itself.

THE NEEDLE AND CANDLE TRUTH SPELL

The needle and candle spell is one of the oldest spells and can be performed for a variety of reasons from drawing luck and love, to warding away negative energy. It is the intent you place upon it that changes the outcome. If you have found that the truth is hiding from you, then bring the truth back into the light by performing this spell.

Take a needle and push it into the side of a candle so it goes all the way in. As you do this, think of the truth that is hidden and imagine it coming into the light. Then light the candle and say these words:

Let the truth come into the light,
That which is hidden come right.

As the candle burns down the truth will find its way out and the clouds and fog begin to clear. When the candle burns down to the needle, the truth will have been exposed and all will come right.

MOOD-BOOSTING COLOURS OF AUTUMN

Energy levels can take a tumble in autumn and we can develop colds and flu. Keep your vitamin C levels up by eating plenty of oranges and drinking fresh orange juice.

If you feel the dark days are getting you down then try some mood-boosting spells. Anything bright yellow or orange has mood-boosting properties to it. Surround yourself with orange and yellow colours. Some ideas are given on the following pages to help.

NOVEMBER HAPPY DISPLAY BLESSING

Create a seasonal display of pumpkins alongside orange or yellow gourds with the black seed heads of *Monarda* or bergamot 'squaw'. Although pumpkins are used predominately for specific autumnal celebrations (such as Halloween and Thanksgiving), they can be used throughout the season as a mood booster. As you create your bright autumn display, say this blessing:

> Bless this sight,
> With happiness and light.
> May I always be,
> Looking at it happy.
> An' it harm none so mote it be.

PUMPKIN ENERGY SPELL

To help boost your mood during autumn, hollow out a pumpkin and cut holes in it to make a lantern. You do not have to make a face. Place a candle inside the pumpkin and light it while saying these words:

Pumpkin bright, pumpkin light,
Boost my energy tonight.

The glow of the candle through the orange skin of the pumpkin will enhance your mood.

AUTUMN HEALTH SPELL

Fruit and vegetables contain many of the vitamins and minerals we need to stay mentally and physically healthy. The harvest fruits and vegetables of autumn are the gifts given by Mother Earth for the long winter ahead. As you enjoy their bounty, say this spell:

Green, yellow and orange be,
Sunflower seeds heavenly.
Heat from the autumn light of the sun,
Boost my energy and health in one.

THE WILD HUNT SPELL

We cannot leave autumn without mentioning the Wild Hunt. As autumn slips away, giving winter its strength, dramatic changes in the weather take place. The winter is ruled by the Norse gods and this spell celebrates them.

In folklore, the Wild Hunt involves ghostly or supernatural hunters sweeping across the land at night, led by Odin riding his trusty steed Sleipnir. The hunt's presence can be felt on wild stormy nights in late autumn and legend holds that if you see or hear the Wild Hunt approaching then some catastrophe such as war or plague will follow, much like the prophecy of the Four Horsemen of the Apocalypse. It is also believed that those encountering the hunt might be abducted to the underworld, so protect yourself by repeating this spell three times at night:

> I do not hear,
> I do not see.
> Hounds of the Hunt,
> Stay away from me.

Winter

WINTER

*'Plenty of holly berries
predict a cold winter.'*

Traditional proverb

Winter is a season of wondrous delights. There are festivals and joyful occasions a plenty, although on dark, damp cold days we may want nothing more than to stay indoors and hibernate like some of our animal friends. During the winter months, we can connect to the sleeping magic that is all around us, building up to burst anew in spring. Yet magic never sleeps and it is just as alive in winter as any other season.

Few plants flower in the winter but those that do are some of the most fragile and beautiful of any season. These include the pure snow-white snowdrops, the vibrant yellow winter aconites, the tiny glory-of-the-snow plant – blue and white star-shaped flowers that have six pointed petals like the snowflake. Despite their fragile beauty, they are the hardiest flowers nature gives.

Winter is dominated by the Norse gods and goddesses, especially those who make up the principle Norse pantheon: Odin, ruler of all, Frigg, the matriarch and Thor, protector of the human realm. Discover their power, along with the beauty of the plants of the winter garden and the spells that harness the energy of this majestic time of year.

THE WINTER GARDEN

The garden is alive in winter just as in the rest of the year. Trees feature very strongly, and while most of them are dormant, there are some that are more alive during the winter than in any other season such as the evergreens. Some plants even flourish in the winter. Here is a selection of the best ones for a winter display.

DAPHNE
A daphne plant can fill a room with its scent and also makes a pretty winter display in the garden. One particular variety that has gained popularity is the *Daphne napolitana*, which has small pink flowers and evergreen leaves followed by berries. Another good variety is the *Daphne odora*, which is also known as the winter daphne. Both are beautiful plants to have in a winter garden.

HIMALAYAN SWEET BOX
Sarcococca hookeriana is perfect for a winter wonder garden. It is an evergreen shrub that produces beautiful white flowers throughout winter. It then develops black berries. The flowers are so sweet that no wonder the plant is known as the 'Himalayan sweet box'. Remember, as the flowers are white, always ask Mother Earth for permission before cutting a sprig to bring indoors for a winter display.

WINTER VIBURNUM

The winter viburnum is a beautiful plant to have in your garden and can flower all winter. *Viburnum bodnantense* 'Dawn' is also referred to as Freya's flower and is a strong, hardy plant with deep green leaves. The clusters of scented blooms begin life as red buds then turn pink before becoming white flowers. It is truly a beautiful plant to have in the garden. Cut them for the house or a midwinter feast or midwinter wedding table decoration. As cut flowers the winter viburnum can last a long time.

CROCUS

One of the most common winter flowers is the crocus. This delicate little flower can bloom in autumn, winter and spring, depending on the species. The species *Crocus laevigatus* can start flowering in late autumn through winter and into early spring so it is a good plant to have in the garden. *Crocus imperati* is another variety that is ideal for your winter garden as it flowers during the colder months.

WINTER BEAUTY

The honeysuckle *Lonicera purpusii* is often referred to as the winter honeysuckle. It is a delightful plant with delicate fragrant white flowers. It flowers in the early winter months and truly is a winter beauty.

These five wonderful plants of such delicate beauty and gentle fragrance help us to remember that life and the gods are always here. There must be a winter in order for the spring and subsequent summer to follow.

The Nordic gods and goddesses, who govern the winter months, would not leave the earth completely void of life and magic at this time. The elves and dwarves of the Norse cosmos, which consists of the nine worlds – Niflheim, Muspelheim, Asgard, Midgard, Jotunheim, Vanaheim, Alfheim, Svartalfheim, Helheim – are welcome in any garden of Midgard (Earth) whatever the weather. So make them welcome by planting the trees and plants as described on the previous pages.

WINTER GARDEN BLESSING

This is a garden blessing to attract the elves and dwarves of the Yggdrasil, the immense mythical tree that connects the nine worlds of Norse mythology:

> Welcome elves, welcome dwarves,
> Welcome to beings of all.
> Enjoy my garden and bring your magic,
> But leave only good wishes for all.
> An' it harm none so mote it be,
> Blessings to both you and me.

THE WINTER CRYSTALS

The winter crystal, the snow quartz, is good for healing a rift in families. It is also beneficial to keep a piece in your purse or handbag if you are experiencing financial difficulties. It is a stone that keeps good luck flowing.

SNOW QUARTZ BLESSING
Blessed be to you snow quartz,
The gifts you bring.
Bless this love, bless this house,
As sure as winter there is spring.
For now and evermore, so mote it be.

Although the snow quartz is the most important winter crystal, there is another stone that can be used during this season. It is amber – the stone associated with the Norse goddess Freya. Amber is formed from fossilized tree resin and has been used for many millennia for its beauty and healing properties. Available in many different colours, from the more common orange and brown to red, green and even blue, it is the blue amber that is extremely rare and precious. An almost deep teal colour in normal daylight, when held up to the sun it becomes the more common yellow or orange colour. It is because of this that the stone is highly sought after by those who work in magic. It is used in glamour spells – a form of magic used to make objects or living things appear different from what they really are – and is often termed the 'gold of the north'.

Amber Blessing Spell

Use this amber blessing spell to invoke the power of the stone, which can also be used as an all-purpose winter charm. Hold a piece of amber in your hands and say:

> Blessed stone of winter's north,
> I ask your powers come forth.
> Bring to me all I desire,
> Wealth, love and passion's fire.
> Send your winter blessing to me,
> An' it harm none so mote it be.

Keep the stone in your purse or pocket for the duration of the winter months.

THE GODS OF WINTER

The deities that preside over winter are the gods and goddess of Nordic mythology with Odin, supreme deity and ruler of all gods, chief of the principle Norse pantheon. The matriarch of the pantheon is Frigg (or Frigga), wife of Odin, who can be compared to the Greek goddess Hera, as she is the goddess of marriage and motherhood. Joining them in the pantheon is their eldest son, Thor, the god of thunder, able to yield the power of lightning with his hammer, which is a symbol of strength and courage. Any spells you do regarding Thor are always best done on a Thursday, which some call Thor's Day. The pantheon is completed by Baldr, god of beauty, peace, innocence and rebirth, and Tyr, though little of this god survives beyond old Norse sources.

The second pantheon consists of a group of gods and goddesses associated with fertility and wisdom. This pantheon includes Freyja (or Freya), the goddess of war, death, love, sex, beauty, fertility and gold. Also within Nordic mythology are elves, dwarves and jotnar, or frost giants, and the valkyries – warrior women who bring their chosen fallen soldiers to Valhalla, the great hall of slain warriors presided over by the Odin (the remaining fallen soldiers being taken by Freya).

The trinity or triad in the Nordic creation myths is comprised of brothers Odin, Vili and Ve, comparable to Zeus, Poseidon and Hades in Greek mythology. Represented as Spirit, Will and Holiness, the triad created the first human couple, Ask and Embla, male and female respectively. Odin gave the couple life by blowing his breath into two tree trunks that resembled human forms. Vili gave intelligence and the sense of touch and Ve gave speech, hearing and sight.

While Vili and Ve are part of the triad, it is Odin that has a more celebrated role in Norse mythology. He has over 200 names but is often referred to as the 'Grey Wanderer' as he is said to wander the land in a grey hooded cloak. Some historians believe his image over the years has turned into Santa Claus. However, others like to believe that Father Odin still walks the land on cold winter nights, making sure his flock are safe and protected.

Father Odin has many correspondences, one of them being pine. There is a marvellous drink called pine nut drink, regarded by some as the champagne of the north. It is a sparkling spruce drink and predominantly made in Finland. If you can, buy some for the Yuletide celebrations, then raise a glass to Odin while saying, 'skal', which is a wish for good health and good fortune.

BELOW: Norse god, Odin

Day	Colour	Deity	Stone
Sunday	Gold	Sol	Goldstone
Monday	White	Mani	Moonstone
Tuesday	Yellow	Tyr	Red Jasper
Wednesday	Blue	Odin	Diamond
Thursday	Red	Thor	Emerald
Friday	Green	Freya	Amber
Saturday	Silver	Loki	Norwegian moonstone (Laravkite)

OPPOSITE: Thor's hammer

ABOVE: Odin's raven

Oil	Tree	Herb
Orange	Yew	Lemon/Thyme
Eucalyptus	Hawthorn	Fennel
Tea Tree	Pine	Parsley
Geranium	Ash	Bay
Spikenard	Oak	Mint
Lotus	Lime/Lindon	Rosemary
Patchouli	Wych Elm	Sage

WINTER SPELLS, BLESSINGS AND RITUALS

THE FIRST SNOW SPELL

When there has been a forecast of snow, take a clean plastic container and place it outside. Try to catch as much of the first snow as possible. If you have had several flurries previously, do not worry – you are trying to catch the first snowfall that will cover the ground. When it has stopped snowing or when your container is full, bring the snow inside, transfer into a freezer bag and say these words:

Pure white snow, nature's innocence,
White and clean shinning vibrance.

Day	Star Sign	Deity	Colour
Sunday	Leo	Sol	Gold
Monday	Cancer	Mani	White
Tuesday	Aries, Scorpio	Tyr	Yellow
Wednesday	Gemini, Virgo	Odin	Blue
Thursday	Sagittarius, Pisces	Thor	Red
Friday	Taurus, Libra	Freya	Green
Saturday	Capricorn, Aquarius	Loki	Silver

Bring me your strength and purity,
In all my magical endeavours.
An' it harm none so mote it be.

Date and label the snow 'first snow' to show that you have captured the snow with the purest of properties, and freeze. The snow can be used for a number of spells, such as the Snow Wish Spell (*see page 182*).

For powerful spells, collect the snow from winter thunderstorms. A winter thunderstorm that accompanies a snow storm is a rare event and a blessing from Thor.

Depending on the day the snow falls, the energy of that day can be used to enhance the snow's power: for example, Monday is associated with home, politics and female power, while Friday is good for money spells. The chart below shows the correspondences of days, gods and goddesses, star sign, stones and colours that can be used throughout the year.

Stone	Rules
Goldstone	Joy, Happiness, Health, Leadership
Moonstone	Home, Politics, Business, Female Power
Red Jasper	Sex, Passion, Desire, Ambition, Work
Diamond	Communication, Magical Ability, Knowledge, Rational Thought
Emerald	Luck, Abundance, Expansion, Career
Amber	Beauty, Money, Marriage, Love, Fertility
Norwegian Moonstone (Laravkite)	Karma, Reincarnation, Work, Reality Past Lives

No Money Like Snow Money Spell

If you collect your snow on a Friday, then it can be used for a money-making spell. Put a few coins in a glass jar, the higher the denomination the better. Cover them with the snow. Then tie a green ribbon round the jar and say these words:

> Blessed be, thankful to thee,
> Goddess Freya on this Friday.
> From now till there again,
> Let this jar fill with money.
> An' it harm none so mote it be.

Let the snow melt in the jar and on top of the money. Do this spell on a Friday and keep it overnight. The following Friday empty the jar of snow water and coins saying:

> Thankful to thee, blessed be
> Thank you, goddess Freya,
> For now, and evermore blessed be.

The snow money water can be kept in a spray-top bottle and used when you need an extra financial boost. Spray a little round yourself perhaps when you are meeting a bank manager or when you are asking for a pay rise.

Fruitful Snow Spell Charm

To make a snow spell charm to attract good fortune, take a green apple and thinly cut across the middle to expose the pentagram inside. Cut at least five very fine slices of the apple, making sure they all have the pentagram in them. Lay the apple slices out on a plate and sprinkle your money snow collected on a Friday (*see opposite*) over the apple slices. Say these words as you do:

> May these gifts of nature
> Pure brilliant snow of winter bright,
> Charm these apple slices
> With financial strength and might.
> Blessed be

Leave the apple slices on the plate for a full seven days until they have withered. They should look and feel a bit like leather. Then take one of the slices and put it in your purse, one in your bank and/or cheque book and others with your credit cards. Keep the apple slices in your financial places until you feel you no longer need them. Then bury them in the garden, giving thanks for all the good they brought.

SNOW WISH SPELL

Use this spell to make a wish for something. If you can be outside when the snow is falling, so much the better. Otherwise, use the first snow that you kept in the freezer (*see page 178*). Over the snow say this little spell:

> Snow light snow bright
> Grant me a wish tonight.
> (*Say what it is you wish for*)
> An' it harm none so mote it be.

You can use this spell every night for seven nights until your wish comes true.

Ice Wand Consecration Ritual

If you are lucky enough to find an icicle, store it in the freezer to use as a wand for your winter spells and rituals. Your magic is within you, but if nature leaves you an icicle, then use it as an extension of your magic. Before you use your icicle wand, purify it and remove any negative energies by perform the ritual below and then return it to the freezer.

Light a smudge stick made of sage and rosemary (*see page 58*) and let the smoke waft around you. Pass your ice wand through the rising smoke seven times while saying these words:

> Blessed water turned to ice,
> A gift from the winter night.
> Let my wand full of magic be,
> An' it harm none so mote it be.

Once your wand is purified, you can use it for magic throughout the year as it gradually gets smaller. When the wand has completely disappeared, the magic from it has been spent.

Snow Travel Spell

Travelling in the snow and ice can sometimes be dangerous, so if you
are embarking on a journey, try this spell. You can say it prior to starting
your journey, or the day before in a car or on a plane. If you have time and
want to use this spell before you travel, light a blue candle as you speak
these words:

Shimmering snow,
Safety please.
Shimmering snow,
Here we go.

FORGIVENESS SPELL

Winter is often a time of reflection, when you may think of things that have happened in the past and begin to make plans for the future. This snow spell can help put you in the right frame of mind to make changes in your life, particularly if you have done things in the past that you are not happy with or feel could have done better. In order to move on and make plans for the future, let go of the past and forgive yourself. Use the power of the pure white snow to move on.

This is a two-part spell. First, let go of the past and move on, then focus on the future and what you need to do in order to achieve the life you want.

Light a white candle and look out of the window as you say this spell:

Sprinkle sprinkle little flakes,
In my life I have made mistakes.
Sprinkle sprinkle forgiving snows,
Please wipe clean all my woes.
Things I have said I now regret,
Things I have done,
I ask forgiveness of me.

After you have said the spell, meditate and think of things you have done, no matter how painful. Imagine the light of the flame illuminating your past sending negative thoughts away.

Once you have meditated for a while, keep the candle burning and turn your mind to the future. What do you want the future to be? Make a plan about where you see yourself in one year, two years, three years and then five years. Give yourself achievable targets for each year.

Write out your plans on white paper with a blue pen. Title the paper 'my goal for one year'. Then, on a separate piece of paper for each, write: 'my goal for two years', 'my goal for three years' and so on. This spell is a good long spell; do not try to rush it. It should take at least two to three hours. When you have written out your plans, place them in front of you and say:

Sprinkle sprinkle little snow,
How far I will go.
Sprinkle sprinkle little snow might,
Let my future be forever bright.
Let my plans come to pass,
My future is right at last.
A good happy future for me,
An' it harm none so mote it be.

Fold each paper, one fold for the first year, two folds for the second year page, three folds for the third year, and so on. Then keep them in a place only you can see every day. Throughout the year, take out your year-one plan and look at it. See where you are with your goals.

A year to the day you cast your spell, take out your year-one plan and, after looking at it, light a white candle, giving thanks for what you have accomplished, then burn your plan and bury the ashes in the garden.

Esbat Ritual

It is your choice how you work with the Norse divine and use the chart of deities (*see pages 176–77*), whether in the winter months or throughout the year, but try the following ritual for a winter full moon, called Esbat. An Esbat is a ritual observance on the night of a full moon, and a time to harness the moon's power for any healing, love or gratitude rituals.

If the full moon begins on a Thursday, take a red candle and oak incense – the symbols of Thor. The candle represents fire, the incense air. You will also need a bowl or cup of water and a winter plant, such as winter aconite or hellebore, a piece of cake and some wine to represent the sweet and good things in life.

As a full moon lasts three nights, you could plan out each night: the first night can be a ritual of gratitude, the second night could be dedicated to healing and the final night of the full moon could be for casting a spell for something you need.

An Esbat ritual is respectful, individual and positive. Make a list of your achievements, successes and all you are grateful for that month. Then raise your arms upwards in a Y shape towards the full moon and say:

Mighty Thor, thank you for your gifts this month,
I am grateful for everything good that has come my way.
Thank you for the strength to continue day by day,
Thank you for (read out your list)

Afterwards, break some of the cake and leave it on the altar for Thor while eating the rest, then do the same with the wine. Always leave some food and wine for the deity you are praying to. On the last night of a full moon, cast any spells you desire on the Esbat and finish the cake and wine.

While eating, meditate and reflect on the past month. If something negative has happened, then acknowledge this and ask Thor for guidance. During the Esbat you could also scry – seeing the future – using Tarot cards, tea leaves, water, or fire, by seeing the images which form in the candle flame.

Tree Spirit Spell

Invoke the gods of the north with this spell to enhance strength for the winter. Pour boiling water into a cup. Add a tablespoon of either maple syrup or birch sap into the water and gently stir clockwise while saying:

> Gods of the north, hear me please,
> Let that which I lack
> Now begin to attract.
> Strong and healthy like the mighty tree,
> Let my strength return to me
> An' it harm none so mote it be.

Then slowly sip your tree water and imagine yourself gaining strength, as if from the earth. Let the strength creep, from your feet up your legs and through your body. You stand firm and strong, bending in the breeze, able to withstand all. Blessed be.

Winter Healing Blessing

Call upon Father Odin to enhance your family's health with this winter healing blessing.

Light a blue candle for healing and keep it alight during your Yule festivities. Place it on the table during your meals to keep the flame of hope and love alive. Over the candle say these words:

Blessed be to one and all,
Those alone and without family.
Father Odin help them through the festivity,
Ease the pain of those suffering.
Bring to them the warmth of spring,
Father Odin thank you and blessed be.

CHARM OF ODIN

Create a good luck charm with symbols of Odin. You will need navy-blue ribbon, three twigs from an ash tree, a pine cone and an image of the symbol called the triquetra (*see above*), which consists of three interlocking triangles. Its magical nature comes from the fact that it is drawn without the pen leaving the paper. It is Norse Viking symbol of protection and so we are asking Odin to protect all those in the house.

Tie the ash twigs together, with the pine cone and triquetra, with the ribbon. The ash twigs should be no more than 10cm (4in) in length. Please do not rip them from the tree, Odin would not be happy with that! Instead look on the ground around the ash tree, as the winter storms will have granted you what you need.

Hang the charm up above your door or hang it on your Christmas tree and see who notices. As you hang the charm say these words:

Father Odin blessed be
Grant me a peaceful festivity,
Let this house be full of love and harmony,
Father Odin thank you and blessed be.

Odin's Magic Salt

Believed to purify and repel evil, the importance of salt and holy, or blessing, water in spell work cannot be underestimated. To make magic salt and blessing water (*see below*) each month, name it for the god corresponding to the day the salt was made. So, if you do this on a Wednesday, it would be regarded as Odin's Blessing Water or Odin's Magic Salt.

To make the magic salt, leave a bowl of sea salt in view of the full moon overnight. In the morning, put the salt in an airtight container and tie a black or grey ribbon around it. This can be used to make the blessing water below.

Odin's Blessing Water

Fill a spray-top bottle with water and then add a tablespoon of Odin's salt. Add 3 drops of pine essential oil. Put the lid on the bottle and shake it up, saying these words as you do so:

> Odin bless this spray
> With your protection and strength.
> Keep evil far away
> Keep me forever safe blessed be.
> An' it harm none so mote it be.

Spray the water around when you feel you need extra protection, either at home or at work. You can make as much as you need but only use it for that month.

A Midwinter Wedding

Midwinter, or the winter solstice, typically occurs between 21 to 23 December in the northern hemisphere and 20 to 23 June in the southern hemisphere depending on the year. The winter solstice is the shortest day of the year and is followed by the longest night. Rejoicing can now begin as the days start to get longer and light returns to the earth.

A midwinter wedding is a beautiful and magical affair. In Norse mythology the trinity of gods, Odin, Vili and Ve, made the first man (Ask) and the first woman (Embla). Odin saw the trees ash and elm and gave them a new form, man and woman, while Vili and Ve gave both the new forms souls and intelligence.

At a midwinter wedding, the ash and elm are therefore present in some form. Saplings may be planted by the couple or a twig from the trees may be placed on the tables of friends and family of the couple. Guests of the groom would have an ash twig and guests of the bride an elm twig.

You can also make gifts of wands from the trees. The bride's bouquet can also have small twigs from the ash and elm encased around holly, ivy and hellebores, which makes a very pretty combination.

PERFORMING A MIDWINTER WEDDING

'Handfasting' is another name for a wedding. It is the joining together of two people, or the binding of their souls together on this earth and for all their lives. Therefore, it is something not to be taken lightly. There is no divorce in the spirit world.

A handfasting ceremony at any other time of the year would involve gold and silver cords. However, for a midwinter wedding, green and silver cords are used to literally bind the couple together. The green represents Freya, the goddess of love. The silver cord is for Odin, the Grey Wanderer.

The handfasting is usually presided over by the High Priest/Priestess. The couple are expected to write their vows to one another. It is a happy and loving occasion that involves the witnesses. An example of a handfasting ceremony is given on the following pages. This can be written out and given to the congregation to use and is also a lovely keepsake of the day.

Midwinter Handfasting Ceremony

High Priest/Priestess

Blessed be to one and all.

All

Blessed be.

High Priest/Priestess

We are here today to join together Ask (groom) and Embla (bride). I ask Odin, father of all, to bear witness to this union. I ask Freya to bless this union with the love of these two souls forever. So mote it be.

All

So mote it be.

High Priest/Priestess

Ask and Embla whose mortal names are (bride's name) and (groom's name). Do you join us here of your own free will this midwinter?

Bride/Groom

I do.

High Priest/Priestess

Then I ask you to now speak your vows in the presence of Odin and Freya as your family and friends bear witness to your union.

Bride/Groom

(Speak their vows to each other.)

HIGH PRIEST/PRIESTESS

As I bind your hands with these cords, you are reminded that you are forever joined, although the cord is not tied as you are also free to grow and support each other with love. In the name of love. In the name of Freya. So mote it be.

ALL

So mote it be.

HIGH PRIEST/PRIESTESS

Now (groom's name) and (bride's name), say your oath together.

BRIDE/GROOM

Heart and mind to thee.
Body and soul to thee.
I love and protect thee.
Forever, so mote it be.

HIGH PRIEST/PRIESTESS

We have now witnessed the joining of Askr and Embla together in love and matrimony. I give thanks to great Odin and blessed Freya for their presence. Blessed be.

ALL

Blessed be.

HIGH PRIEST/PRIESTESS

I now pronounce (bride's name) and (groom's name) husband and wife. Blessed be.

ALL

Blessed be.

I Don't Feel the Cold Spell

In many parts of the world we expect harsh cold weather in the winter months. The snows and bitter frosts are actually helpful to us as they kill germs and bacteria. The delightful saying, 'a green winter makes a full churchyard', makes the point very well.

Try this spell if you are feeling particularly cold. Clap and stamp your feet three times as you say:

> I do not feel the cold,
> My teeth do not jitter back and forth,
> My feet are warm and toasty,
> My fingers are not frosty,
> Heat and warmth come to me,
> An' it harm none so mote it be.

WINTER'S MORN STRENGTH SPELL

Energy levels may wane during the cold winter months, and with each passing week it can get harder to be energized. Try this spell on a winter's morn to gain vitality. If it is a sunny snow day, that will give you an added boost, although it will work just as well on a grey day too. You will need an orange cut in half, and a yellow candle. Light the yellow candle and say:

Winter's morn, winter's day,
Send heat and light my way.
Return to me my energy,
An' it harm none so mote it be.

Squeeze the orange halves into juice. Then, sip the juice slowly with your eyes closed and feel your energy return.

CHARM OF THOR

Create a charm of Thor to hang in the house for protection throughout the long months of winter. You will need red ribbon, three twigs, 10cm (4in) in length, from an oak tree, and some acorns. Tie the twigs and acorns together with the red ribbon and hang in the kitchen or above the door. Please do not pull the twigs or acorns from the tree; nature will have granted what you need so please look on the ground. As you hang the charm, say these words:

> Blessed Thor protect all in this house,
> None shall enter who brings harm.
> Mighty Thor please protect me,
> Mighty Thor blessed be.

BATTLE AHEAD SPELL

Call upon Thor if you are facing a battle or challenge, or if
you need to overcome the darkness felt in the winter months.
Invoke the help of the gods, but always be respectful and
mindful – they are deities after all! Light a red candle on a
Thursday (Thor's Day) and say this spell:

Mighty Thor big and strong
Help me fight the negative one,
Grant me victory in the battle ahead,
Mighty Thor grant me success
Let me be simply the best.
Mighty Thor blessed be
An' it harm none so mote it be.

LIFT MY SPIRITS SPELL

If, on any winter's day, negativity and darkness descend,
counteract it with this spell. Place a yellow candle, an orange
candle and a red candle in a triangle and light them. With
your hands open and palms turned up to the universe, say
these words:

> Light chase the darkness away,
> Free me from the blues today.
> No more with winter chill,
> Take away your woe and ills.
> I embrace the light,
> I embrace the day.
> No more this eternal night,
> From depression let me be free.
> An' it harm none so mote it be.

Keep the candles burning for as long as you can and absorb
their light. Embrace the illumination of the candles lighting
up the dark corners in your life.

MIDWINTER TEA

This tea can help soothe mind, body and soul and is used as a blessing. To make midwinter tea you will need:

1–2 teaspoons black tea leaves or green tea leaves
2 cloves
Handful of almonds, walnuts and cranberries, chopped
Orange peel, if desired

Add all the ingredients, except the orange peel, to a tea pot and pour boiling water over. Allow to brew for about 5 minutes. Try to avoid artificial sweetener. Add an orange peel for a winter feel.

Now, sit down in a quiet place where you know you will not be disturbed. Pour the tea, and have a pen and paper at the ready in case any visions come for you. Say these words:

> Blessings to the passing
>   season,
> Of summer's orange and
>   autumn's fruits.
> In mind, body and soul let
>   this tea soothe me,
> Blessings to the land and
>   blessing of the north.
> To the gods of midwinter,
>   one and all, blessed be.

THOR'S MAGIC SALT AND BLESSING WATER

This is similar to Odin's Blessing Water (*see page 194*) and is made in the same way. Leave a bowl of sea salt overnight in view of a full moon. In the morning, put the salt in an airtight container and tie a red ribbon round it. To make Thor's Blessing Water, fill a spray-top bottle with water, add a tablespoon of Thor's salt and 3 drops of juniper essential oil. Put the lid on the bottle and shake it up, saying these words as you do:

Mighty Thor bestow your strength upon me,
Great Thor scatter my enemies.
Keep those who would do harm far away from me,
Though it harm none so mote it be.

Remember, only use this for one winter month. You can spray Thor's blessing water around the home or at work if you feel there is an enemy near you.

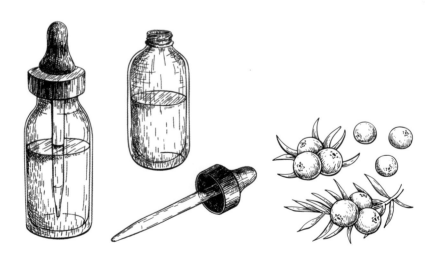

IMBOLC

In February in the northern hemisphere and August in the southern hemisphere, the delightful festival of Imbolc gives us hope and renews our strength. Translated from Old Irish, Imbolc literally means 'in the belly' and is the beginning of the lambing season. The earth starts to burst with life as the sweetness of spring begins to envelop us once more. Welcome the changing of the season by saying these few words on the first sun-filled day of February or August:

Imbolc sweet and bright,
Leave winter behind and out of sight.
Envelop us with blooms and sun,
Winter is now gone and done.

IMBOLC RITUAL

This is a beautiful little ritual of acknowledgement that light is returning and warmer weather is not far away. On your altar place a plant pot of snowdrops or white crocuses that are still growing, a white candle and a green candle. On the day of Imbolc, which usually occurs between 1–2 February in the northern hemisphere and 1–2 August in the southern hemisphere, light your candles and say these words:

Welcome to the blessed spring,
My arms are open to the goodness you bring,
Lady in robes of white grace our land,
With all your might.

At your altar have a pen, some paper and star anise to hand. Write down all the things you hope to do in the coming spring, such as save money, lose weight or get healthy. Afterwards, fold up the paper, with the star anise enclosed, and keep in a safe place until spring has passed. Then give thanks to Mother Earth and bury in the garden.

NORTHERN LIGHTS HEALING SPELL

If you are far away from your friends and you want to send them healing thoughts, send them on the northern lights, or aurora borealis. It's like casting your thoughts on the wind, which is what aurora borealis means. Coined by Galileo, the name comes from the Roman goddess of the dawn (Aurora) and the Greek name for the north wind (Boreas).

Imagine your healing thoughts being carried throughout the universe on the dancing, glowing wind of dawn.

Look up at the stars and cast a spell of healing to a friend in need by saying these words:

> Blessed be to the night sky
> Dancing lights of centuries past,
> Grant me a wish at last.
> My friend (name) is suffering,
> On medicines they rely,
> Dancing northern lights of the night skies,
> Send your magic healing blessed be.

CHARM OF FREYA

To bring love and beauty into the last days of winter, make a charm of Freya. This Norse goddess is associated with the alder tree, apples, mint, roses, feathers and amber. For this charm we will use three twigs 10cm (4in) in length that have fallen from an apple tree, some sprigs of mint, a red rose and a feather. Tie all these up in a pretty bundle with green ribbon and hang either in your bedroom or bathroom. As you do say these words:

> Goddess Freya blessed be,
> Please bring your gifts to me.
> Let love, passion and beauty
> In this home wander free.
> An' it harm none so mote it be.

You can keep your charm from year to year, or make a new one. It is also worth making a charm as a little gift to like-minded friends for birthday presents.

Vanadinite Charm Necklace

Vanadis is one of Freya's many names and is the root source for the chemical compound extract vanadium. Vanadinite, called the passion stone or the sex stone, is a stone of the sacral chakra where sexuality lies. As Freya is also known as the goddess of sex, this stone is often associated with her. Strong and forceful, Freya pursues whatever or whomever she desires. Try to make a necklace of crystal vanadinite, or keep a piece of it in the bedroom. On a Friday, say these words over your vanadinite:

Bless this night,
Love that feels so right.
Let me have the passion tonight,
Goddess Freya bless this vanadinite.

Freya's Blessing Water

This is similar to Odin and Thor's Blessing Water (*see pages 194 and 208*) and it is made in the same way. Leave a bowl of sea salt overnight in view of a full moon. In the morning, put the salt in an airtight container and tie a pink and white ribbon around it. To make Freya's Blessing Water, fill a spray-top bottle with water, add a tablespoon of Freya's salt and 3 drops of rose essential oil. Put the lid on the bottle and shake it up, saying these words as you do:

Goddess Freya please bestow your gifts,
Love, passion and desire come to me.
Let love be present in every room,
Let my desires come to be.

THE WHEEL OF THE YEAR

The festivals of the Turning of the Wheel are celebrated at different times around the world. Here are the typical dates for the north and south, but the dates may change slightly from year to year:

NORTHERN HEMISPHERE

LAMMAS
2 FEBRUARY
FIRST HARVEST

MABON
20–21 MARCH
AUTUMN EQUINOX

LITHA
21 DECEMBER
SUMMER SOLSTICE

SAMHAIN
30 APRIL – 1 MAY

BELTANE
31 OCTOBER
MAY DAY

NEW YEAR

MIDWINTER
20–23 JUNE
WINTER SOLSTICE

OSTARA
22–23 SEPTEMBER
SPRING EQUINOX

IMBOLC
1–2 AUGUST
SPRING BEGINS

THE WHEEL OF THE YEAR

Imbolc sweet and fair
Blessed maiden with flowers
 in her hair,
Snowdrops of pure white
Bless the world on this cold night.

Ostara wise and strong
Winter winds be gone,
New life you bring
Glory to the spring.

Fires burn at Beltane
May the sunshine remain,
Maypole magic prevail
In a world's fairy tale.

Midsummer fires burn bright
As fairies dance this night,
Lovers jump over broomsticks
Joy at Litha the summer solstice.

Lammas brings first harvest
First fruits are the best,
Offer your finest bread
To keep the winter fully fed.

Mabon brings a harvest festival
Leaves colour for an autumn carnival,
Mabon equinox day and night
Mabon equals dark and light.

Samhain wishes a Happy New Year
Halloween ghosties give a cheer,
Ancestors walk the world tonight
As children give trick or treat fright.

Turning seasons turning round
Snows will soon be on the ground,
Giving Yule a frosty bright
Granting all a midwinter's night.

REFERENCES

Binney, R., *Wise Words & Country Ways: Weather Lore*, David & Charles, 2010

Castleden, R., *The Element Encyclopedia of the Celts: The Ultimate A to Z of the Symbols, History and Spirituality of the Legendary Celts*, Harper Collins, 2012

Conway, D.J., *Norse Magic*, Llewellyn Publications, 1990

Conway, D.J., *Celtic Magic*, Llewellyn Publications, 2002

Day, B., *A Chronicle of Folk Customs*, Hamlyn, 1998

Duggan, E., *Autumn Equinox: The Enchantment of Mabon*, Llewellyn Publications, 2005

Eason, C., *The New Crystal Bible: 500 Crystals to Heal Your Body, Mind and Spirit*, Carlton Books Limited, 2010

Forty, J. (Ed.), *Classic Mythology*, Grange Books PLC, 1999

Harding, M., *A Little Book of The Green Man*, Aurum Press Ltd, 1998

Kershaw, S.P., *A Brief Guide to The Greek Myths: Gods, Monsters, Heroes and the Origins of Storytelling*, Constable & Robinson Ltd, 2007

Leland, C.G., *Aradia: Gospel of the Witches*, David Butt, 1899

Macbain, A., *Celtic Mythology and Religion*, A. & W. Mackenzie, 1885

March, J., *The Penguin Book of Classical Myths*, Penguin Books, 2008

Matthews, J., *The Quest for the Green Man*, Quest Books, 2001

Meadows, K., *The Little Library of Earth Medicine: Wolf*, DK Publishing, 1998

INDEX

ACKNOWLEDGEMENTS

AUTHOR ACKNOWLEDGEMENTS:

Thank you to Lisa Dyer, Managing Director of Eddison Books, for believing in my work and seeing the potential in words on a page. And to Nicolette Kaponis, Managing Editor, who with passion and vision has helped to create a truly beautiful book of magic.

PICTURE CREDITS:

ShutterstockphotoInc. 4–5 (background) tbmnk; 4 (winter aconite) Cat_arch_angel; 4 (pelargonium and bluebell) arxichtu4ki; 4 (dianthus) Potapov Alexander; 5 (iris) Dmytro Balkhovitin; 5 (crocuses) Ekaterina Koroleva; 5 (barberry) Ollga P; 5 (autumn bouquet) Depiano; 7 Le Panda; 8 Kudryashka; 10–11 ildab; 12 Eisfrei; 15 (gypsophila) Irina Violet; 15 (hyacinth) anemad; 15 (lily of the valley) Galyna Gryshchenko; 16–17 Pawaris Pattano09; 20 Anita Ponne; 21 Artishok; 26 Anastasia Lembrik; 28–29 Aepsilon; 31 amalia19; Yudina Anna; 34 JasminkaM; 36–37 Color Symphony; 38 Ratana21; 39 Thoom; 41 krisArt; 42 GoodStudio; 43 ArtMari; 44 Ase; 47 Meawstory15; 48 S.Borisov; 49 ArtMari; 50 hello808; 51 Katja Gerasimova; 53 Ianrward; 54 KostanPROFF; 56 Rafal Kulik; 58 QinJin; 59 Alina Briazgunova; 60–61 ildab; 62 Pawaris Pattano09; 64 Zhanna Smolyar; 65 (small dianthus) Africa Studio; 67 arxichtu4ki; 68–69 Creaturart Images; 70–71 Gannie; 72–73 Simple ThingsHere; 74–75 sondem; 78 EleniKa; 81 Natalypaint; 82–83 jakkapan; 84 Pruser; 85 TandaPanda; 87 SONTAYA CHAISAMUTRA; 88–89 ilolab; 90 Rafal Kulik; 83 Amka Artist; 92–93 Rafal Kulik; 94 romeo61; 95 AkimD; 96 MightyRabittCrew; 97 mexrix; 99 Erik Svoboda; 100–01 Color Symphony; 102 Katja Gerasimova; 103 somchaiP; 105 maljuk; 106–07 Yury Bobryk; 109 silver tiger; 110–11 Anton Watman; 112–13 ilolab; 114 Violet Gin; 116 (oxalis versicolor) fotosanka; 117 (saffron crocus) ann diidik; 117 (bergamot) Zadiraka Evgenii; 118 Ellerslie; 124 Philip Silver (background); 124 Macon (pentacle); 126 Shavood; 128–29 pixeldreams.eu; 131 Astro Ann; 132 Depiano; 133 bamamaba; 134 mart; 135 Helena-art; 136–37 Aepsilon; 138 Attitude; 139 Alkestida; 141 Jka; 143 Romolo Tavani; p145 Lenorko; 148 Gorbash Varvara; 150 PrasongTakham; 151 HorenkO; 152–53 Simple ThingsHere; 154 Rafal Kulik; 155 Trifonenkolvan; 157 Daniiel; 158 Gringoann; 160 Gribanessa; 161 ilolab; 163 IgorZh; 164–65 ilolab; 166 IMR; 168 Hein Nouwens; 169 (viburnum) P.S.Art-Design-Studio; 169 (crocuses) Royalty-free stock illustration; 169 (honeysuckle) Anastasiia_Shliago; 170–71 Sergey Gerashchenko; 172–73 ilolab; 175 patrimonio designs ltd; 176 1008; 177 Bourbon-88; 180 Tatiana Ol'shevskaya; 181 logaryphmic; 183 Kite_rin; Vlad Sokolovsky; 186–87 tomertu; 189 (glass) MoreVector; 189 (cake) vector_ann; 189 (candle) Azurhino;189 (flower) Gringoann; 191 oriontrail; 193 Anar Babayer; 194–95 javarman; 196 Liubabasha; 197 Tamara Kulikova; 198–99 Muamu; 201 Michael Sapryhin; 202–03 LilKar; 207 dzujen; 208 (essential oils) logaryphmic; 208 (juniper berries) Epine; 209 Stephanie Frey; 210–11 Lyudmila Miklailovskaya; 212 J. Helgason; 214 Pacrovka; 215 Shyvoronkova Kateryna; 216–17 icemanphotos; 218–19 (background) ilolab; 218–19 (wheel) moibalkon; 220 Daria Ustiugova; 224 Depiano.

EDDISON BOOKS LIMITED

Managing Director Lisa Dyer
Managing Editor Nicolette Kaponis
Copy Editor Nicola Hodgson
Proofreader Nicky Gyopari
Indexer Christine Shuttleworth
Designer Lucy Palmer
Production Sarah Rooney